Business Skills 1

Mark Faraday

with illustrations by Linda Hardwicke

Osborne Books

the author

Mark Faraday has had wide experience of office administration, both in London and also in Worcester where he held a management position in a large and busy office for a number of years. He is also a qualified lecturer with considerable experience of writing and teaching BTEC courses in Business and Finance.

acknowledgements

The author would like to thank the following individuals and organisations for their advice and assistance: Carole Clark, David Cox, Anne and Michael Fardon, Barbara and Glynne Jones, Sarah Musgrave, Catherine Parry, the Administrative Business and Commercial Training Group, BTEC, City of Worcester Community Services Department, Pitney Bowes plc, the Post Office, Worcester College of Technology.

bibliographical details

Published by Osborne Books Limited,
Gwernant, The Common,
Lower Broadheath, Worcester, WR2 6RP.
Tel 0905 333691

Printed by Ebenezer Baylis & Son Limited,
The Trinity Press,
London Road, Worcester, WR5 2JH.

British Library Cataloguing in Publication Data

Faraday, Mark, *1951 -*
  Business skills. 1.
  I. Title
  658

ISBN 1-872962-15-7

contents

about this book

Business Skills 1 is designed as a basic and practical text in office skills for

• BTEC First Level Award in Business and Finance
• NCVQ accredited courses in Business Administration, Levels I and II

The way in which the text may be used on these courses is explained on the next two pages.

The book is divided into self-contained Units which cover the competences specified by the Administrative Business and Commercial Training Group (ABC). The Units also cover the BTEC First Level Business Support Systems 1 requirement and provide material required in Business Support Systems 2. The principal ABC competences are:

> • filing
> • communicating information
> • data processing
> • processing petty cash and invoices
> • stock handling
> • mail handling
> • reprographics
> • liaising with callers and colleagues
> • health and safety

The first Unit of the book covers the Work Role requirements of the BTEC First Level Award and is also invaluable material for the work induction requirements of other NCVQ accredited courses in Business Administration. At the start of each Unit (except the introductory Unit 1) is set out the ABC element covered and the appropriate performance criteria under the heading 'NCVQ coverage'.

The aim in writing *Business Skills 1* has been to provide a clear and down-to-earth text which will instil the basic knowledge required for developing competence in office skills. The Student Activities which follow all the Units will enable the student to satisfy the requirements of the standards laid down by the Administrative Business and Commercial Training Group. In addition, specific 'Skills Development' sections have been included which explain in straightforward terms the 'Common Skills' required as an essential element of BTEC courses. Each of these sections is followed by an assignment which will provide further assessment material.

Two useful appendices have been included. *Appendix 1* contains specimen forms and documents which may be photocopied freely for use in the Assignments and Student Activities. *Appendix 2* contains the catalogue and price list of Wyvern (Office Products) Limited, a fictional organisation featured in the book.

In writing this book many real-life incidents and situations have been recounted. Office work provides its fair share of stress and many moments of humour. Dull it never is!

Mark Faraday
Spring 1991

BTEC First Award - how to use this book ▬▬▬▬▬▬▬

coverage and assessment of the First Level Modules

The BTEC First Award in Business and Finance contains three Delivery Support Modules which are fully covered in this book: Business Support Systems 1, Common Skills and Work Role.

The table set out below explains how this coverage is achieved. *Business Support Systems 1* is covered in a logical sequence of Units starting with 'liaising with colleagues' and progressing to the more specialised competences. In addition, many of the aspects of the Industry Standard Module *Business Support Systems 2* are covered in the text of these Units and the Student Activities which follow the text. There is ample assessment material in these Student Activities and the supporting Assignments.

The Common Skills are explained in full in the seven special 'Skills Development' sections and then practised in the Assignments which follow. It is suggested that lecturers and trainers might like formally to assess each skill on the basis of these assignments because each assignment concentrates (although not exclusively) on a single Common Skill.

The 'Work Role' Module is covered in Unit 1 'Work Role - you and your job' and developed further in the Common Skills Development Section 'Managing and Developing Self' and the two assignments which follow. These form useful assessment material for the 'Work Role' Module.

BTEC Module	coverage in the book	pages
Work Role	Unit 1	1 - 18
Business Support Systems 1		
Filing	Unit 10	140 - 154
Communicating information	Units 4, 5, 6, 7	51 - 92
Data processing	Units 8, 9	105 - 134
Processing petty cash & invoices	Units 13, 14	196 - 225
Stock handling	Unit 15	226 - 239
Mail handling	Unit 12	168 - 185
Reprographics	Unit 11	155 - 167
Liaising with callers and colleagues	Units 2, 3	27 - 33, 39 - 50
Health and safety	Unit 16	257 - 266
Common Skills		
Managing & developing self	Skills Development, Assignments 1 & 2	19 - 26
Working with and relating to others	Skills Development, Assignment 3	34 - 38
Communicating	Skills Development, Assignment 4	93 - 104
Applying technology	Skills Development, Assignment 5	135 - 139
Managing tasks & solving problems	Skills Development, Assignment 6	186 - 195
Applying numeracy	Skills Development, Assignment 7	240 - 256
Applying design & creativity	Skills Development, Assignment 8	267 - 272

NCVQ courses in Business Administration - how to use this book

Trainers using this book for NCVQ Levels I and II accredited courses in Business Administration, such as those offered by LCC or RSA, will find that their requirements for the nine basic ABC elements are fully covered. The Student Activities at the end of each Unit fulfil all the requirements for simulated work activities. In addition, the Assignments throughout the book will provide further assessment material.

The table set out below shows how the nine elements are covered in the Units of this book.

ABC Unit	Unit in this book	pages
1 Filing	Unit 10	140 - 154
2 Communicating information:		
- telephone calls	Unit 4	51 - 60
- oral and written messages	Unit 5	61 - 70
- supplying information	Unit 7	84 - 92
- routine communications	Unit 6	71 - 83
3 Data processing:		
- text processing	Unit 8	105 - 121
- update database records	Unit 9	122 - 134
4 Petty cash and invoices:		
- petty cash transactions	Unit 13	196 - 205
- invoice processing	Unit 14	206 - 225
5 Stock handling	Unit 15	226 - 239
6 Mail handling	Unit 12	168 - 185
7 Reprographics	Unit 11	155 - 167
8 Liaising with callers & colleagues:		
- with colleagues	Unit 2	27 - 33
- with callers	Unit 3	39 - 50
9 Health and Safety	Unit 16	257 - 266

1 Work role - you and your job

introduction

you and your situation
When you read this book, you may be

- at school studying how businesses and offices are organised
- at College full-time studying on a business course
- at work gaining qualifications to help you in your work

One factor is common to all these situations: you will be looking at how organisations work, and how you can develop your *business skills* and improve your competence. Whether you are already at work, or whether you will gain experience of the office environment through work placement, you will encounter a variety of clerical tasks - covered in later Units of this book - which involve the use of business skills. What then, are these skills - or *common skills* as they are often known?

common skills

self development	you must come to terms with your own role at work, learn to manage your activities, adapt to change, and be aware how you can develop your career
working with others	working involves teamwork - you must learn how to fit in with others, how to benefit from others, and how to relate yourself to the organisation as a whole
communicating	you will come into contact with colleagues and outside callers - in person, over the telephone, through writing letters - and will need to get your message across and understand others; this is *communicating* and an essential skill in the workplace
numeracy	you will need to deal with numbers in the workplace - performing calculations using your head or a calculator, making estimates, interpreting figures and presenting figures - all these require *numeracy* - the ability to deal with figures
managing tasks and problem solving	work involves problems - being overwhelmed by paperwork, making decisions between courses of action, meeting deadlines, sorting out priorities, dealing with awkward colleagues or outside callers - these all cause pressure on the individual, and it is an important skill to learn how to manage a variety of tasks and how to solve problems

technology   the modern workplace is constantly changing with the introduction of new technology - computers, computer software, communications - and it is an important skill to be aware of these changes and to be able to master them

design   you may think that design is the job of the art student, but if you think about it, many of the everyday office tasks involve design - setting out a letter, preparing publicity material, organising your desk and work area, even bringing in a pot plant - all these help efficiency and job satisfaction

These skills will be developed in the clerical tasks practised in this book, and also in the grey-tinted sections of the book.   These grey-tinted sections contain full explanations of each of the common skills and full-length assignments. We will now turn, however, to the different types of office with which you may be familiar, either through employment or through work placement.

office work

what is office work?

You may consider this to be rather an obvious question. Office work might be compared to the bloodstream of the human body.   It is taken for granted all the time, yet it provides the necessary support for all parts of the organisation; if it fails, or becomes inefficient, the whole 'body' - the organisation - suffers. What does office work involve?   In looking at skills we have already mentioned some of the functions; the following list is more comprehensive, and you might like to compare it with the types of office work of which you have experience:

external communications
- receiving and greeting visitors
- receiving and sending letters, telephone calls, faxes, telexes

internal communications
- receiving and sending messages, memoranda and notes
- telephone calls
- meetings

dealing with information
- dealing with the incoming and outgoing mail
- filing, photocopying (reprographics)
- operating a computer database

financial transactions
- operating a petty cash system
- processing invoices

dealing with resources
- maintaining stock for the office (e.g. stationery)
- ordering stock for the office

types of office

There are many different types of office because there are many types of organisation. For example:

a 'one person' office   for example, in a small business, where someone does all the office tasks, from making the tea to dealing with visitors

a central office   *either* a small organisation, e.g. an estate agent, employing two or three staff to carry out all the clerical tasks

                              or a large organisation, e.g. a large manufacturing company, consisting of many departments which centralise all the clerical functions in special sections - typing, reprographics, reception, mail handling

departmental **offices**	a large organisation, e.g. a local authority, which has an office for each department rather than one central office for all departments

types of organisation

If you are working in the office of an organisation, it is important to realise what type of organisation your employer is. The first distinction to be drawn is that between the *public sector* organisation and the *private sector* organisation.

public sector organisations

These are government owned or government controlled, and include large public corporations such as the Post Office or British Rail, bodies such as the Civil Service and more local organisations such as County, Metropolitan or District Councils.

private sector organisations

These are not owned by the government, but either directly or indirectly by private individuals. They include one-man businesses (sole traders), partnerships and limited companies.

sole trader	*A sole trader is an individual trading in his or her name, or under a trading name.*
	The advantages of being a sole trader are simplicity and cheapness of operation, freedom (you are your own boss) and control. Very often a sole trader will carry out some of the office tasks himself or herself, and possibly employ part-time clerical assistance.
partnership	*A partnership is a group of individuals working together in business, aiming to make a profit.*
	The advantages of forming a partnership are added expertise in the business, more money available to run the business, and relief for holidays. Common examples of partnerships include dentists, doctors, solicitors and accountants. Normally there are between two and twenty partners in a partnership. Because of the more elaborate nature of the business, a partnership is more likely to employ full-time office staff.
limited company	The largest business organisations are limited companies.
	A limited company is a separate legal body, owned by shareholders and managed by directors.
	There are two types of limited company: a *private limited company* and a *public limited company.*
	private limited companies, which have 'Limited' (abbreviated to 'Ltd') in the name, are usually small or medium-sized businesses, and often family-owned. They raise their finance from shareholders in return for *shares* which are *not* for sale through the Stock Exchange.
	public limited companies, which have 'plc' in their name are larger limited companies whose shares can be traded on the Stock Exchange.
	Companies are major employers of office staff; the type of office used by a company will depend on its size and requirements.

your place in the organisation

Your first day at work or on a work placement can be very confusing. Not only do you have to find your way about the building, you also have to remember a great many faces, and remember what those people *are* and what they *do*. It will be useful if you are able to obtain - or even draw up for yourself - a structure chart of the organisation. This will enable you to see

- the different levels of management
- the different departments or areas of work
- the names of people you should know about - supervisors, managers, the managing director
- *your* place in the organisation

The structure chart set out below is that of Wyvern (Office Products) Limited, an organisation used in this book for exercises and assignments. By the end of your studies you will get to know well the staff, the products, and the way 'Wyvern' operates. The company is a stationery wholesaler: it buys office equipment and stationery, and sells these products to other organisations, normally at a discount price.

Wyvern (Office Products) Limited: Structure Chart

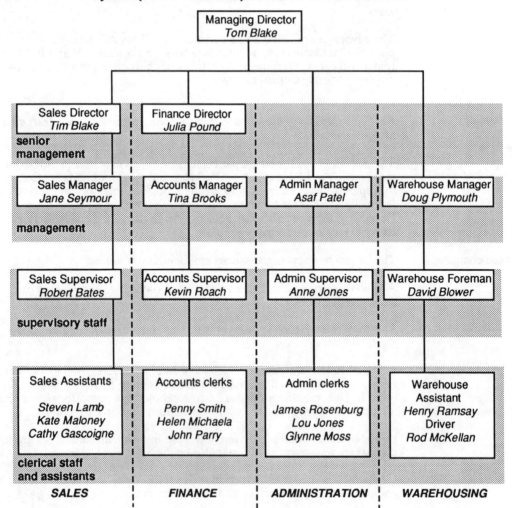

points to note from the structure chart

departments

Each vertical column represents a separate department:

- *sales* - responsible for the marketing and selling of the office products
- *finance* - responsible for the everyday financial transactions such as invoicing the customers, getting the money in, paying for purchases and running expenses,
- *administration* (abbreviated to 'admin') - the day-to-day running of the company - employing staff, payroll, running the building
- *warehousing* - storing the stocks of office equipment, arranging for its delivery and despatch to customers

You should note that larger organisations will have more operating departments, e.g. production, marketing, personnel, purchasing, while smaller organisations will have fewer.

management levels

Each horizontal level represents a step in the level of importance and responsibility of the staff:

- the *managing director* is responsible for everything in the company
- the senior management, the *directors* are appointed in the important money-making areas of the company - sales and finance
- *managers* are in charge of the departments, take important decisions and liaise with the senior management
- *supervisors* are in charge of the day-to-day running of the departments and normally work alongside the clerical staff
- *clerical staff and assistants* are the people who, as we have seen earlier, are the lifeblood of the organisation; their activity enables the company to function and to communicate effectively both internally and externally.

levels of authority

Each horizontal level represents a level of authority which must be respected and used in cases of
- *instructions* - these are passed down the line of authority
- *problems* - if you cannot deal with a problem, you should refer it to your immediate superior
- *disciplinary matters* - if you need to be disciplined, the person above you will deal with the matter in the first instance, and then pass it higher up the line if necessary
- *complaints* - if you have a complaint against the organisation, you should take it first to your immediate superior; if you do not obtain satisfaction, you should then take it higher

promotion and career path

When you join an organisation you should have an idea of a career path which will take you up through the levels of responsibility shown on the structure chart; this may involve taking qualifications, in-house training, and even moving from one organisation to another. Your career path is an important subject to discuss at job interviews. Applying for a new job is covered in Assignment 2 'The Job Application'.

contract of employment

what is a contract?

A contract is a legally binding agreement between two people. If you buy goods or rent a room you enter into a contract: you pay money and expect goods or a room in return. Similarly, if you get a job you enter into a contract with your employer. This will establish

• your employer's rights and duties
• your rights and duties

In other words, a contract of employment sets down what your job is, what you will be paid, what you must do if you are ill, and how you can be disciplined.

forms of employment contract

The contract may be a formal written document - an example is illustrated on the next page. But it does not have to be in writing; it may be a combination of terms
• agreed at your interview
• set out in a letter from your employer accepting your application
• set out in a written job description
• contained in a work 'rule book'
• agreed between the Union and your employer

Whatever the form of the contract, your employer should, by law, give you a written statement of certain terms within thirteen weeks of your starting work, if you work at least sixteen hours a week. The statement should set out
• the names of the employer and employee (i.e. you)
• the date when employment began
• the amount of pay, and when you are paid (weekly or monthly)
• the hours to be worked
• holiday entitlement and holiday pay (if any)
• procedures for reporting sick, and sick pay arrangements
• details of any pension schemes
• length of notice required if you are leaving (or are being asked to leave!)
• what to do if you have a grievance
• the disciplinary rules and procedures
• the title of your job

legal duties of an employer

The law states that the employers must

• pay you the agreed wages and provide you with an itemised pay slip
• provide sick pay (most of which is then reclaimed by the employer from the Government)
• take care over your safety, health and welfare
• provide work if you are paid on commission (based on the amount of work done) - otherwise the employer does *not* have to provide work (but he does have to pay you!)

Note: these duties are explained in more detail later in this Unit

legal duties of an employee

The law states that you must

• use reasonable skill and care in your work
• carry out lawful and reasonable instructions (e.g. you do not have to drive an uninsured van!)
• give faithful service (i.e. not letting out trade secrets or confidential information)

Note: these duties are explained in more detail later in this Unit

CONTRACT OF EMPLOYMENT
Particulars of Terms and Conditions of Employment pursuant to the Employment
Protection (Consolidation) Act 1978

Employer.......... *Wyvern (Office Products) Limited* ....

Employee.......... *Katherine Maloney* ....

1. **Continuous Employment**
   You are on a fixed term contract of .... *2* ....years

   Your continuous service dates from.......... *21 January 1989* ....

2. **Job Title**
   You are employed as.......... *Sales Assistant* ....

3. **Salary**
   The rate of your salary is..... *£ 8,400* ....per annum, paid monthly

4. **Hours of Work**
   Your normal hours of work are ..... *35* ... hours a week, worked over a five day period
   (Mondays to Fridays inclusive)

5. **Leave**
   You are entitled to..... *22* ....days paid holiday per annum in addition to statutory
   holidays. The leave is to be taken at a time convenient to the employer.

6. **Sickness**
   Notification of absence should be made on the first day of sickness, in writing or by
   telephone.
   If you are absent for a period in excess of five working days, a doctor's certificate
   must be submitted to the employer.
   Regulations for payment during periods of sickness or injury may be inspected on
   request in the Administration Manager's Office.

7. **Notice**
   The length of notice for termination of employment required from employer or
   employee is...... *4* ....weeks, subject to statutory requirements.

8. **Grievance Procedure**
   In cases of dissatisfaction with disciplinary procedure you are to apply in the first
   instance to the Manager of the Sales Department. Details of the rules of the
   Company and disciplinary procedures may be obtained from the Administration
   Manager's Office.

9. **Pension Scheme**
   Details of the contributory Company Pension Scheme, for which you are eligible,
   may be obtained from the Administration Manager's Office.

Signed this...... *21* ....day of.... *January* .19. *89* ......

T J Blake

T J Blake, Managing Director and Company Secretary

Example of a Contract of Employment

your rights as an employee

As an employee you will have certain rights and protections in situations such as

- discrimination against you on the grounds of sex, race or because you are married
- belonging to a Union
- dismissal and redundancy
- Health and Safety at Work
- Sick Pay and Maternity Rights
- receipt of a pay statement (payslip)

You should in your own interest be aware of these rights, and it is an important area of your training that you should know about these rights, and be able to discuss them with colleagues. We will now examine your rights in more detail.

discrimination

It is against the law for an employer, or a prospective employer, to discriminate against you on the grounds of sex, race or because you are married, in the following situations:

- recruiting you or considering you for a job
- in the terms on which a job is offered, e.g. hours, fringe benefits
- making you redundant or dismissing you

If the employer infringes any of these rights, the employer can be taken to court.

While the areas of discrimination listed above are provided for *in law,* there are a number of areas which you will encounter which are *personal attitudes* which it will be up to you to deal with on a *personal level.* You might like to think about the attitude of employers to employees who are

- handicapped
- gay
- married women with children

belonging to a Union

As an employee you have the right to join a Trades Union, although not every employee is a Union member. An employer cannot prevent you from joining a Union. The only reason for which an employer could sack you for Union activity is if you go on strike, provided everyone who goes on strike is sacked by the employer!

the benefits

- protection of working conditions (hours, pay, holidays, heat, light and safety in the workplace)
- protection against redundancy, unfair disciplinary action, discrimination
- social activities, training and education

some terminology

closed shop   a *closed shop* is a place of work where it is compulsory to join a Union;
                       normally 80% of the employees have to be in favour before this can become
                       legal, and an employee cannot be dismissed if they object to being a Union
                       member on the grounds of religion or deeply-held belief

collective bargaining the Union organisation enables the Union officials (representatives, shop
                       stewards) to negotiate with the employer on behalf of the members on matters
                       of pay, hours, working conditions; this negotiation process is known as
                       collective bargaining

dismissal and redundancy

As a full-time employee you are protected in law against *unfair* dismissal, and you also have certain entitlements to redundancy pay.

notice of dismissal

Your contract of employment (see page 7) may state the period of notice the employer has to give you. If there is no provision in a written contract, you should expect at least a week's notice if you have worked for the employer for more than a month. If, however, you are guilty of *gross misconduct* (being caught stealing or breaking your manager's nose, for example) you can be dismissed without notice.

dismissal procedure

The employer must follow a strict procedure before dismissing you:

* you must be given a warning of conduct which could result in your dismissal
* you must be given a written warning before your dismissal
* if you have worked for at least six months for an employer you must be given *written* reasons for your dismissal

why could you be dismissed?

You could be dismissed in a number of situations:

* redundancy
* misconduct, e.g. persistent lateness, insubordination, drunk at work
* gross misconduct (see above), e.g. theft, assault
* poor job performance (lack of training, qualification, competence)
* illegal employment (a driver who has lost his licence)

You will see that in the case of redundancy, dismissal is not your fault. All the other reasons stated are *fair* reasons for dismissal - the fault lies with you. If you consider that you have been dismissed *unfairly* through victimisation or discrimination you can seek help from your Union (if you are a member) or the Citizens' Advice Bureau (who can introduce you to legal advice) and then take the case to an Industrial Tribunal if you have a sufficient case.

health and safety at work

Employers must by law (the Health and Safety at Work Act 1974) provide a safe and healthy environment for their employees. The law also states that employees have responsibilities for the health and safety of their colleagues. This subject is covered in full in Unit 16 (pages 255 - 264). For the present you should note that an employer should

* provide a safe and healthy working environment for employees
* ensure that all machinery - including office equipment - is safe to use
* provide training in safety for employees

Accident Book

All places of work should have an Accident Book in which are recorded full details of any accident - the name of the victim, details of the injury and *how* it happened. This book is very important:

* if you suffer an injury, it is evidence which can be used if you are claiming against the employer
* it makes the employer aware of hazards in the workplace - e.g. dangerous stairs, badly lit areas

If you are in employment or on work placement you should make it a priority to find out who looks after the Accident Book.

sick pay

Statutory Sick Pay (SSP)

If you are off sick your employer should have an arrangement with you to pay you - possibly at full rate - for the hours which you have lost. Your employer is also *legally bound to pay you* if you are sick for four or more days in a row. This pay is known as *Statutory Sick Pay (SSP)*, and is in essence a State benefit: the employer pays the employee and then recovers most of the money from the Government. SSP is

- available for employees aged 16 or over
- payable only for four or more days' sickness (including weekends - i.e. if you are away ill Friday to Monday inclusive you are entitled to SSP even if you don't normally work at weekends)
- payable from the fourth day of sickness (the first three do not qualify)
- payable for a maximum of 28 weeks

notification of sickness

If you are in employment or on work placement you should ensure that you know what to do about informing your employer when you are off sick. A typical arrangement is

- notify the employer by phone if you cannot come to work
- complete a self-certification form on your return to work (saying what was wrong with you and when) - these forms will be available from your employer
- bring your employer a doctor's note if you are off work for more than seven days

maternity rights

employers schemes

Many larger employers (e.g. local authorities, banks) operate schemes whereby pregnant women are paid during the time they are away from work in the latter stages of pregnancy and after the baby is born; this is known as *maternity leave*. Some enlightened employers also give the *father* a limited amount of paid leave; this is known as *paternity leave!*

Statutory Maternity Pay (SMP)

Your employer is also legally bound to pay you Statutory Maternity Pay (SMP), which like Statutory Sick Pay, is a State benefit paid by the employer and recovered by the employer from the Government. The features of Statutory Maternity Pay are

- the woman must have been continuously employed for 26 weeks
- Statutory Maternity Pay is payable for up to 18 weeks
- payments normally start 11 weeks before the baby's arrival date

the right to return to work

An employee who has had a baby has the right to return to her job, or if the job no longer exists, a comparable job. If the employer refuses to take her back, she has effectively been dismissed and may have a claim against her employer for unfair dismissal.

payslip

An employee must by law be given an itemized pay statement (payslip) when the wages are paid, or in advance of payment of wages. This payslip must show

- gross pay, i.e. the pay before any deductions are made
- the deductions that are made, e.g. income tax, National Insurance, pension payments
- the method of payment, e.g. cash, to bank account, to building society account

An example of a payslip is illustrated on the next page.

Wyvern (Office Products) Limited		**Pay Statement** May 199-	
	£		£
Basic Pay	700.00	**Income Tax**	112.75
Overtime	50.00	**National Insurance**	53.50
		Pension	45.00
TOTAL GROSS PAY	750.00		
		TOTAL DEDUCTIONS	211.25
		NET PAY	538.75

CUMULATIVES		**EMPLOYEE DETAILS**
Taxable earnings	901.82	
Tax to date	225.25	Miss K Maloney
NI to date	107.00	Staff No 0178653425
Pension	90.00	NI No YT 77 77 01 A
		Tax Ref 792/W1
NET PAY	1077.75	Payment BACS

Payslip of Kate Maloney, employee of Wyvern (Office Products) Limited

notes

❏ **gross pay** is shown on the left hand side (upper half), and is calculated by adding basic pay and overtime

❏ **net pay** is shown in the box on the right hand side - this is calculated by subtracting income tax, National Insurance Contributions and pension from gross pay

❏ **deductions** for income tax, National Insurance Contributions and pension are itemised and totalled

❏ **payment method** - to a bank account through a computerised system known as BACS - is shown in the 'Employee Details' section

❏ **cumulatives** is a section on the left hand side (lower half) showing the totals for the tax year (which starts on 6 April) of pay which is taxed, income tax, National Insurance Contributions and pension payments.

responsibilities of the employee

As an employee you should also be aware of *your* responsibilities

* *to your organisation* - to the outside world you *are* the organisation, and reflect its efficiency
* *to yourself* - you need to develop personal skills as an employee to enable you to progress

In this section we will examine

* presentation and behaviour
* the need for efficiency
* the importance of organising your work area, organising your time and coping with deadlines
* preparing for promotion

presentation and behaviour

As an employee you will have dealings with your colleagues and also possibly with outside callers, either on the telephone or in person. You will need to bear the following points in mind:

image

You represent your organisation to the outside world and should try to project a helpful and efficient image. How would you rate yourself in these qualities:
* politeness?
* cheerfulness at all times?
* helpfulness?
* level-headedness (do you panic in crises?)
* knowledge of your organisation's products or services?

How do you score? Obviously no person is perfect, but all of these qualities should be developed by the employee.

presentation

When you deal with colleagues or callers, you should take care about even the most obvious points of personal presentation. You might be put off by people with these problems:
* *voice* - mumbling or talking too loudly
* *manner* - the over-cheerful (too much of an act), the miserable moaner
* *hands* - dirty hands, bitten nails
* *hair* - greasy, unwashed, unbrushed, hanging over the face
* *breath* - smelling of drink, garlic, onion and other strong foods
* *body odour* - you can use your imagination in this case

These problems paint a fairly unpleasant picture, and it is clearly unlikely that any one person will have them all! Nevertheless, you should look at yourself critically and see how you can improve your own presentation to your colleagues and callers.

dress

Organisations will normally have a stated policy on dress. Some, such as retail stores, banks and building societies have uniforms; others are less formal. Whatever the circumstances dress should be:
* clean
* well fitting
* appropriate
* tidy

Dress expresses your individuality, and you can still achieve this in the workplace - a choice of scarf or tie, for instance - but not at the expense of smartness or the organisation's stated policy.

behaviour

The word 'behaviour' may remind you unpleasantly of schooldays, but it is an important area of your workplace personality which will be noticed by outside callers and also by your supervisors. The following conduct would undoubtedly be frowned upon
- lateness
- extending coffee breaks and lunch hours
- rudeness to colleagues, superiors and callers
- coming in drunk
- taking days off 'sick' when you feel like it

Many of these offences may be treated with disciplinary action, and may even be grounds for dismissal. It must be stressed however that an office should not be a miserable place in which to work: an office with a *relaxed* atmosphere, where the employees and supervisor can enjoy a good joke or laugh, is often the most efficient and hardworking. It is all a question of using common sense and a sense of proportion.

the need for efficiency

Time, space and resources mean money to an organisation. If you can be efficient and save any of these, you will be a valuable employee. The following resources are areas where savings can be made:

time

Your time is a cost to your employer. Can you improve your daily routine - fill in slack periods, carry out tasks for colleagues, use the word processor or computer to carry out tasks which take you a long time, cut down on overtime?

people

Can you improve the efficiency of the office by carrying out tasks which someone else would otherwise have done? This is a sensitive area as you may deprive someone of a job.

materials

Can you see where materials can be saved - is printed matter being photocopied unnecessarily, are certain files redundant, are you ordering material or publications which are not required? Tell your supervisor.

energy

Can you save the electricity bill - are lights being left on unnecessarily, photocopiers used wastefully?

space

Office space is expensive. Can you reorganise (with the permission of your supervisor) you own office space, both to improve it and also to allow extra workspace and additional equipment to be installed?

You will doubtless point out that decisions about improving efficiency come from management rather than office staff. Nevertheless your management will be pleased to receive suggestions about improving efficiency and saving money. Some organisations operate 'staff suggestion' schemes and reward good suggestions with money payments.

organisation of environment and time

To be an efficient employee you need to organise

- your working environment
- your time

organisation of working environment

Your working environment in the case of most employees means your desk. You may have noticed if you have worked in an office that the most efficient members of staff have the most organised desk layouts; they can always find the letter or file you ask them for. If you are a student you will notice in the same way that the better students have the more organised files and are the most up-to-date on assignments. The same principle of *organisation* applies.

The normal desk will be organised into task areas:

tasks given	Incoming tasks - the morning's post to deal with, memos and notes from colleagues, telephone messages requiring you to ring back. These are normally placed in an 'in tray' and require immediate attention, and a decision on whether they are urgent or non-urgent
tasks pending	Tasks which cannot be completed at present, either because you are too busy, or because you are waiting for further information in order to complete them. Tasks pending are often placed in a 'pending tray'.
tasks completed	The most satisfying area of the desk is the space allocated to completed tasks e.g. letters ready for signing, memos and notes written. Completed tasks are often placed in an 'out tray'.

The desk of an efficient person will be organised and divided in this way. If you are not organised you will get in a mess: urgent tasks may go into the pending tray, or worse still, be buried under piles of paper and neglected entirely! The illustration on page 15 will give you an idea of the importance of the organisation of your work area.

organisation of time: deadlines and priorities

Work involves deadlines. Dealing with deadlines is an important skill which can determine whether you are successful at work, or whether you just manage to cope. There are two basic character extremes:

• the cool calm efficient type who is never flustered when faced with deadlines
• the excitable type who rushes here and there in a crisis and achieves little

Most people fall somewhere between the two. How do *you* rate yourself?

Most jobs involve the process of giving tasks priority. Each task has its own level of importance and a deadline. Tasks may arrive with the morning post or be generated by the everyday business of the office. It is your job to sort the tasks in order of priority and to make an 'action list', either in your mind, or better still, on paper. Place the paperwork on your desk in this order of importance. Your 'action list' will, of course, change during the working day as new tasks arrive.

Do you think the following tasks are in the correct order of priority?

• reporting a suspicious package left in the reception area
• finding a telephone number for the Sales Director
• replying to a customer who has requested a Sales Catalogue
• replying to a memorandum asking for your stationery requirements

Yes, they are, and for reasons which are obvious.

organisation of time: time management aids

So far we have looked at work as it occurs in a single working day. Office work, however, involves a continuing process: tasks continue over a period of time and need to be monitored from time to time. There are a number of aids which can help you organise your time and plan ahead

action lists	As noted above, make a list of things you have to do during the day and head it up 'TO DO' if you wish. When the tasks are completed, cross them off, or tick them

an example of a badly organised work area

an example of a well organised work area

diaries	You may have your own work diary or may share an office diary which will, depending on the type of work your office carries out, contain important information such as • appointments with customers • bookings to be made for senior staff (travel, meals) • information to be given to other staff (e.g Sales figures) • follow up tasks (e.g telephone a customer to whom you have sent sales literature) In addition to a desk diary, *copies* of letters and other written communications which require a follow up may be placed in a date order diary file and taken out on the appropriate date for action.
electronic diary	Some offices operate diary systems which are recorded on computer file. This type of system, known as the *electronic diary* has the advantage that access is available to a greater number of people, and as long as the *input* is efficient, the system works well.
charts	Some offices record forward planning on a wall chart - a 'Year Planner' which shows each day individually, and displays each month on a new line. Required actions can be recorded on the chart with special pens and other stick-on devices. These charts can be useful for organisations which operate along the lines of separate projects. They are often also used for recording staff holidays - a very important function!

delegation and asking for assistance

There will be times when you know you cannot complete all the tasks within the given deadlines. It is then your responsibility to

• *delegate* - to pass on tasks to other colleagues (if you have the authority, or can persuade them), or
• *ask for help* - your supervisor is employed to ensure the efficient running of the office; if you are overloaded with work, it is your supervisor's responsibility to find someone else to do it

You may think that these solutions sound very well in theory but are difficult or impossible in practice. It is up to you to use your communication skills to persuade your colleagues of your problems, as long as you do not make a habit of it!

preparing for promotion

It is up to you as an employee to prepare yourself for promotion: you will be benefiting yourself, and also your organisation because your efficiency will (or should) improve as a result.

You should bear the following points in mind:

attitude	Without becoming the office 'creep' you should • be smart in appearance, be punctual and produce good work • show enthusiasm and take the initiative (volunteer for difficult tasks) • be well informed about the organisation's products or services
training	• offer yourself for in-house training if the opportunity arises • ask about the possibility of studying for qualifications
career path	You should map out on paper the jobs and levels through which you would like to progress. Link them wherever possible with qualifications for which you could undertake a course of study.

student activities - work role: you and your job

1. Which of the Common Skills listed at the beginning of this Unit do you use at work (employment or work placement)? Set out a table stating
    (a) the skills used
    (b) the areas in which they are used
    (c) your assessment of how proficient you are in their use (good/satisfactory/could be improved)

    Suggestion for table layout:

Skill	Use (Yes/No)	Areas of Work	Self- Assessment
Numeracy	*Yes*	*Petty Cash/ invoice processing*	*Good*

2. Using as a basis the organisation which employs you (or an organisation which has given you a work placement)

    (a) state what type of organisation it is (private sector or public sector; sole trader, partnership or limited company)
    (b) state what type of office it has (one person, central or departmental)
    (c) draw up a structure chart (see page 4 for an example) showing the different management levels and the different operational areas (e.g. Sales, Finance)

3. State the terms of employment which an employer by law is obliged to give to an employee within 13 weeks of starting work.

4.

Rushwick Frozen Foods			Pay Statement	
Payments		**Deductions**		
	£		£	
Basic Pay	80.00	Income Tax	12.50	
Overtime	24.00	National Insurance	6.39	
		TOTAL DEDUCTIONS	18.89	
TOTAL GROSS	104.00	NET PAY	85.11	
Gross pay to date	184.00	Income Tax to date	19.00	
Taxable Pay to date	76.72	National Insurance to date	10.62	

Date	Employee's name	Tax Code	Payment method
20 Apr. 199-	R V Williams	305L	BACS

Mr Williams has been at work for two weeks. Explain to him how his payslip tells him
(a) his gross pay
(b) his net pay
(c) his deductions
(d) the method of payment
In each case explain to him what the figures or items in question represent.

5.   List the benefits to an employe of belonging to a Trades Union.

6.   Why is an Accident Book maintained at work? Explain the procedure for recording an accident at work.

7.   What as an employee would you do in the following situations:

(a)   You are female, and your employer promotes a male colleague rather than you. You remember that you asked about maternity leave in a recent interview wth your employer.

(b)   Your employer says he is going to sack you because you are persistently late for work.

(c)   Your employer says he is going to sack you because you recently lost your temper, punched your supervisor and knocked two of his teeth out.

(d)   You are off sick for two weeks in succession.

(e)   You become pregant.
Note: male readers should use their imagination here.

8.   You are talking to a friend and learn that she is about to start work with your organisation. She has been appointed trainee Sales Assistant, a post that requires contact with the general public. She is understandably nervous, as this is her first job. List the points that you would mention to her about
(a) the way she should deal with the general public - the type of image she should project
(b) her presentation and dress (she does not wear a uniform).

9.   You start work in an office, and are told on the first day by a colleague that the supervisor is soon to retire, and that generally 'anything goes.' You are told that it doesn't matter
(a) if you are late for work
(b) if you extend your lunch-hour by ten minutes
(c) if you help yourself to stationery from the stationery cupboard for private use.
What would you do, and why?

10. A new employee, John, starts work in your office. He claims that he has done the type of work before - answering customers' product queries by letter and telephone - and so he is left to get on with the job at a desk of his own after a morning's training.

After a couple of days, John is starting to leave the office late looking bothered; his desk is a mess, and one or two important customer queries have been 'mislaid' by him. He has appeared to be very busy, but surprisingly has not asked any further questions about the job.   Your supervisor is concerned, and asks you to go and sit with him and 'sort him out'.

(a) how would you start to clear up the muddle - what would be your priorities?
(b) what advice would you give John about organising his work environment - i.e his desk?
(c) what advice would you give John about organising his time?

 # linking assignments

Common Skills Assignment 1
Work Role: guide to new employees, page 22

Common Skills Assignment 2
Managing and developing self: the job application, pages 23 to 26

Common Skills development:
Managing and developing self

Skills developed
The skills developed in this section are as follows
- *managing own roles and responsibilities*
- *managing own time in achieving objectives*
- *undertaking personal and career development*
- *transferring skills to new and changing situations and contexts*

These skills, together with the appropriate performance criteria will be examined in turn.

1. managing own roles and responsibilities ▬▬▬▬

performance criteria
If you are to manage your roles and responsibilities in the workplace you should be able to
- agree and accept work roles and responsibilites
- identify the constraints of work roles and responsibilities
- set goals for your achievement, monitor them and adjust them if necessary

what this means
If you have a job, go on work experience, or 'shadow' someone at work you will appreciate that each job has its own particular activities and areas of responsibility. It is possible that the job activities and responsibilities are set out in a 'job description', a written statement of what you are expected to do. Clearly if you accept the job, you must accept the job specification as well. Other less specific responsibilities to your fellow employees may *not* be written down. These include many of the points raised in the last Unit under the heading 'responsibilities of the employee' (see pages 12 to 14), for instance:

organising your work area
Your desk should be tidy and well organised so that it could be taken over by a colleague should you be absent for any reason. Use 'in', 'out' and 'pending' trays for your tasks. Compare the pictures of good and bad practice on page 15: the message should be very clear.

observing the Health and Safety at Work regulations
You should make the workplace safer both for yourself and your colleagues - do not leave drawers open or electrical leads trailing. Your responsibilities are set out in Unit 16 'Health and Safety'.

seeking assistance if you cannot cope

It often happens that the unexpected occurs and you are faced with a difficult decision to be made, or a customer outside your range of experience or responsibility. Do not panic or try to bluff your way through the difficulty. Ask for help from a more experienced colleague or your supervisor. Contrary to what you might think people are ready to help and will not think you stupid or ignorant.

promotion and career path planning

It is your responsibility to think ahead about the direction your job and career is taking. This is part of your job role, and will be dealt with in more detail later under the heading 'undertaking personal and career development' on page 21.

setting goals for achievement at work

Goals for achievement at work include

- specific *workload* targets - e.g. finishing your work for the day without working overtime
- specific *skills* targets - e.g. being able to increase your typing speed, being able to master a particular computer program used in the office
- *personal* targets - being able to get on with a person at work whom nobody else can stand, improving your punctuality, standard of dress, telephone manner, and so on

The process of setting targets and examining your success rate is a very important personal skill. You should be able to monitor your success rate and adjust your targets accordingly. Of course the process may well be shared by your employer who will be assessing your performance, suggesting training courses, discussing your periodic reports with you and possibly talking about your progress with your training body. In this way you are in control of the process of *managing and developing yourself*.

2. managing own time in achieving objectives ━━━━━

performance criteria

If you are to manage your time effectively in the workplace you should be able to

- plan your objectives (what you have to do) within a set timescale
- use specific techniques for planning your work
- achieving what you set out to do within a set timescale

what this means

The management of time is the key to efficiency and self-management. In the last Unit under the headings 'organisation of time' (pages 14 - 15) we have already explained the skills that need to be developed and the time management aids which exist. Reread those two pages now.

You will see that organisation of time is a mental discipline involving

- establishing deadlines
- establishing priorities

You will see that *self-discipline* is essential and also that there are many aids and office systems to help you in the task. These include action lists, diaries, and charts.

Managing time is a skill which improves with experience. It is also a skill which is invaluable outside the workplace, and can lead to a balanced lifestyle which mixes work and relaxation, study and going out with friends or a partner. People who are all work and no play, or all play and no work, run into trouble. Organisation of time normally leads to having a good time!

3. undertaking personal and career development ▬▬▬

performance criteria

If you are to develop your character and career you should

- identify areas for development
- produce an action plan
- enhance your performance in line with the action plan

what this means

Your future is important to you and it is therefore essential that you are able to assess yourself, to identify your strengths and weaknesses, and to plan your career. It may be that you are studying full-time, in which case your College or training body will advise and counsel you whether to go straight into a job or undertake further study.

It may be that you are already in a job, in which case you should plan ahead by considering a variety of options:

- staying in the same organisation - planning your career progression through the various levels and possibly changing areas of work, e.g. moving from Accounts to Sales
- moving to a different organisation doing similar work
- moving to a different area of work following a period of retraining

In all of these options you should consider the possibility of studying for qualifications either at a College on a work-release basis or on an open-learning (work at home) basis. Remember that self-improvement leads to advancement.

Assignment 2 'The Job Application' on pages 23 to 26 develops this theme of career planning in a practical way.

4. transfer skills gained to new and changing situations and contexts ▬▬▬

performance criteria

If you are to change your job, either by progressing within the same organisation, or by moving to a different organisation, you will need to transfer your existing skills to the new job. You will need to

- identify and value your existing skills and knowledge
- apply them to differing situations and contexts (i.e. a new job)
- identify new skills and knowledge that will be needed

what this means

If you apply for a new job in a different organisation you will need to take stock of your existing skills and knowledge to see if they are acceptable for the new position. A good way of achieving this is to write up a CV (curriculum vitae - latin for 'history of your life') which will summarise your achievements and abilities (see Assignment 2, pages 23 to 26 for practical guidance). If you are hoping to move within your own organisation you should investigate the practical skills and knowledge required for the new position, and find out how *different* the job is. Talk to the people involved in that area, and if possible obtain a job description for the post. How far do you fulfil what is required? To what extent will you have to undertake further training or study? Do you need to do this in your own time, or will the organisation provide you with on-the-job training? These are some of the many questions which will have to be answered before you can consider a move.

Common Skills Assignment 1
Work role:
Guide to new employees

Areas assessed

This assignment covers the following areas
- *Work Role Unit*
- *Common Skill: managing and developing self*

Scenario

You are a clerical assistant in the Administration Department of Wyvern (Office Products) Limited. Your supervisor, Anne Jones, knows that you are an experienced member of the Administration staff, and asks you to draft a guide for new entrants to the company. She has in mind particularly the needs of school leavers who have no knowledge or experience of the working environment. She asks for a preliminary draft containing word processed text and diagrams. This will form the basis of the document. It will then be checked by her and then produced in final form by the in-house publishing system.

Tasks

You are to set out the guide in the following sections

1. A structure chart of Wyvern (Office Products) Limited showing the members of staff, the departments and management levels. (Note: guidance for this may be found from the chart on page 4).

2. A copy of the Contract of Employment signed by new entrants with explanatory notes of what it is, and what the terms mean. The Contract of Employment may be completed with details of a member of staff. (Note: see page 7 for guidance).

3. A sample payslip with explanations of what the various sections mean. (Note: see page 11).

4. The rights of the employee with respect to Union membership and dismissal.

5. Instructions on what to do if an employee has an accident in the workplace.

Notes on completion of the Assignment

You are to provide a draft format only. The text should be word processed, but the charts and illustrations may be line drawings with labelling done by hand. If you have access to more sophisticated equipment such as a desk top publishing package, you may use it. Try to keep the text as simple and jargon-free as possible. Remember that the guide is to be read by a new employee on the first day in the workplace. A blank contract of employment and payslip, both of which may be photocopied, are reproduced in Appendix 1 at the end of this book.

Common Skills Assignment 2
Managing and developing self:
The job application

Areas assessed
This assignment covers the following areas
- **Work Role Unit**
- **Common Skill:** *managing and developing self*

Scenario
*You are **either***

- *leaving College and applying for a job, **or***
- *you are already employed and now looking for another job.*

You see a suitable job advertised in the the local newspaper or in an employment agency. You are asked to apply in writing and enclose a curriculum vitae.

Tasks
You are to

1.   Consider carefully what type of job you would like to apply for. Examine the career paths open to you and enquire what your entry level into that particular type of job would be.

2.   Find an advertisement in the local paper or details in an employment agency for a job which you think would be suitable for you.

2.   Write a letter of application for the post in question, in your own handwriting.

3.   Draw up a draft curriculum vitae appropriate to your circumstances. Word process or type it out.

Notes on completion of the Assignment
On the next few pages you will find

- an advert for a vacancy in the Accounts Department of a local firm
- a sample letter of application, together with hints on how letters of application should be composed
- a completed curriculum vitae, together with explanatory notes

It should be stressed that these specimens are set out for guidance purposes only. You might like to consult other sources of information: if you are in employment your personnel staff may be able to help you, if you are at College your Communications lecturer or Careers tutor should be able to assist.

Dynatechic Limited
Accounts Clerk

A vacancy exists for a trainee Accounts Clerk to deal with cash book and double-entry ledger systems.

Salary based on age and experience. Please apply in writing with CV to

Mr N Farrant, Personnel Manager,
Dynatechnic Limited,
Unit 14, Oak Industrial Estate, Stourminster MR8 5TG

an advertisement for a job

7, Mill Lane,
Broadwater
Mereford MR6 8JP

7 May 199–

Mr. N Farrant, Personnel Manager,
Dynatechnic Limited,
Unit 14, Oak Industrial Estate,
Stourminster, MR8 5TG

Dear Mr Farrant,

I am writing in reply to the advertisement in "The Evening Echo" dated 5 May 199– for a vacancy for a trainee Accounts Clerk. I would like to apply for this post, and have pleasure in enclosing my curriculum vitae.

I am at present studying for a BTEC First Level Award in Business and Finance at Mereford College, and am very interested in working in the field of accounting. As you will see from my CV I have already spent three weeks on a work experience placement with MRC Electronics, working in their Accounts Department. At Mereford College I have been active in the student-run College Bookshop, helping with the accounts.

My course finishes in June of this year, and I would be free to start full-time employment from 1 July. I will be available to attend for interview at any time convenient to you.

Yours sincerely

Alice Peters

Alice Peters (Miss)

a letter of application for the job from Alice Peters

CURRICULUM VITAE

Personal Details

Name   Peters, Alice Joanne

Address   7, Mill Lane, Broadwater, Mereford, MR6 8TP

Telephone   0605 456729

Date of birth   20 January 1975

Nationality   British

Marital status Single

Education

1986 - 1990   Henry Bulstrode High School, Mereford
                GCSE's: English Language (B); Mathematics (B);
                French (C); Geography (C); Home Economics (C).

1991 - 1992   Mereford College, Mereford
                BTEC First Award in Business and Finance
                Final Assessment June 1992.

Positions of Responsibility

School   Form captain and member of Under 11's netball team.

College   Student representative on Course Liaison Committee.
                Book-keeper to Student-run College Bookshop (a Young
                Enterprise Scheme).

Work Experience

July - August 1991   Part-time assistant in the shop at Peters Garage, the
                      family business.

November 1991   Work placement (part of BTEC course). Three weeks
                      spent at MRC Electronics Limited, Mereford. Work in
                      the Accounts Department, processing invoices for
                      payment, cash book and payroll.

Interests

Sports   Canoeing , orienteering, swimming.

Leisure   Jazz music, science fiction.

the curriculum vitae drawn up by Alice Peters

notes on job application letters

written or typed? Employers prefer letters of application to be in the applicant's own handwriting. Handwriting will form part of the employer's assessment of the applicant, and so it is important that the letter is neat and tidy. If your handwriting is very poor (for instance you may have a dyslexia problem) you should type or word process the letter, but only as a last resort.

presentation The way the letter is set out will make a great deal of difference to the impression made on the employer. If you are not sure of the correct layout, e.g. where the addresses and date are placed, you should refer to the example here and to Unit 6 for guidance. The letter on page 24 is a common format for a letter of application. Use good quality paper, preferably A4 size.

advert and post State in the first paragraph where you saw the advert, and refer to the post for which you are applying. Quote any reference number given in the advert.

CV State that you are enclosing a CV, and remember to enclose it! If the advert does not mention a CV, still enclose one, and mention it in the letter.

selling yourself The letter must summarise your achievements and skills which relate the post being advertised. Do not be modest, sell yourself. Do not, on the other hand, sound bigheaded.

length The letter should be short and to the point. A single sheet of A4 is quite sufficient.

copies Do not forget to take a copy of the letter and the CV, and to keep the original advertisement.   If you are called to interview you will need to remember what you said, and when you wrote the letter.

notes on the completion of a CV

presentation A CV should either be typed or word processed. If it is word processed there is the advantage that you can update it from time-to-time without having to retype the whole document. A CV should be set out with clear headings, as in the example on page 25. Notes on some of these headings follow below.

education Schools, Colleges, dates, qualifications and grades should be included, plus any special awards. You can omit primary education (i.e up to the age of 11).

employment If you are already in employment, include your present job. Give the name and address of your present employer in case a reference is needed. Give details of your job, emphasising aspects relevant to the job being applied for.

interests Be specific. Writing 'sports, reading and listening to music' sounds wet and half-hearted. Write instead 'Playing squash. Crime fiction. Traditional jazz.' if those are your interests.

other information If you can drive and have had no convictions, add an additional heading 'Other Information' and write 'Clean driving licence'.

2 Liaising with colleagues

NCVQ coverage
8.2 maintain business relationships with other members of staff
Performance criteria
- *responding to colleagues' requests willingly*
- *explaining clearly and politely if you are unable to respond to a request*
- *discussing and resolving difficulties in working relationships*
- *knowing when to refer unresolved difficulties to a higher authority*

introduction

If you work in an office, you work in a group, and must be able to adjust to the needs and pressures of that group. You may not like your colleagues - you may not like your supervisor! - but you have no choice in the matter and must learn to develop business relationships with other members of staff. If you are unable to work in your group, you, your colleagues and the work will suffer.

If you are not working full-time, the same principles of group work can be applied either to a College situation - you may be working on a group assignment - or to experience gained in a work placement.

In this Unit we look at
- the types of group that you are likely to encounter
- how to adapt to the needs of that group
- the problems encountered with the giving and receiving of oral and written requests
- the ways in which you can resolve those problems

---

 linking assignment

Common Skills Assignment 3
Working with and relating to others: Teamwork - a sales promotion, pages 37 to 38

---

working in a group

group characteristics

A group has a number of characteristics of which you should be aware:

identity

If you work in an organisation you are member of a number of different groups, each with its own identity. You should normally have loyalty to these groups, although your strongest loyalty will be to your most immediate group - possibly the people you work with on a day-to-day basis:

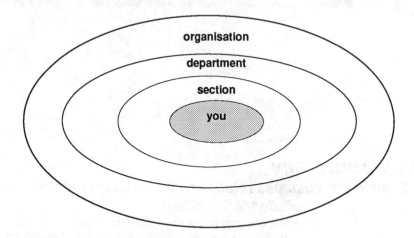

belonging

If you belong to a group you have a sense of 'belonging' to that group. If someone starts work in your section, they will lack that feeling, and it will be up to you to make them feel welcome and develop that sense of belonging to what is in essence a work environment 'family'.

hierarchy

In any group there will be strong members and weaker members; and as a result there will be defined levels of authority and seniority - a *hierarchy* - which is normally refelected in work gradings. It is normal, for example, for the supervisor to be the 'strong' member. If the supervisor is overshadowed by a junior but dominant member of staff, there could be problems! The important lesson for a member of a group - particularly for a new member - is to recognise and respect the hierarchy.

objectives

All groups have objectives, and all the groups mentioned in the section 'identity' (see above) will have their particular aims:

- *the organisation* will aim to provide a service, be profitable, and look after its staff
- *the department* will aim to fulfil efficiently a certain function within the organisation - sales, accounts, administration, and so on
- *the section* in which you work will have its own particular role to play, and it is up to your supervisor to ensure that you perform your work efficiently and well

It is up to *you* to be aware of these group aims.

how to be a successful group member

Groups at work, like families at home, involve communication and misunderstanding, conflict and compromise.   If you have been in different work environments you will know the different 'atmospheres' that can exist: some offices are relaxed and the work goes well, some are tense and unpleasant because of tensions between individuals, and the work suffers. It is up to you as a group member - and particularly if you reach a supervisory role - to adopt the right attitude and create the right working atmosphere.

Consider how the following attitudes help an office to function more efficiently

cooperation	working with other members of staff, helping them and giving them advice, even if the work involved is not your responsibility; this is particularly important where a new member of staff is involved
listening	pay attention to other people's opinions and suggestions, even if you do not agree with them; be prepared to *change* your opinions and working methods as a result of listening to others
meeting deadlines	if you are given tasks to do, do them on time, otherwise you will let your colleagues down; be prepared to work extra time and extra hard when the office is under pressure and the work has to be done
no backbiting	if you do not like a colleague or a colleague's opinions, confront the colleague; do not complain to your other colleagues - backbiting is one of the surest ways to destroy trust in a working environment
accept responsibility	if something goes wrong in your section or department, you should be ready to accept responsibility; it is no help to say to someone with a complaint 'It's not my fault, someone must have sent the information to the wrong address.'
knowledge	knowing your organisation - its staff, structure, products and services

dealing with requests from colleagues

During the course of a working day you will receive many requests from colleagues - spoken (oral) requests and written requests - and these should be dealt with willingly and efficiently.

These requests can include

- being asked to undertake a routine task by a colleague in your department
- being asked to do something by a colleague in another department
- responding to a written request - e.g a note - from a colleague in your department
- responding to a written request - e.g. a memo (see page 80) from another department or senior management

Normally you should be able to deal with these requests, having given them the appropriate priority (as discussed in Unit 1). There will, however, be times when you do not have the time available to deal with a request or you might consider that it is not your job to do that particular task. In these circumstances you should know how to deal with the situation without - to use the modern expression - 'losing your cool'.

On the next page are listed some problem situations and suggested ways of dealing with them.

request	reply
someone puts a note on your desk asking you to ring back a caller - you are very busy	*You should assess the urgency of the call - if you are not sure, ask the person who dropped you the note - then give the call the appropriate priority. If you simply do not have time to call, ask a colleague to do it for you, or as a last resort tell the supervisor.*
a colleague goes home with a bad migraine - the supervisor asks you to finish your colleague's filing for her, but you know that you do not have the time available - you are already staying late to finish an important task.	*Tell the supervisor about your present workload. Do so in a calm and polite way - do not appear to panic or complain: if you show a negative attitude, your supervisor will think that you are either incapable of working under pressure, or just unwilling to take on extra work.*
you receive a memorandum from another department in the organisation requesting information - a task which you consider boring and not your responsibility anyway	*This is a task which has to be done. Assess the urgency of the request; if a deadline is given, deal with it as appropriate. If you think that the request is not part of your normal duties, or not part of your department's normal work, refer it to your supervisor who will give it to the appropriate person or query it with the sender.*
you have just arranged to meet your husband/wife/boyfriend/girlfriend after work, and are asked to do overtime because an office deadline has to be met	*Do not complain, but show willingness to carry out the work. Mention the problem to your supervisor who should give you permission to telephone the person, and may even let you off in good time if you show a positive attitude. Do not just sulk and complain to your colleagues - it will get you nowhere!*

poor liaison with colleagues - how to resolve the problems

The examples set out below show how bad communications and poor staff attitude can result in messages

- getting lost
- being ignored
- being misinterpreted

In each of the cases set out below, a suggestion has been given of how to resolve the problem. Do you agree with the solutions?

problem - a message not received . . .

A colleague has spoken to a customer over the telephone; the customer was returning your call of earlier in the day and asks your colleague to suggest to you that you ring back. Unfortunately your colleague is about to go to lunch at the time and forgets to give you the message. Your colleague remembers the following morning but is too embarrassed to tell you. The customer then telephones, very annoyed that you have failed to return the call the previous day.

solution?

Your immediate concern is to pacify the customer, and deal with the <u>customer's</u> problem. You should then afterwards find out who failed to give you the message by asking around the office. If the culprit does not admit the fact, you should make some general announcement to the office about the importance of passing on messages. If the culprit does admit the fact you should tell him or her about the importance of dealing with customer enquiries, rather than making it into a personal issue.

problem - a message ignored . . .

Two members of staff - Penny and Helen - are in strong competition for promotion. They have both been in the same section for five years and are hoping to get the supervisor's job when he retires at the end of the year. At times there is considerable friction between the two. One Friday afternoon the supervisor is going to a meeting and asks Penny to pass on a message to Helen to finish typing an important report which the manager needs to see on Monday. Penny and Helen have just had an argument, and Penny decides not to pass on the message. The report is not ready on Monday morning when the manager asks for it . . .

solution?

The immediate solution is for the report to be completed as soon as possible, possibly by Penny, who is at fault. Penny and Helen should try and resolve their difficulties and establish some sort of a working relationship, as clearly the situation where the work of the department suffers cannot continue. The supervisor could help by talking to them individually and perhaps look into the possibility of one of them being promoted or transferred to another section, as they cannot both be promoted in the same section.

problem - a message misinterpreted . . .

Steve, a rather 'scatty' disorganised member of staff takes a telephone call from a customer, and writes a note and hands it to you. How many things are wrong with it? What opportunities are there for misinterpretation and mistakes?

> *Mr Smith telephoned and asks if you can call him back. He wants to know the price of paper as soon as possible. Thanks.*
>
> *Steve*

solution?

It is up to you to speak to Steve and find out

- *when the message was taken (there is no date or time)*
- *which Mr Smith called (there are no initials or telephone number to help you)*
- *whether it was you that Mr Smith wanted to talk to (there is no indication on the message)*
- *when Mr Smith wanted you to call back*
- *what type of paper was it that Mr Smith was interested in - typing, computer, photocopy paper?*

There is clearly plenty of opportunity for misinterpretation in this message. You should take Steve on one side and politely explain to him the problems he has caused. You should not make it a personal issue because he may react in a negative way and go off in a huff.

resolving disputes

The examples given in the previous section contain situations which are potential disputes: the person who is inconvenienced by a lost, delayed, or misinterpreted message will feel fairly put out by the experience and may confront the person responsible. The solutions given in the previous section suggest instead that conciliation and compromise are better alternatives than picking an argument. You will doubtless point out that it is easy to say this in theory, but more difficult to do it in practice!

There are situations, however, where conciliation and compromise are not possible and the matter has to be resolved by a superior authority. Whom do you approach?

- in the first instance approach your supervisor with the problem
- if the supervisor *is* the problem, you may need to take the matter to a higher authority, a departmental manager, for instance
- if the matter is a grievance covered by your contract of employment, you will need to find out the necessary procedure

It is part of your skills development to be able to work in a group and to be able to resolve disputes. These skills are summarised in the Action Points set out below.

✓ action points - liaising with colleagues

○ be aware of the different types of group - the organisation, the department, the section

○ be aware of the objectives of the different groups

○ accept responsibility for the group, even if a mistake is not your fault

○ cooperate with your colleagues

○ listen to your colleagues and appreciate their points of view

○ be aware of - and meet - deadlines wherever possible

○ communicate clearly with your colleagues, whether orally or in writing, and pass on messages

○ do not let personal rivalries and other considerations affect your efficiency at work

○ avoid disputes - try to resolve problems in a calm and reasonable way

○ if you cannot resolve a problem, refer it to your supervisor, or to the appropriate authority

student activities - liaising with colleagues

Performance criteria

The student activities in this section test competences in the following areas:

- *responding to colleagues' requests willingly*
- *explaining clearly and politely if you are unable to respond to a request*
- *discussing and resolving difficulties in working relationships*
- *knowing when to refer unresolved difficulties to a higher authority*

1. What separate groups can you identify in the organisation in which you work or the organisation which has given you work experience? Draw a suitable diagram to illustrate the groups.

2. What are the objectives of the groups identified in Question 1?

3. List the personal qualities which you think are necessary for someone working in a group.

4. What types of messages and requests are you likely to receive from colleagues during the course of a working day?

5. List three reasons why a message from a colleague might be lost or delayed.

What is the problem in each of the following situations, and how would you resolve it?

6. A colleague - Jake - is having personal problems (a divorce) and has delayed giving you a telephone mesage asking you to call a customer about faulty goods supplied.

7. A colleague - Lucy - who does not like you, failed to give you a message asking you to go and see the Personnel Manager to discuss your career.

8. Your supervisor seems to be victimising you. You discuss the matter with your colleagues, and they agree with you. On Monday your supervisor gives you a warning about lateness to work when you were only two minutes late because the bus was delayed.

9. A new member of staff - Jason - has been turning up for work in an untidy state, with soiled clothes and dirty shoes. When you mention it, he says he 'doesn't care a toss' about his appearance or his work. As Jason deals with the public, working with you on an enquiry counter, your supervisor asks you to have a word with him.

10. You find that one of your colleagues - Linda - with whom you had been very friendly, is telling other members of staff details of your personal life and also about mistakes you occasionally make in your work.

 ## linking assignment

Common Skills Assignment 3
Working with and relating to others: Teamwork - a sales promotion, pages 37 to 38

Common Skills development:
Working with and relating to others

Skills developed

The skills developed in this section are as follows

- *treat others' opinions, values and beliefs with respect*
- *relate to and interact effectively with individuals and groups*
- *work effectively as a member of a team*

These skills, together with the appropriate performance criteria will be examined in turn.

1. treat others' opinions, values and beliefs with respect

performance criteria

If you are working with other people it is important that you are able to understand their point of view. You should be able to

- be aware of your own values, beliefs and opinions
- be aware of the values beliefs and opinions of others
- deal sensitively with others who have different values, beliefs and opinions

what this means

When you are working in an organisation you encounter many different types of people; some you like, some you are less enthusiastic about. Why is this? Largely because you like the people who think the way you do and those who are easy to get on with, and you do not like the people who are *different* in some way. This difference often lies in the way these people think and speak, because of their values, beliefs and opinions. It is an important personal skill to be able to see *where* this difference lies, if there is a disagreement - to know what your position is and why the other person's viewpoint is different.

what are your own values, beliefs and opinions?

Values, beliefs and opinions can involve

- the way you approach your work in terms of application and loyalty
- your religious and political views
- your moral viewpoint

How would you react in the following common workplace situations?

Try to classify your reaction into one (or more) of these three categories:

- the situation is something which is against the workplace regulations
- you object to the situation on moral grounds
- in your opinion you cannot agree to what is going on

1.   *You see a colleague putting some pens and pencils from the stationery cupboard into his bag to take home.*

2.   *You find a colleague photocopying on the office copier some dirty jokes from a magazine.*

3.   *You find out that a married colleague is having an affair with one of the secretaries.*

4.   *Your colleagues ask you to contribute £5 towards a fridge for the rest room. You do not think a fridge is necessary, and would not use one.*

Your answers will probably include a mixture of reactions: a moral or even a religious reaction against the affair, a clash of opinion against the £5 donation, an acknowledgement of a breach of rules (pilfering of pens and pencils). The important factor is how you would *manage* the situation. Would you do nothing? Would you confront the people involved? Would you tell your supervisor? It is all a question of coming to terms with your own values, beliefs and opinions. You will probably be very aware of your own popularity in the group before taking any unpopular action.

how do you treat the values, beliefs and opinions of others?

If you are working in a group, you will need to be tolerant of the other group members, and sensitive to their views. It is very easy, and a group characteristic, to be intolerant and to isolate the individual who is different and thinks differently. Examples of situations which might require restraint include

- a colleague with a different ethnic origin
- a colleague with a different sexual persuasion to yourself
- someone who has not joined the Union when most people are members
- a colleague who dresses differently

Whether you are at work or at College, how do you rate yourself in terms of tolerance and sensitivity?

2.   relate to and interact effectively with individuals and groups

performance criteria

When you work in a group, either in the work-place or at College, you should be aware of the resources of the group in terms of the knowledge and skills of the group members. You should be able to

- identify and value the knowledge and skills of others in the group
- listen to and observe others in the group
- help and support others, and in turn be helped and supported by others
- adjust your behaviour in response to feedback from the group

what this means

If you are working in a group, of say, two to six people, either at in the workplace or at College, you may be faced with a problem or a new situation involving change, and have to tackle it *as a group*. In the workplace this could include the introduction of a new computer system which changes the office routine; at College it could involve the setting of a new group assignment which will involve the allotting of tasks among group members. In both cases members of the group must

- be aware of the knowledge and skills possessed by other group members
- be prepared to listen to the views put forward by group members
- be prepared to change their own views accordingly
- be prepared to change the ways in which they act

an example of a group accepting change

Suppose you work in a small solicitor's office staffed by six: one supervisor and five assistants. The office is old-fashioned and does not have any computer equipment. The Managing Partner of the firm decides that a word processor must be installed, together with a database to hold clients' details and an accounting program to send out the bills to the clients. What is the effect on the group? The first step will be a discussion in which various questions will be asked. Has any of the staff had any experience with computers? It turns out that two of the typists - the juniors of the office - have been trained on a word processor. The supervisor and the older colleagues will have to listen to the juniors and benefit from their experience. Working methods will have to be changed, and so too will the attitudes of the older staff towards the younger members.

3.   work effectively as a member of a team _____

performance criteria

In Unit 2 we saw that an organisation is made up of a number of different groups based around the individual. In the workplace you will probably be a member of a *section*, working in a *department,* which is itself part of the *organisation*. If you are at College, you are likely to work within a *group*, within a *class*, within a *Department* or *Faculty*, within the *College*. Each group is in effect a team with specific objectives. If you are to work as part of a team you must be able to

- recognise and accept the importance of the team
- identify the strengths and weaknesses of team members
- participate in the allocation of team tasks
- make sure you know what your allotted tasks are
- complete your tasks to the required standard and deadline
- help others and ask for help from others as necessary
- adjust what you are required to do in response to feedback from the group

In Unit 2 'Liaising with colleagues' we have already examined in detail (pages 28 to 29) how to work effectively as a member of a team. You should reread those pages now. You will see that being a successful group member requires

- an awareness of the group's objectives
- a readiness to cooperate and avoid conflict within the group
- the ability to listen to colleagues
- the ability to meet deadlines
- loyalty to the group
- the ability to accept responsibility for group decisions

Assignment 3 'Teamwork - a sales promotion' will explore working with others in a practical way.

Common Skills Assignment 3
Working with and relating to others:
Teamwork - a sales promotion

Areas assessed

This assignment covers the following areas
- **Clerical Task:** *liaising with colleagues*
- **Common Skills:** *principal skill - working with and relating to ohers; other skills - communicating, applying numeracy, applying design and creativity*

Scenario

You work in the Sales Department of Wyvern (Office Products) Limited in a small team of three or four under the supervision of Bob Bates, Sales Supervisor.

You have been asked to prepare a product and price list for a special promotion of certain items of office furniture for next month (See Appendix 2 at the end of this book for Wyvern's catalogue and price list). The list is to be produced on a single A4 sheet showing:

- *the company name, address and telephone number*
- *the heading 'Special Offer'*
- *an overall 10% reduction on the list price*
- *the offer being available for one calendar month only (e.g. September or October)*
- *catalogue numbers for the selected items to be quoted*
  (these are: F1005, F1006, F1007, F1022, F1023, F1024, F1070, F1071, F1072, F1090, C1010, C1030)

You have been set a specific deadline by Bob Bates for the production of the promotional sheet, and also to think up ideas of how and where the sheet could be circulated. You are to work in a team to complete the work. The team does, however, encounter some problems which it will have to discuss and resolve.

Tasks

You are to form a group of three or four. Use your own names, or, if you prefer, the names of the sales assistants set out on the structure chart on page 4. Choose a group leader who will coordinate the job.

Task 1: defining of tasks

Discuss in your group how the work is to be tackled. The tasks can be grouped under four headings:

1.   Extracting the information from the Sales Catalogue and Price List for the selected items (see Appendix 2) and working out discounts.

2.   Designing the promotional leaflet.

3.   Deciding on the people to whom the leaflet should be sent (suggestions: businesses in the area,

existing customers, educational establishments,) and how the leaflets should be sent (suggestions: mailshot, insert in the local business magazine).

4.   Typing out or word processing the leaflet into a draft form for checking by Bob Bates, Sales Supervisor.

As noted above, each group should discuss how the tasks are to be defined.
The Group Leader should keep a written record of the defined tasks and give a copy to the assessor.

Task 2: allocation of tasks
The group should discuss how the tasks are to be allocated to group members. A *suggested* allocation is:

•   all members could extract product details and prices from the catalogue and price list (Appendix 2) and calculate the 10% discount (as a check on the calculations)

•   all members could draw up a draft design for the leaflet and the group could decide which was the best

•   each member could research separately target areas to which the leaflet could be sent, and then the ideas could be combined in group discussion

This is only a suggestion. It is up to the group to ensure that all members are fully occupied at all times, so that the group resources are employed to the full.
The Group Leader should keep a written record of the task allocation and give a copy to the assessor.

Task 3: carry out tasks and assess success
The tasks should then be carried out as far as the production of the final draft design which is to be shown to Bob Bates, Sales Supervisor. The members should then formally discuss how successfully they performed as a group. They should pinpoint their strengths and weaknesses. For instance

weaknesses
- breakdown in communication between members
- individual members not having enough/having too much to do
- individual members letting the group down by not completing allocated tasks

strengths
- making the most of individuals members' skills
- being aware of the opinions expressed by others
- changing a plan of action as a result of someone's opinion on what should be done

A group member should make a written summary of the discussion and give a copy to the assessor.

Task 4: encountering and solving problems
During the course of a project, a group often encounters personal problems which have to be resolved. You are to discuss as a group how to deal with the following problems:

1.   The person who is calculating the discounts comes in a late one morning with a hangover - not for the first time; as a result a number of the calculations are found to be incorrect.

2.   The person who is dealing with the design of the leaflet is having serious boyfriend/girlfriend problems and is often on the office telephone agonising over the relationship rather than getting on with the work.

3.   The person who is in charge of typing up the leaflet is off sick, and has disappeared with the final draft.

4.   The person who is in charge of deciding on the distribution of the leaflets has strong opinions and will not listen to anyone else's ideas.

It is suggested that this discussion is videotaped so that each group member as well as the assessor can literally 'see' and pass comment on the contribution of individual group members.

3 Liaising with callers

NCVQ coverage

8.1 receive and assist callers

Performance criteria

- *greeting all callers promptly and politely, and identifying their needs*
- *giving callers disclosable information only*
- *directing or escorting callers to the correct destination*
- *explaining politely the reasons for any delay or non-availability of assistance*
- *identifying situations outside your job's area of responsibility and asking for assistance promptly*

introduction

The initial impression of a caller at an organisation is based on the reception he or she receives. Is the person who meets the caller polite and helpful, or is the person unhelpful and not interested in the caller's request? The result will be a good impression - or a bad impression - of the whole organisation. If you work in an organisation, permanently or on work placement, you will probably have to deal with callers, either at a reception desk or elsewhere on the premises. The skills you need to develop - listed in the section above - are to be able to greet callers, to direct them and to deal with difficult situations. In explaining these skill areas, we will also look at how to deal with problem callers - people who are difficult and aggressive - by interpreting their body language (gestures and expressions) and by reacting accordingly.

You will also need the basic knowledge required when receiving visitors, including:

- the structure of the organisation and the jobs of the members of staff
- the rules for the security of the building

---

 linking assignment

Common Skills Assignment 4
Communicating: getting the message across, pages 100 to 104

making an impression

impressions of the receptionist

If you greet a caller, you make an impression. The type of impression that you give depends on a number of factors:

appearance   We have already seen in Unit 1 (page 12) that one of the responsibilities of the employee is to pay attention to one's personal presentation. In particular
- voice
- hands
- hair
- breath and other possible sources of odour
- dress

personality   You should aim to give a positive and efficient image of your organisation to the outside world. You should try to be
- polite
- cheerful (but do not overdo it!)
- helpful
- calm (do not panic)

efficiency   No caller likes dealing with an incompetent! Ensure that you know
- who your staff are, and what their jobs areas are
- how the staff can be contacted if required
- what your products and/or services are

impressions of the reception area

An organisation will normally have a specially designated reception area or public area with a reception desk. The scale of this area will depend on this size and type of the organisation. Consider the types of reception areas provided by
- doctors
- banks
- car show rooms
- large industrial companies
- small factory units

You will see that there is no 'standard' reception area as such; they can vary from the well-provided reception areas of large companies to the sliding frosted glass window in the office wall of a small factory unit.

For the purposes of this Unit we will take as an example a medium-sized manufacturing business which has a specific reception area with a receptionist sitting at a desk. The illustration on the next page shows how this area can be set out well (giving a good impression) and how it can be a disaster.

The receptionist's desk and reception area will often be equipped with
- a telephone
- a structure chart of the organisation with all the appropriate telephone extension numbers
- catalogues and publicity material about the organisation's products
- a list of appointments for the day (so that callers can be anticipated)
- a caller's book (so that callers can 'log in' and 'log out')
- a card index file to contain the visiting cards of callers

The reception area should be welcoming, comfortable, clean and, in the case of larger organisations be equipped with reading material (trade magazines, newspapers), a drinks dispenser, a payphone and cloakroom. All these factors will put a caller at ease when he or she calls, or has to wait.

a poor receptionist and a badly organised reception area

a good receptionist and a well organised reception area

greeting callers

types of caller

The way in which you greet a caller will depend on the *type* of caller.

callers with appointments

Callers with appointments should be included in the list of appointments for the day (sometimes written in a special Appointments Book). They might include:
- salesmen wishing to sell to you
- existing customers
- potential customers
- potential employees attending for interview
- technicians to service or install equipment

callers without appointments

Callers without appointments will clearly not be listed in the list of appointments. They might include
- salesmen calling by chance
- existing customers calling by chance
- potential customers calling by chance
- general enquiries about products, jobs

regular callers who do not need an appointment

These will normally be familiar figures such as
- delivery men
- couriers
- the postman
- cleaners
- maintenance staff for pot plant displays, drink dispensers, photocopiers

greeting the caller

Greeting callers is a skill that must be practised. It is up to the receptionist to decide what approach is necessary.

Regular callers who do not need an appointment may be dealt with on an informal basis; the receptionist may well be on first name terms with individuals such as the postman or the photocopier engineer.

For other callers who call with or without appointments, a more formal approach is called for. Organisations have their own ideas about the specific way a caller is greeted : the 'house style'. The example given below is a typical method of greeting a caller

stages in the conversation	dialogue	
initial contact	Receptionist	*'Good morning. How may I help you?'*
	Caller	*'I have come to see Mr Hopkins.'*
	Receptionist	*'Do you have an appointment?'*
	Caller	*'Yes, at 9.30.'*

establish the caller's name	Receptionist	Consults the appointments list *'That will be Mr Drew, won't it?'*
	Caller	*'Yes, that's right.'*
		Hands her his visiting card
take action	Receptionist	*'I will let him know you are here, Mr Drew.'*
		Speaks to Mr Hopkins' secretary on the telephone, and arranges for Mr Hopkins to collect the caller
		'Mr Hopkins will be with you in a minute. Would you like to take a seat?'
	Caller	*'Thanks..'*
		Sits down

Note the following points:

- the initial contact is made in a polite and friendly manner
- the name of the caller is established at an early stage, and is then *used* by the receptionist
- if the caller did not have an appointment, the receptionist could ask further questions to establish the identity of the caller:

     'May I ask your name?' - the caller may then produce a card

- action is taken by the receptionist to arrange for the caller to be collected by, or escorted to, the appropriate person within the organisation
- if the caller has to wait, he or she should be made comfortable

calling people names?

As we have already mentioned, it is important to establish the name of the caller as soon as is practicable. But how do you address a caller and refer to your own colleagues? There are certain guidelines which you should follow:

- *before* you establish the name of the caller, you *may* use the words *'Sir'* or *'Madam'* - you should find out whether this traditional form of address is used by your organisation
- *after* you have established the name of the caller, you should use the words *'Mr . . Mrs . . Miss . . Ms'* as appropriate before the surname; *never* use the first name - it will sound over-familiar
- if you are able to obtain the caller's business card, file it on your desk for future reference
- if you refer to a colleague when speaking to a caller, use the *'Mr . . Mrs . . Miss . . Ms'* form of name; for instance:

	Caller	*'May I see <u>Mike Hopkins</u>?'* or . . . *'May I see <u>the boss</u> now?'*
	Receptionist	*'I will see if <u>Mr Hopkins</u> is available.'*

caught on the telephone?

A receptionist will inevitably be faced from time-to-time with the problem of speaking to someone on the telephone when a visitor calls. What is the procedure?

- make contact with the visitor, i.e. smile and indicate politely that you are speaking, then
- when there is a pause in the telephone conversation, say *'Sorry, I won't be a minute,'* then
- conclude the telephone call as soon as possible; or arrange to telephone back later

communicating with callers - identifying needs

Communicating is an important skill to be developed - as we have seen in Unit 2 - when you liaise with your colleagues. You also need to communicate with callers, both by speaking and listening to them (verbal communication) and also by non-verbal communication (body language).

verbal communication - speaking and listening

It is essential for the person receiving a caller to be able to find out what the caller wants. It may be that the caller is not very clear about what he wants, or is not able to express his intentions very well (his English, for instance, may be limited). It is up to the receptionist to

listen
- the caller must be given the chance to say what he wants to say
- the receptionist must not interrupt - it is considered rude - unless the caller is beginning to ramble away from the point

respond
- the receptionist may insert encouraging phrases into conversation, e.g. *'I see'* ... *'I understand'* ... *'Yes'* or even *'Mmm.'*
- the receptionist may ask questions if they will help, e.g. *'Is it Mr Hopkins you want to see?'*

confirm
- the gist of the message should be confirmed by the receptionist, e.g. *'So, you would like to see Mr Hopkins. I will telephone and see if he is available.'*

non-verbal communication - body language

If you receive a caller you must be able to interpret his or her mood and intention from expressions, gestures and posture. These collectively are known as *body language*, a means of communication you can see clearly in animal behaviour (wagging tail, tail between the legs, and so on!) Human beings have their own versions of these body signals.

A person receiving a caller will

- *interpret* the body language of the caller - is it an enquiry? a complaint? a routine call?
- *respond* to the caller by using body language - encouraging, questioning, confirming

Body language involves a combination of complex signals. How would you intrepret the following?

- *facial expressions* - smiles, frowns, clenching teeth, raised eyebrows, narrowing eyes,
- *gestures* - use of the hands, nodding and shaking the head, tapping feet, shrugging shoulders
- *posture* - standing stiffly upright with arms crossed, sitting hunched up, sitting sprawled out

When you receive a caller you should instinctively use body langauge to make the person feel at ease:

- nod your head periodically in encouragement and agreement
- relax if you consider the caller is tense or nervous - your calm will 'rub off' on the other person
- look the caller in the eye when you are speaking or listening, but do not overdo it - it will make them feel nervous!

Later in this Unit we will explain how to deal with a difficult or aggressive caller, a situation which calls for the exercise of all your communicating skills.

directing and escorting callers

When you have identified the needs of your caller you will either be able to deal with the matter yourself, or you may have to refer the caller to someone elsewhere on the premises. For example, the caller may have an appointment with one of your managers, or they may have called to sort out a jammed photocopier. Your action - to direct them or to arrange for an escort - will depend on the type and size of organisation for which you work. What procedure would you adopt in the case of

- a bank (where security is of paramount importance)?
- a car showroom (which is open-plan)?
- a large manufacturing company (which has a well-equipped reception area)?
- a small one-man business who employs a part-time receptionist/typist/accounts clerk/tea-maker (who has no reception area, but greets visitors through a sliding glass panel)?

Clearly there is no set procedure. The following factors, however, should be borne in mind

the security risks - escorting the caller

The bank mentioned above will be very security conscious, as large sums of cash are readily to hand for unescorted visitors to the premises! Other organisations also have need for security:

- organisations holding sensitive material on computer file
- research establishments and organisations developing new products
- Government establishments (e.g Ministry of Defence)

What are the security procedures the receptionist employs?

- the visitor's identity must be established
- the visitor should sign the caller's book (see the illustration on page 50)
- the visitor should be provided with an identification tag (usually a lapel badge) if required
- the visitor should be escorted to the correct location by a person other than the receptionist, e.g. a messenger (security guard), a secretary, an assistant receptionist, or even by the person the caller is visiting
- the escort should be told clearly where the visitor is to be taken and the person they are to see

Note that the receptionist *never* leaves his or her desk unattended - that would be a flagrant breach of security. The receptionist should be familiar with the security regulations for the premises: which areas are restricted, which areas should be locked, how to raise the alarm if an unauthorised person gains access, what to do when faced with an armed raider.

directing the caller

There will be situations where the caller does not need an escort:

- there is no security risk on the premises
- the caller knows and is known by the organisation (e.g. the photocopier engineer)

If the caller *is* familiar with the organisation, all that is required is a telephone call from the receptionist to the person or office the caller is visiting. The caller will then proceed alone.

If the caller *is not* familiar with the premises, the receptionist should give clear instructions on how to get to the required location:

- the directions should be given clearly and at a pace which the caller can manage
- the receptionist should ask if the message is understood
- the caller (preferably) should then repeat the directions briefly
- the receptionist should ensure that the caller knows the name of the person and department for which he or she is heading
- the receptionist should telephone the person the caller is visiting to say that the caller is on the way

problems with callers - delays and complaints

Things never do run smoothly, and inevitably a person receiving a caller will encounter problems:

- the person the caller is visiting is delayed, and the caller has to wait
- the person the caller is visiting is unavailable, and there is no chance that the caller can see them
- the caller is difficult or aggressive, or both, and will not take 'no' for an answer

These problems call for the use of all the tact and communication skills that the receptionist can muster. We will deal with each of these problems in turn.

delays

Given the complexity of the working day it is inevitable that appointments may run late. A caller with an appointment will expect you to run to time, and if you are dealing with the caller and a delay occurs, you have a number of responsibilities:

apologise	You are in the wrong if you delay a caller, and must admit the fact
	'I am sorry, Mr Drew.'
explain	There is nothing more irritating to a caller than not knowing the cause of a delay
	'I am sorry, Mr Drew, but Mr Hopkins has been delayed in a meeting.'
estimate the delay	The caller will appreciate an estimate of how long the wait will be
	'Mr Hopkins should be with you in ten minutes.'
make the caller comfortable	The caller should be made as comfortable as the reception area permits
	'Would you like to take a seat, Mr Drew? Would you like a coffee?'
update the caller	The caller, who may have a busy schedule ahead, will appreciate being updated after a period of time if the delay is extended
	'I am sorry to keep you waiting, Mr Drew, I have telephoned Mr Hopkins, and he will be with you in five minutes.'

unavailability

There will also be awkward occasions when the person whom the caller has arrived to see is not available. The person may have been called away elsewhere, may have been taken ill, or may even be at an extended lunch! It is your responsibility

- to explain the unavailability tactfully and politely to the caller
- to try to arrange a further appointment, or an appointment with someone else in the office

> *'I am sorry, but Mr Hopkins has been called away to another office, and we were unable to contact you in time. Would you like to make another appointment, or would you like to see his colleague, Miss Maddocks? I am sure she will be pleased to help you.'*

Avoid, at all costs, saying things like 'I am sorry, but Mr Hopkins is still having his lunch' or, as someone once told the author 'I am sorry you can't speak to Mr M............; he is in the toilet.' As an employee you have a loyalty to your staff and organisation; this involves using tact and discretion!

difficult and aggressive callers

You will from time-to-time encounter callers who are difficult, rude or aggressive, or all of these. Some individuals feel thay have a mission in life to be as unpleasant as possible, and it is occasionally your bad luck to have to deal with them. Nevertheless you should be prepared.

The situations you may encounter include

- a caller who has been kept waiting because appointments are running behind time
- a caller who finds that the person he is due to see is unavailable
- a caller who refuses to leave because he cannot get what he wants (usually an appointment)
- a caller with a complaint about your product or service

How should you deal with these situations?

listen
You should let the angry person explain the problem, however rude and aggressive they are in the process. By venting their anger and frustration they will start to get the problem out of their system. You should use all your skills of body language to listen and sympathise.

be detached
Do not get drawn into the argument, otherwise a 'slanging match' will result which gets nobody anywhere, least of all your organisation

assess the situation
Can you deal with the situation yourself, or does the situation require the caller speaking to a colleague? Can you make an appointment for a caller who calls unannounced? Can you offer the caller an alternative solution? For instance, if the caller wishes to see the Managing Director with a complaint, will the Sales Manager be able to help? If the caller is abusive, will you need to get help?

take action
Be decisive.

If you can deal with the problem yourself, do so calmly and efficiently; if the person has to be kept waiting, ensure that he or she is looked after - given coffee, made comfortable, and updated with the situation.

If you need to pass the person to a colleague (a complaint, or a rapidly arranged appointment), ensure that the colleague is adequately briefed about the situation.

If the person cannot be dealt with immediately, becomes abusive and refuses to leave, you may need to obtain assistance from a security guard or a large colleague to persuade the caller to leave. On no account should violence be used!

Remember that there may be other callers in the reception area witnessing the incident, and assessing the way *you* are dealing with the situation.

armed raiders

The most difficult callers you will receive are criminals raiding your premises. If you work in a bank or building society you will be well briefed about how to deal with individuals carrying firearms and wearing black stockings over their heads. The golden rule is to cooperate and *not to put yourself at risk*. It may be that an alarm system will be activated and video cameras will record the incident for the benefit of the police, but it is in your interests to stay alive, so do exactly what the raider asks you to do, quietly and efficiently. Remember that the raider will be as nervous as you are, and may react with violence if you try to be clever. Hopefully it will never happen.

confidentiality

Confidentiality is the duty of the employee to ensure that certain information about the organisation and its dealings with others is not 'leaked' to the outside world. This information includes:

- details about your staff - their activities, pay, private life
- financial details - your banking arrangements, payroll details, sales figures
- details about customers with whom you deal, particularly their ability to pay!
- security arrangements for your premises - when they are locked, who looks after them, and when

If you receive callers you may be approached with enquiries which *seem* innocent, but may be an invitation to breach your duty of confidentiality. For example:

- an investigative journalist asking if a certain person works with you
- a fraudster asking what your bank account number is
- a competitor asking for deatils of a product which you are developing
- a debt collector asking whether one of your customers has paid up recently
- a thief posing as a detective asking about the security arrangements of your building

You should also remember your duty of loyalty to your colleagues and organisation, and avoid 'letting the side down' by revealing details which would reflect badly. For instance

NOT   *'I am sorry Mr Hopkins is not in today. He's off sick again - it's a real pain.'*
but . . . *'I am afraid Mr Hopkins is not available. Can I make an appointment for another day?'*

NOT   *'Mr Hopkins is not here; he's at a leaving party and so he's probably had one or two drinks, and may be held up.'*
but . . . *'I am sorry Mr Hopkins is not available at the moment; would you like to wait?'*

NOT   *'I am sorry Mary didn't call you back. She's new here and makes a lot of mistakes.'*
but . . . *'I am sorry nobody called you back. Can I get someone to help you now?'*

✓ action points - liaising with callers

- ○ make a good impression by presenting yourself as being smart and efficient

- ○ ensure the reception area is tidy, well-equipped and welcoming

- ○ greet the caller politely, using their name as early as possible

- ○ when receiving a caller, identify their needs: find out whether they have an appointment or not, or whether they need one - escort or direct them to their destination as required

- ○ respect the security of the building

- ○ be aware of your caller's body language - and your own

- ○ if there is a problem, remain calm, assess the problem and take the necessary action

- ○ do not get drawn into an argument, even if you know that the caller is in the wrong!

- ○ remember your duty of confidentiality to your organisation and your colleagues

student activities - liaising with callers

Performance criteria

The student activities in this section test competences in the following areas:

- *greeting all callers promptly and politely, and identifying their needs*
- *giving callers disclosable information only*
- *directing or escorting callers to the correct destination*
- *explaining politely the reasons for any delay or non-availability of assistance*
- *identifying situations outside your job's area of responsibility and asking for assistance promptly*

1. What advice about personal presentation would you give to a colleague who is new to the task of receiving callers?

2. What facilities would you expect to see
    (a) on a receptionist's desk?
    (b) in a reception area?

3. What would be your response if a caller approached you when you were sitting at a reception desk?

4. What would be your response if a caller approached you when you were speaking on the telephone at a reception desk?

5. What is body language? What body language would be used by
    (a) an aggressive caller?
    (b) a nervous caller?
    (c) a receptionist dealing with these two callers?

6. How would you deal with a customer who calls with a complaint, but without an appointment?

7. How would you deal with a customer who calls with an appointment, but you find that the person they have come to see is
    (a) going to be delayed for half-an-hour at a meeting with the Managing Director
    (b) unavailable because they have gone to the hospital to see a member of the family

8. How would you deal with a caller who demands to see the Managing Director and is not satisfied with your explanation that he is at an important meeting for the next hour. The caller will not leave, and threatens that he will interrupt the meeting?

9. Choose an office or building with which you are familiar. Write down the directions to a specific room in the building
    (a) as you would explain them (i.e. your actual words) to a caller
    (b) in the form of a sketch plan which you could give to the caller
    If possible try out these directions on another person, and ask for their comments on how clear they are.

10. State what you think is is wrong with the following, and say how you could do better:

    'I am sorry Mr . . . er . . . , sorry, I didn't catch your name. So you want to see Mr Halifax. Not a chance, I'm afraid; he's far too busy. There's been a lot of trouble over one of our customers - Mintern Electronics - they're going bust, and it could be big trouble for us - they owe us a packet. Mike - that is Mr Halifax - is with them now. Would you like to come back tomorrow? I am sorry, there is no need to look at me like that, it's not my fault!'

11.   Log Book Exercise

For students who already work in an organisation, or for students who are given work placements, a useful exercise is to keep a 'log book' of callers to the organisation. It is suggested that you record at least twenty callers, both routine and non-routine callers, using the format set out below as a model.   If you do not actually work on the reception area yourself you could examine the organisation's caller's book and *with permission* use that as a basis for your own log book (you might, for example, change the names).

Note: if the format below is different from your caller's book, use your own format.

date	caller & organisation	reason for visit	time	seen by	action taken
199- Jan 27	L Jones Wyvern Foods	enquiry	09.00	R Snell (Sales)	
	C Smith Electra Alarms	sales visit	09.35	J Small (Admin)	will send brochure to Admin Dept

 linking assignment

Common Skills Assignment 4
Communicating: getting the message across, pages 100 to 104

4 Communicating - the telephone

NCVQ coverage

2.1 process incoming and outgoing business telephone calls

Performance criteria:

- *answering calls promptly and clearly, using the approved organisation manner*
- *identifying callers correctly and establishing their requirements accurately*
- *answering callers politely and/or transfering the call to an appropriate authority if necessary*
- *giving only disclosable information to callers*
- *obtaining external numbers correctly and establishing contact*
- *conveying clearly the purpose of outgoing calls*
- *identifying faults and reporting them promptly to an appropriate authority*

introduction

You will from time-to-time receive and make telephone calls from an extension line, or you may even operate a switchboard. Telephones may seem intimidating if you are inexperienced, but practice will enable you to develop confidence and competence.

In this unit we will look at the practicalities of

- dealing with routine incoming calls - answering and transfering
- dealing with difficult calls - wrong numbers, disconnected calls, angry or suspicious callers
- making outgoing calls
- dealing with answerphones
- dealing with faulty phones

---

 linking assignment

Common Skills Assignment 4
Communicating: getting the message across, pages 100 to 104

incoming calls

the switchboard

Most organisations use a telephone switchboard. If you operate a switchboard you are in a critically important position because you represent the organisation. Your telephone skills and manner reflect the competence and attitude of the organisation to the outside world - if you get out of bed on the wrong side, it should not show! To be competent in this area you should be familiar with the following:

know how the switchboard works

This may sound an obvious point, but it can be overlooked and will give a poor impression of your organisation if you delay or lose calls. Make sure you receive proper training and know where the reference manual is kept.

be safety minded and prepared for emergencies

Make sure the telephone is set up safely and in the manner recommended in the manual - avoid trailing leads and loose connections. Ensure that you have the numbers to call in case of emergencies in the office, personal injuries, fire or break-in or raid (you may work in a bank or building society).

dealing with incoming calls

Whether you deal with incoming calls at a single telephone handset or at a switchboard, the same basic skills are required:

answer calls promptly in a standard way

Always use the standard answering format, for example

'Midshires Electronics, good morning, may I help you?'

Speak naturally and pleasantly, without overdoing it. An over-enthusiastic 'parrot-like' response can irritate a caller beyond belief.

Do not keep the caller waiting before you answer ; waiting on the end of an unanswered line can be very annoying for a busy customer.

identify the caller and the caller's requirements

Establish the name of the caller, the organisation for which he or she works (if any) and the nature of the enquiry. If you are not sure of the names quoted, ask the caller politely to repeat them or to spell them. If you can deal with the enquiry yourself, e.g a request for your fax number, do so ; if you cannot deal with the enquiry, either
• take a message (see below), or
• transfer the call (see below)

know your organisation

Keep an up-to-date list of names, job titles and extension numbers by the telephone. *Know* your organisation. The list will be invaluable if someone else has to fill in or 'temp' for you. Be familiar with your organisation's products or services - have a catalogue or publicity material to hand.

keep a message pad and pencil to hand

Make sure that you are able to take a message if the person the caller wishes to contact is unavailable. Some organisations use preprinted pads for messages (see illustration on page 66).

transferring calls

If you transfer the call to an extension it is essential to communicate to the caller that you are dealing with the call, using phrases such as

'Trying to connect you, Mr Clarke'
'Sorry to keep you waiting.'
'Putting you through now.'

Before the transfer is made, make sure that you have established
• the name of the caller
• the caller's organisation
• the nature of the call
If the person the caller wishes to contact is not available you should give the caller the option of holding the line or calling back:

'I am sorry, the line is engaged. Would you like to hold, or call back later?'

Some switchboards play music to a call 'on hold' in order to make the caller feel relaxed. The important factor is to make sure that the caller is made to feel that *something* is happening.

If the person the caller wishes to contact is *definitely* not available (he may have gone out), you should give the caller a choice of options:

'I am sorry Mr Ramsay is not available, can anyone else help, or can I take a message?'

wrong numbers and misdirected calls

Problems can occur if callers accidentally dial the wrong number, the telephone system wrongly routes a call to you, or the caller has the wrong number. In all of these cases you will probably have to deal with an embarrassed or exasperated caller. The situation calls for tact and courtesy:

'I think you have the wrong number. This is Midshires Electronics 0605 - 152426.'

If you know the correct number, or if you can help the caller find it, you will give a good impression of your organisation.

problems with angry callers and disconnected callers

If your caller is obviously angry and upset and has a complaint or problem, keep calm yourself and do not be tempted to join in a slanging match. Stay cool. If you can deal with the problem yourself, do so; if you have to transfer the call, be courteous and prompt. The sound of a helpful and soothing voice may well calm the caller.

If a caller is somehow disconnected (it happens!), wait for him to call back, then apologise (*'I am sorry, we seem to have been cut off.'*) Do not ring back yourself - it will result in further delay as you both try and contact each other on engaged lines!

disclosable information

You may receive calls which attempt to obtain confidential information from your organisation. These calls may be from competitors seeking restricted information about your products; they may even be from people trying to perpetrate a fraud. You should be very clear what constitutes 'restricted information.' For example:

- details about your staff
- your banking arrangements or credit card merchant information
- details about customers with whom you deal
- security arrangements relating to your premises

If you receive calls of this nature, try and obtain details of the caller, and pass the information to your supervisor without delay.

receiving internal calls

Internal telephone calls between extensions are very common; they normally have a different ringing pattern from external calls - you should learn to distinguish an internal call from an external call.

You should answer calls by naming your department and yourself:

'Accounts, Parry speaking.'

✓ action points - incoming telephone calls

○ know your telephone system

○ make sure the telephone is set up safely - no trailing wires

○ know the emergency numbers

○ have a message pad and pencil to hand

○ know the organisation - have a list of the names, positions and extensions

○ answer incoming calls promptly

○ greet the caller politely and pleasantly with the organisation's standard greeting

○ identify the caller, the organisation and the purpose of the call

○ deal with the matter promptly, or transfer the call, or take a message

○ do not keep the caller waiting

○ do not get drawn into arguments or disputes - stay calm - remember the customer is always right (even if he or she is obviously wrong!)

outgoing calls

If you are making outgoing calls you will normally do so from an extension by dialling a numeric code before the required telephone number. In some circumstances the switchboard operator will obtain an outside number for an internal caller on an extension. It is useful to have a list of frequently used numbers by the telephone and essential to have an up-to-date telephone directory to hand.

As we have covered the basics of telephone technique in the previous section, we list below a number of Action Points which you should bear in mind when making outgoing calls.

✔ action points - outgoing telephone calls

O   make sure you have the correct number and code - do not ring the fax number by mistake

O   have all the relevant information to hand, e.g. a letter, an invoice you are querying, the correct file, sales information, and so on

O   make sure you have the correct name of the person to whom you wish to speak

O   have paper and pencil to hand to make notes

O   when connected, identify yourself and your organisation

O   be brief and courteous

O   record on paper relevant outcomes: information gained, contacts made

O   ensure that any follow-up is acted upon, e.g. written confirmation of the conversation, correction of mistakes, a note in the diary for follow-up calls

O   ring off when you have finished - discussing the weather costs your organisation money

O   make sure you know the charge rates for the different times of the day - use the cheapest period (normally the afternoon) for calls *if they are not urgent*

O   if you are disconnected, ring back

answerphones

An answerphone is a machine which automatically answers calls when the telephone is left unattended. It plays a taped message to the caller and will enable the caller to record a message which can be played back when the owner of the answerphone returns.

It is a commonly accepted fact that nobody likes answerphones: speaking to a machine understandably makes people feel uncomfortable. Answerphones are nevertheless an essential means of communication, especially for the competitive small business which cannot afford (and does not need) a permanent telephone operator.

Only use an answerphone if you have to. Do not switch it on just because you want a break (as in the illustration on the next page): you are not likely to impress the caller, in fact you are likely to make the caller rather cross.

'Do not switch on your answerphone just because you feel like a break - you are not likely to impress the caller.'

outgoing messages: setting up the answerphone

If you are setting up an answerphone in your office you should record a short but helpful message. For example:

'This is John Eliot of Midshires Electronics. I am sorry there is no-one available to come to the telephone. If you would like me to call you back, please leave your name, organisation and telephone number, after the tones. Thank you.'

If you leave a general message of this type on the answerphone you will be able to go to lunch or concentrate on an important meeting without having to answer the telephone in person. If you have a fax (facsimile transmission machine) you could incorporate the fax number in your message and invite the caller to send you a fax.

dealing with the answerphone on your return

It is essential on your return
• to listen to the messages
• to write down the messages (you may have to listen more than once)
• to act upon the messages
It gives a very poor impression of an organisation to a caller if an answerphone message is not responded to.

leaving a message on the answerphone

If you make a call which is answered by an answerphone, follow the instructions given in the message on the machine. This will normally involve you giving your name, organisation and telephone number. Be brief and speak up - some machines do not record very well. If you suffer from answerphone 'stage fright,' i.e. being tongue-tied, try and picture a person at the other end rather than a cassette tape, and direct your message to that imaginary person.

faulty phones

Faults can occur both in your telephone equipment, and also in the line. These faults include:

• not being able to dial out
• noise on the line
• getting the unobtainable signal (constant tone)

You should

• test first for simple faults (your manual may include a 'troubleshooting' section)
• advise your supervisor of any problems you cannot deal with
• have to hand the contact name and number for the supplier of the equipment
• know the directory number for a faulty line (151 for British Telecom)

If your own telephone is faulty you will have to make contact on another line. If you have a fax with a telephone handset, use it.

student activities - the telephone

Performance criteria

The student activities in this section test competences in the following areas:

- *answering calls promptly and clearly, using the approved organisation manner*
- *identifying callers correctly and establishing their requirements accurately*
- *answering callers politely and/or transferring the call to an appropriate authority if necessary*
- *giving only disclosable information to callers*
- *obtaining external numbers correctly and establishing contact*
- *conveying clearly the purpose of outgoing calls*
- *identifying faults and reporting them promptly to an appropriate authority*

1.   Obtain a local telephone directory and code book (if the codes are not incorporated in the directory). What numbers would you ring for
   (a) directory enquiries
   (b) the emergency services
   (c) the operator
   (d) reporting faults on the line
   (e) your organisation's bank
   (f) the nearest rail information service
   (g) the Post Office's Datapost service
   (h) road travel information

2.   What actions would you take if the telephone line went dead?

3.   Write down the standard greeting that would be used by you if you received a call at work.

4.   Draw up a table showing the times for peak, standard and cheap rate telephone calls.

5.   What areas of information would you treat as confidential when answering the telephone in your organisation?

6.   You work as a switchboard operator for a D-I-Y firm, Supatools. Write down what questions you would ask and how you would deal with a customer (Mr Colin Plane) who had bought some faulty equipment from you and telephoned as follows:

   'Hello there. It took you enough time to answer didn't it? Don't you people know I have got better things to do with my time? Well, I've bought this drill, and it must be the third thing I have bought from you which doesn't work. I don't know what British workmanship is coming to. I want to speak to your managing director. NOW!'

   Your Managing Director is on holiday.

7.   You work in a small business, Malvern Windows (tel 0684 729816, fax 0684 729801), and have just purchased a fax and answerphone to improve your image, as you spend a lot of time out of the office. Write down the text of a message which you could leave on the answerphone to cover the occasions when the office is unattended. (Use your own name).

   Optional task: record the message on a real answerphone or cassette recorder and ask your assessor to assess your message.

8. **Telephone Practice: simulated exercise**
   Wyvern (Office Products) Ltd is a family firm selling office supplies. The structure of the company is set out below. The catalogue and price list of its products are to be found in Appendix 2 in this book.

Wyvern (Office Products) Limited

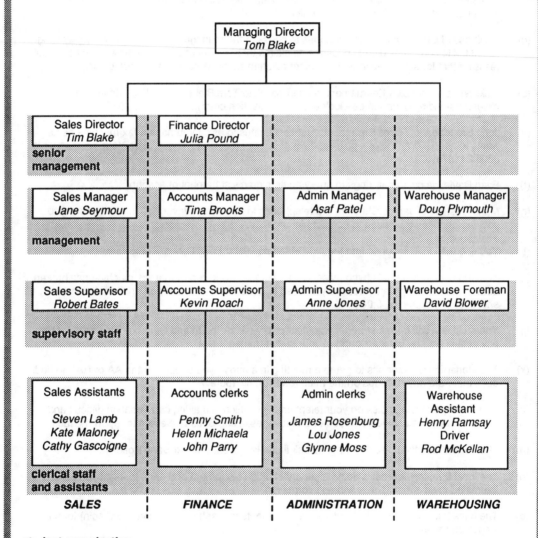

	Managing Director *Tom Blake*		
senior management	Sales Director *Tim Blake*	Finance Director *Julia Pound*	
management	Sales Manager *Jane Seymour*	Accounts Manager *Tina Brooks*	Admin Manager *Asaf Patel*	Warehouse Manager *Doug Plymouth*
supervisory staff	Sales Supervisor *Robert Bates*	Accounts Supervisor *Kevin Roach*	Admin Supervisor *Anne Jones*	Warehouse Foreman *David Blower*
clerical staff and assistants	Sales Assistants *Steven Lamb Kate Maloney Cathy Gascoigne*	Accounts clerks *Penny Smith Helen Michaela John Parry*	Admin clerks *James Rosenburg Lou Jones Glynne Moss*	Warehouse Assistant *Henry Ramsay* Driver *Rod McKellan*
	SALES	*FINANCE*	*ADMINISTRATION*	*WAREHOUSING*

student organisation
   Divide into pairs.

   - *one student will be the outside organisation or individual*
   - *the second student will be Wyvern (Office Supplies) Ltd (the telephone operator in the first instance and also the required individual within the organisation)*

   After the calls have been made, the roles should be reversed, and the calls repeated.

practical suggestions
   The best scenario would be for two internal extension lines within an organisation to be used; alternatively two 'mock up' telephones could be used.

situations

(a)   Henry Young of Plaster Mouldings Ltd telephones to enquire the cost of fax rolls.

(b)   David Rich, Managing Director of David Rich Marketing, telephones to enquire about black leather executive swivel chairs for his office.

(c)   Ian Cross of Cross Wires Ltd telephones to speak to the Managing Director about a faulty filing cabinet. He complains bitterly because he claims that he cannot open two drawers at once (not realising that for safety reasons the cabinet mechanism prevents you from doing this.)

(d)   Vicki White of Manplus Recruitment rings to speak to Tom Blake, Sales Department (a misunderstanding over names - look at the organisation chart).

(e)   John Broadbent of Harris Broadbent, Architects, rings to ask if you have a fax machine as he wants to send a drawing of a proposed warehouse extension to Tom Blake. Your fax number is 0605 241879.

(f)   Evan Davies, a customer, rings to query an item on his statement of account.

(g)   Mario Castello of James Cheshire Ltd telephones to ask if their driver has made a delivery to your warehouse; they need to contact him urgently.

(h)   You ring the local station to find the time of the earliest train to London tomorrow.

(i)   You ring Northern Rentals (who lease you a photocopier) to report that the machine has broken down. You are desperate because you need to get some financial reports (25 copies of 10 sheets of A4) copied by 5.00 p.m.

(j)   You receive a call from a stranger who claims to work for the Inland Revenue. He asks for the pay details (salary, bank account) of your senior management.

(k)   The Managing Director has to get to a meeting in a hurry: you telephone the AA or RAC to find out if there are any hold-ups on the main roads on his route.

(l)   You are experiencing noise on your telephone line which is making conversation difficult and prevents the fax machine from receiving messages. Ring British Telecom to report the fault.

(m)   Mrs Porter, the office cleaner, rings to ask if she is to work on next Bank Holiday.

(n)   The local Evening Journal is doing a survey of office equipment and rings to ask if you are interested in advertising or providing information.

(o)   The bank telephones to ask about your requirements for cash (i.e. the notes and coin) for the wages on Friday.

 linking assignment

Common Skills Assignment 4
Communicating: getting the message across, pages 100 to 104

5 Communicating - oral and written messages

NCVQ coverage
2.2 receive and relay oral and written messages
Performance criteria
- *obtaining relevant information courteously from callers*
- *verifying relevant information with callers*
- *passing on messages to the appropriate person or location*
- *communicating all relevant information accurately*

introduction

If you work in an organisation you may be in a position of having to take a message from an *external* caller - over the telephone or face-to-face, or from an *internal* caller - someone from another department or area of work. You will find yourself in the middle of a communication line and therefore need to develop the skills of listening, interpreting and explaining information. You will need to develop accuracy - to ensure that you have got the correct message and are able to pass it on in an intelligible way.

 linking assignment

Common Skills Assignment 4
Communicating: getting the message across, pages 100 to 104

why are messages important?

If a customer telephones you - or calls personally - and finds that the person to whom they wish to speak is not available, you should take a message to that person, the *recipient*. This message can be

* in *written* form (normally on a pre-printed pad), so that it can be handed to the recipient
* in *oral* form, in other words you can tell the person by word of mouth

It is crucial that the message should be

* clear and accurate
* communicated without delay to the recipient
* acted upon immediately by the recipient

If this does not take place - if the message is lost or forgotten - then communication has broken down and the organisation is seen to be inefficient.

oral messages

Oral communication can involve:

* communicating with someone when you meet them face-to-face, e.g. at an enquiry counter
* speaking to someone on the telephone

Different communication skills should be developed for these two situations, as can be seen from the Action Points set out on the following pages.

 action points - listening to someone face-to-face

○   listen, and *look* as if you are listening

○   relax and look at the speaker

○   take note of body language (gestures and facial expressions) and react - smile, nod, etc.

○   do not interrupt, unless the speaker is rambling away from the point

○   concentrate on the key points of the message

○   write down important details - the person's name, the organisation, telephone number, the details relating to the message

○   when you speak to the person, use his or her name

○   if you don't understand, or if you need further details, ask the caller politely to repeat or explain

✔ action points - giving a message face-to-face

○ think of what you have to say before you say it

○ have to hand any relevant written material such as letters, files and figures

○ speak clearly and precisely - do not rush

○ be pleasant and polite

○ ensure that the message has got through by asking relevant questions:

   'Are you happy with that?'

   'Do you want me to repeat any of that?'

○ after you have given the message, make a note of any follow-up actions - do you need to tell anyone else? - do you need to raise any paperwork?

telephone messages

We have explained the skills needed for communicating over the telephone in the previous Unit, and you should have practised these skills in the exercises on pages 58 to 60.

The Action Points listed below relate specifically to
• *taking* a message over the telephone
• *understanding* that message so that you can tell another person or pass on its meaning in writing
• *giving* a message over the telephone, either to an individual or to an answerphone
• ensuring that the message is *understood*

✔ action points - taking a telephone message

○ listen carefully - if you cannot hear what is being said, ask the caller politely to speak up

○ have a pad and pencil to hand to write down the essential points and details

○ some people gabble away on the telephone - if you do not hear or grasp details, ask them politely to slow down and repeat those details

○ repeat all important details at the end of the conversation to ensure that you have 'got the message'

○ query any unusual spellings by spelling out the words

○ remember that the caller will respect you for checking the details - it is a a sign of efficiency rather than incompetence

✔ action points - giving a message over the telephone

○ think of what you have to say before you say it - write points down if necessary

○ have all the relevant information to hand - e.g. files, catalogues - before you telephone

○ speak clearly and distinctly

○ if you give long numbers (e.g. telephone numbers) over the telephone read them slowly and in groups of two or three digits; the recipient will then normally repeat them

○ take care over similar sounding letters; letters that are often confused are

F & S,   M & N,   D & T,   B & P

If you are spelling a word involving these letters or any letter which you think may be unclear, use words from the telephonist's alphabet to illustrate them. The telephonist's alphabet (see below) provides a word for each letter.   If, for instance, you are spelling 'FAME' say

'F for Frederick - A for Alfred - M for Mary - E for Edward'

○ if you are answered by an answerphone, speak clearly, speak up, and be brief - always follow the instructions given in the recorded message

the telephonist's alphabet			
A	Alfred	N	Nellie
B	Benjamin	O	Oliver
C	Charlie	P	Peter
D	David	Q	Queen
E	Edward	R	Robert
F	Frederick	S	Samuel
G	George	T	Tommy
H	Harry	U	Uncle
I	Isaac	V	Victor
J	Jack	W	William
K	King	X	X-ray
L	London	Y	Yellow
M	Mary	Z	Zebra

written messages

Notes and written messages are frequently used as a means of communication within an organisation

- for passing on information received as a result of a personal visit or telephone call by an outsider
- for passing on information *within* the organisation

printed message forms

Most organisations have message forms in pads. These are either specially printed with the organisation's name or may be obtained pre-printed from commercial stationers. An example of a pre-printed message form (together with a message) is illustrated on the next page.

Note the following details on the form:

- the time that the message was taken - a very important factor
- the name of the person who took the message
- the details of the person to whom the message is to be given
- full details of the caller, and most importantly, the telephone number
- boxes which can be ticked according to the situation - these act as a useful checklist for the person taking the call
- a space for the message itself

The form can either be typed or handwritten. If it is typed, it should not be delayed in the process. If it is handwritten, it should be clear and legible.

✓ action points - taking and passing on written messages

O   tick all the appropriate boxes on the pre-printed message pad

O   check (with the caller if necessary) that all the details are correct, *especially* the telephone number

O   think about the actual message before you write it down - write it down in rough first if you prefer

O   write the message clearly and legibly, or type it if you prefer - be brief

O   check the message by reading it through as if you were the recipient - does it make sense, and is the action to be taken made clear?

O   get the message to the recipient as quickly as possible, either by taking it yourself or using your office distribution system

O   ensure that the message is placed prominently on the recipient's desk - not in the 'out' tray or under his sandwiches

O   remember that communication has only taken place when the message is *read, understood and acted upon*

MESSAGE

while you were out

date...12/12/ 199–.. time......12.30.........taken by.........Kate Maloney.........

to..........Tim Blake........

from............Helen White.........of....Warwick China Promotions...

phone..............(0232) 976015.........

☐ telephoned   ☑ please telephone

☑ returned your call   ☐ wants to see you

☐ will telephone again   ☑ **URGENT**

☐ called in person

message

Helen has got the quotation for the mugs
for the exhibition, and wants to discuss
quantity discounts — as soon as possible.

situation

*Helen White, who works for Warwick China Promotions, is returning Tim Blake's call.
She works for a company which produces special promotional china mugs. Wyvern (Office
Products) Ltd is soon to take a stand at a trade exhibition and hopes to have some mugs
made with the Wyvern name printed on them. Tim Blake is trying to obtain a discounted
price for the mugs. Helen White has telephoned while Tim Blake is out at lunch and Kate
Maloney has taken a message for him and placed it on his desk.*

internal written notes

Informal handwritten or typed notes can often save time and speed up communication.

Penny

5.12.199- 12.45

Have had to go out unexpectedly on a customer visit. Not back until tomorrow. Please

1. *Ensure cheques are banked by 3.30*
2. *Post off the monthly statements by First Class - they are late!*
3. *Sign my letters - they are already in for typing*

Any problems - refer to Mrs Brooks. Thanks.

Kevin

situation

Kevin, an Accounts Supervisor, has had to go out, and is entrusting supervisory duties to his Accounts Assistant, Penny. She has jotted down the details on a sheet of paper.

Note the following:

- the note is brief but clear
- the note is informal - first names are used and the simple 'thanks'
- the time and date are stated - to prevent any confusion should the note reappear at a *later* date
- the note is signed
- a point of contact is given in case of difficulties - very important if the writer of the note is leaving the office and entrusting responsibility to a junior

student activities - oral and written messages

Performance criteria

The student activities in this section test competences in the following areas:

- *obtaining relevant information courteously from callers*
- *verifying relevant information with callers*
- *passing on messages to the appropriate person or location*
- *communicating all relevant information accurately*

The situation in these activities is based on the office equipment wholesalers, Wyvern (Office Products) Limited. The structure of the organisation is set out below; the catalogue and price list are printed in Appendix 2 at the back of this book.

Wyvern (Office Products) Limited

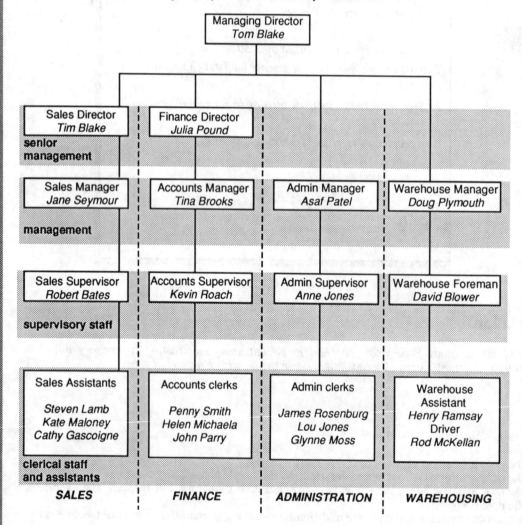

For a number of these activities you will need an internal telephone system and an answerphone. If you do not have access to the telephones, arrange a 'mock up' system; if you do not have an answerphone, use a cassette recorder. You can either draw up your own message forms, or you can obtain pre-printed forms from commercial stationers.

outside visitors - oral messages

1. Required: two students and an assessor. The students play the roles of the receptionist and the visitor; it is recommended that they change roles for (a) and (b). The assessor will receive the verbal message.

(a) Alan Perkins of Perkins Recruitment (Tel 0605 722731) calls at 10.30 a.m. to see Mrs Brooks, as he has an accounts clerk Mario Paluzzi, aged 22, part AAT qualified, whom he thinks she may wish to take on. Mrs Brooks is out on a visit. The receptionist is to pass on the message personally to her at 2.00 p.m.

(b) Mandy Bold of Bold Properties (Tel 0605 210723) calls at 11.00 a.m. with a batch (144) of faulty ball point pens (Catalogue number W1030). She has had a number of problems with your firm recently (late deliveries, wrong deliveries) and wants to make a strong complaint. No-one is available, but the receptionist promises to raise the matter personally with Jane Seymour in the afternoon.

outside visitors - written messages

2. Required: two students and an assessor. The students play the roles of the receptionist and the visitor; it is recommended that they change roles for (a) and (b). The receptionist in both cases has to prepare a written message as a result of the interview. The assessor will receive the written message.

(a) Derek Norbury of Norbury Training (Tel 0605 891706) calls at 11.45 a.m. wanting to open an account with you (i.e. buying goods and paying later). He wants to discuss details of your products and delivery times. There is no-one senior in Sales to answer the query, so you write a message to Jane Seymour.

(b) Fred Luckless, a driver from Martley Transport Hire (Tel 0816 824691), calls at 12.30 to collect ten parcels which are being returned by Wyvern (Office Products) Limited to one of its suppliers. You telephone the warehouse, but the warehouseman is out at lunch and no-one knows about the collection. The driver goes away complaining, but saying that he will be in the area tomorrow.

telephone enquiries - written messages

3. Required: two students and an assessor. The students play the roles of the caller and the switchboard operator; it is recommended that they change roles for (a) and (b). The assessor will receive the written message.

(a) Olga Moziewicz of Schwartz Holdings plc (Tel. 0605 629173 extension 4675) telephones at 12.45 to query her statement (account 639). An invoice (no. 107916 for £126.93) appears on the statement but does not relate to any transaction with her company. She wants an explanation, but there is no-one in Accounts to help her.

(b) Henry Davies of Garden Enterprises (Tel 0605 729107) wants to order some chairs for his office. He needs to discuss specifications with Robert Bates from Sales. Robert Bates is out on a call, but will be back after 3.00 p.m.

telephone enquiries - oral messages

4.   Required: two students and an assessor. The students play the roles of the caller and the switchboard operator; it is recommended that they change roles for (a) and (b). The assessor will receive the oral message.

(a)   Mrs Porter, the office cleaner, telephones (Tel 0729 616859) at 2.15 p.m. to query her payslip - she cannot agree the hours of overtime worked. Mr Patel is interviewing a member of staff.

(b)   Rod McKellan, one of your drivers, has broken down and rings at 2.30 from a call box. He won't be able to deliver his goods to Garden Enterprises (tel. 0605 729107) until tomorrow. Doug Plymouth cannot be contacted because he is supervising a delivery.

answerphone enquiries - taking and leaving messages

5.   Each student listens to the following messages left on the Wyvern (Office Products) Limited answerphone. Each student should write down a message on a message pad to the appropriate person in the Wyvern organisation:

(a)   *'Hello, this is Jack Knott of Webbs Catering, telephone 0605 682534. Please can you send me a copy of invoice 1073, we've mislaid the original. Thanks. '*

(b)   *'Um - pause - this is Fellows Transport about a missing consignment..............'* (the line is cut off at this point).

6.   Each student, using an answerphone or cassette recorder should leave messages on the Wyvern (Office Products) Limited's answerphone as follows (invent names and other details):

(a)   You want a copy of the sales catalogue and price list.

(b)   You want to speak to Mr Patel urgently; you ask him to call back.

internal informal notes

7.   Each student should write the following notes:

(a)   Write a note from Doug Plymouth, Warehouse Manager, to David Blower, his foreman. Doug is going to be away in the afternoon from 2.00 p.m. He expects deliveries from Horsefall Supplies and Contex Computers; he is anxious that the delivery notes (the documents that come with the goods) should be signed and put in the correct file in his office. The notes are filed alphabetically in the name of the supplier. The goods coming in should be checked against the delivery note. He also wants the warehouse checked and locked at 5.30 p.m.

(b)   Write a note from Kevin Roach (Accounts) to Robert Bates (Sales) requesting details of any changes in addresses and telephone numbers of their customers, as he needs to update his accounts files (Sales Ledger). He needs the information within a week, because customer statements are then due to go out.

 ## linking assignment

Common Skills Assignment 4
Communicating: getting the message across, pages 100 to 104

6 Communicating - routine business communications

NCVQ coverage

2.4 draft routine business communications

Performance criteria
- drafting legible letters and memos containing all essential information within specified deadlines
- presenting draft communications in an approved format

introduction

You will find it necessary from time-to-time to communicate with colleagues and with outsiders by means of written documents in a specified format, often within deadlines. You will need to develop the skills to do so concisely and clearly.

The written documents covered in this Unit are

- the letter
- the memorandum
- the fax message

Although the NCVQ requirements do not specify the fax message at this level, the format is included in this Unit because of its increasing popularity and importance as a form of routine business communication.

---

 linking assignment

Common Skills Assignment 4
Communicating: getting the message across, pages 100 to 104

forms of written business communication

Communicating in written form both within and outside the organisation is an essential skill which

- promotes the internal efficiency of the organisation
- presents the organisation to the outside world in a favourable way

Traditional forms of written communication are

- the *letter* - used for communications with the outside world
- the *memorandum* - used for communications within the organisation

A more recent technological advance is the *fax* (facsimile transmission machine) which enables an exact reproduction of an image on a page to be sent over the telephone line to a fax machine in another organisation, or to a department of the same organisation. Transmission of fax messages requires a specific format for the written information.

We will deal with the letter, the memorandum and the fax mesage in turn.

the letter

house style

If you work in an organisation or receive letters from an organisation, you will note that the appearance and format of each letter is (or should be!) in a uniform 'house' style, a style which readily identifies that organisation, and is common to all letters which it sends.

The letter will be normally be

- sent on standard printed stationery showing the name, address and details of the organisation
- printed or typed in a standard style of print ('typeface')
- set out with headings, paragraphs, signatures - the 'elements' of the letter - in a uniform way

A uniform house style gives the impression that the organisation is run efficiently.

presentation formats

There are three main ways of setting out the text of a letter:

- *fully blocked* - the most common method - illustrated and explained on the next page
- *semi-blocked* - a more traditional style - illustrated and explained on page 74
- *fully displayed* - less common, and the most traditional style - illustrated and explained on page 75

The example letters on the next three pages have been prepared by a firm of electrical contractors, Wyvern Electrical Services. A potential customer, Mr J Sutton, has enquired about the possibility of having his house rewired.

**Elements of
the letter**
*(see page 76 for a
full explanation)*

**Wyvern Electrical Services
107 High Street
Mereford MR1 9SZ**

Tel 0605 675365 Fax 0605 675576

reference

Ref DH/SB/69

date

14 December 199-

name and address
of recipient of
letter

J D Sutton Esq
23 Windermere Close
Crofters Green
Mereford MR6 7ER

salutation

Dear Mr Sutton

heading

<u>Rewiring: 23 Windermere Close</u>

Thank you for your letter of enquiry dated 10 December.

body of the letter

We are pleased to enclose a brochure detailing our services
and will be pleased to give you a quotation for rewiring
your new extension. In order to do this we will need to send
our estimator to see your property, and shall be grateful if
you will telephone us to arrange a visit at a time which is
convenient to you.

We look forward to hearing from you

complimentary
close

Yours sincerely

signature

name and job title
of sender

Derek Hunt
Sales Manager

enclosure
indicator

enc

fully blocked letter

Characteristics of a fully blocked letter

- the most commonly used style of letter
- all the lines start at the left margin
- use of *open punctuation*, i.e. there is *no* punctuation, except in the main body of the letter, which uses normal punctuation
- a fully blocked letter looks neat and clean (no untidy punctuation)
- a fully blocked letter is easy to type as all the lines are set uniformly to the left margin

**Elements of
the letter**
*(see page 76 for a
full explanation)*

reference and date

name and address
of recipient of
letter

salutation

heading

body of the letter

complimentary
close

signature

name and job title
of sender

enclosure
indicator

**Wyvern Electrical Services
107 High Street
Mereford MR1 9SZ**

Tel 0605 675365 Fax 0605 675576

Ref DH/SB/69   14 December 199-

J D Sutton Esq
23 Windermere Close
Crofters Green
Mereford MR6 7ER

Dear Mr Sutton

<u>Rewiring: 23 Windermere Close</u>

Thank you for your letter of enquiry dated 10 December.

We are pleased to enclose a brochure detailing our services
and will be pleased to give you a quotation for rewiring
your new extension. In order to do this we will need to send
our estimator to see your property, and shall be grateful if
you will telephone us to arrange a visit at a time which is
convenient to you.

We look forward to hearing from you.

                            Yours sincerely

                            D Hunt

                            Derek Hunt
                            Sales Manager

enc

---

semi-blocked letter

The semi-blocked style is more traditional and is the same as a fully
blocked style, *except that*

- the date is at the right margin and on the same line as the reference
- the heading is centred
- the complimentary close and the name and the job title of the sender
  start at the centre of the letter (a typist would use a tab stop)

**Elements of
the letter**
*(see page 76 for a
full explanation)*

reference and date

**name and address
of recipient of
letter**

salutation

heading

body of the letter

**complimentary
close**

signature

**name and job title
of sender**

**enclosure
indicator**

**Wyvern Electrical Services
107 High Street
Mereford MR1 9SZ**

Tel 0605 675365 Fax 0605 675576

Ref DH/SB/69   14 December 199-

J D Sutton, Esq.,
23, Windermere Close,
Crofters Green,
Mereford. MR6 7ER

Dear Mr Sutton,

                    <u>Rewiring: 23 Windermere Close</u>

        Thank you for your letter of enquiry dated 10 December.

        We are pleased to enclose a brochure detailing our
services and will be pleased to give you a quotation for
rewiring your new extension. In order to do this we will
need to send our estimator to see your property, and shall
be grateful if you will telephone us to arrange a visit at a
time which is convenient to you.

        We look forward to hearing from you.

                        Yours sincerely,

                        D. Hunt

                        Derek Hunt
                        Sales Manager

enc.

fully-displayed letter

The fully-displayed style is very traditional, and is less common than the
blocked and semi-blocked styles:
- the date is at the right margin and on the same line as the reference
- the heading is centred
- the first line of every paragraph is *indented*, i.e. it starts five spaces in
  from the left margin
- the complimentary close and the name and the job title of the sender
  are centred
- punctuation is used in full; it is known as *full* or *standard* punctuation

Elements of the letter

The references next to the left of the letters on the preceding three pages describe the *elements of a letter*. These are explained more fully below.

printed letterhead

This is always pre-printed. All the typist need worry about is whether it is up-to-date. An out-of-date letterhead looks inefficient, and could have serious legal consequences if the letter is important.

reference

The reference on the letter illustrated -*DH/SB/69* - is a standard format
- DH (Derek Hunt), the writer
- SB (Sally Burgess), the typist
- 69, the number of the file where Mr Sutton's correspondence is kept
Note: if you need to quote the reference of a letter to which you are replying, the references will be quoted as follows:
'Your ref. TR/FG/45   Our ref. DH/SB/69'

date

The date is typed in date (number), month (word), year (number) order.

recipient

The name and address of the person to whom the letter is sent. This section of the letter may be displayed in the window of a window envelope, so it is essential that it is accurate. Note the difference between the open and full punctuation in the recipient section of the letters; the open punctuation in the blocked and semi-blocked styles appears much 'cleaner.'

salutation

'Dear Sir. . . Dear Madam' if you know the person's name, use it, but check that it is spelt correctly - a misspelt name will ruin an otherwise competent letter.

heading

The heading sets out the subject matter of the letter - it will concentrate the reader's mind.

body

The body of the letter is an area where communications skills can be developed. The text must be
- laid out in short precise paragraphs
- start with a point of reference (e.g. thanking for a letter)
- set out the message in a logical sequence
- finish with a clear indication of the next step to be taken (e.g. please telephone, please arrange appointment, please buy our products, please pay our invoice).

complimentary close

The complimentary close (signing off phrase) must be consistent with the salutation:
'Dear Sir/Dear Madam' followed by *'Yours faithfully'*
'Dear Mr Sutton/Dear Ms Jones' followed by *'Yours sincerely'.*

name and job title

It is essential for the reader to know the name of the person who sent the letter, and that person's job title, because a reply will need to be addressed to a specific person.

enclosures

If there are enclosures with the letter, the abbreviation 'enc' or 'encl' is used.

continuation sheets

(not shown in the illustrations)
If the text of the letter is longer than than one sheet of paper will allow for, the letter will conclude on a continuation sheet, a matching plain sheet of paper headed with the recipient's name, the page number and the date.

envelopes

The presentation of the envelope is as important as that of the letter itself. Sometimes an organisation will use window envelopes which contain a transparent panel which displays the address typed on the letter. For the purposes of your studies and training it is best to assume that you will have to type the envelopes yourself.

Normally the style in which you type the letter will reflect the format of the envelope:

- *fully blocked and semi-blocked letter styles - open punctuation - no indentation*

```
J D Sutton Esq
23 Windermere Close
Crofters Green
MEREFORD
MR6 7ER
```

- *fully displayed letter style - full punctuation - indented lines*

```
J. D. Sutton Esq.,
   23, Windermere Close,
      Crofters Green,
         MEREFORD.
            MR6 7ER
```

Note that the envelope styles follow the letter styles very closely. The only exception to the rule is the lack of a full stop following the postcode of a fully displayed style envelope. The reason for this omission is that the postcodes are read by an automatic sorter at the Post Office, and a full stop might confuse the machine.

special instructions

It will sometimes be necessary to type special instructions on the letter and envelope. These are normally typed in capital letters, or in ordinary type and underlined. For example

- private and confidential
- for the attention of
- personal
- urgent

Where are the instructions typed?

- *on the envelope* - two lines above the address
- *on the letter* - two lines above the address

The exception to these rules is 'for the attention of' which can be typed (followed by the name) either above or below the address.

Note that you should never open letters marked 'personal' or 'private and confidential' unless they are addressed to *you*.

letter tone and style

You will know from personal experience that if you are writing to your boyfriend/ girlfriend/husband/wife you will use a different tone and style than you would if you were writing to the bank manager or writing an application letter for a job. In writing business letters you should use a tone and style appropriate to the situation. You should always

• have a mental picture of the person to whom you are writing
• be aware of his or her status in the organisation
• adopt the appropriate tone for the situation: are you writing an enquiry, an apology, a complaint?

Here are some suggested approaches to different types of letter

type of letter	*tone and style*
enquiry	• a polite and precise letter • an indication of where the information is to be sent • a deadline if the enquiry is urgent
complaint	• a firm, informative, and polite letter • do not be abusive, even if you feel angry • state what action you want taken: refund, replacement, compensation?
apology	• a helpful and polite letter stating the reason for the problem • accept responsibility - do not blame other people • apologise but do not overdo it - an over-apologetic letter sounds insincere • state what remedy you are making available
selling	• a persuasive and interesting letter • state the facts relating to the product or service • set out the benefits of the service • conclude with an invitation to buy

✓ action points - letter writing

O plan your letter before writing it - jot down the main points on rough paper

O make sure that you are familiar with the house style

O be concise - use short paragraphs rather than one rambling block of text

O be accurate - check the recipient's name and address

O avoid jargon e.g. *'We are in receipt of your I.F.O. and have passed it to the R.S.I.'*

O adopt the right tone for the situation

O make sure the recipient knows how he is to respond (write, telephone, order goods?)

O check your work thoroughly for spelling (use a dictionary), punctuation, and detail (e.g. if you are quoting prices from a catalogue)

the memorandum

format

The *memorandum* (plural *memoranda*) is a formal written note used for internal communication within an organisation. It may be typed or handwritten, and will often be produced in a number of copies which can be circulated as necessary. It can be used for situations such as

- giving instructions
- requesting information
- making suggestions
- recording of opinions
- confirming telephone conversations

A memorandum is normally pre-printed by the organisation with all the headings in place, and can be half page or full page in size. A blank and a completed memorandum are illustrated on the next page.

elements of the memorandum

Most of the headings on the pre-printed memorandum form are self-explanatory, as they are also to be found on business letters. You should, however, note the following:

heading	the name of the organisation may be printed above the word 'Memorandum', although this is not strictly necessary, as the memorandum is an internal document
'to' and 'from'	the name and job title of the sender and the recipient are entered in full, and as a consequence the salutation 'Dear......' and complimentary close 'Yours ....' are not necessary
copies to	memoranda are frequently sent (as in the example on the next page) to a large number of people; the recipients will be indicated in this section of the document
reference	as in a business letter the reference indicates the writer, the typist, and the file number
date	as in a business letter the order is day (number), month (word), year (number)
subject	the subject matter of the memorandum must be concisely stated
text	the message of the memorandum should be clear and concise
signature	a memorandum can be signed, initialled, or even - as is often the case -left blank
enclosures	if material is circulated with the memorandum, the abbreviation 'enc' or 'encl' should be used

MEMORANDUM

To

From   **Ref.**

Copies to   **Date**

Subject

a blank memorandum

MEMORANDUM

To Tim Blake, Sales Director

From K Roach, Accounts Supervisor   **Ref.** KR/AC

Copies to Directors and Managers   **Date** 7 July 199-

Subject COMPUTERISATION OF ACCOUNTING RECORDS

Please attend a meeting on 14 July in the Conference Room. Attendance is
vital as the new system comes on line on 1 September. Summary details of
the new system are attached.

enc

a completed memorandum

the facsimile message (fax)

the technology
Fax is an abbreviation of *facsimile transmission*. A fax machine scans a document and sends an exact (facsimile) image of the document through the telephone system. A receiving fax machine will decode the message and print out an exact copy of the document. A fax machine will therefore enable a copy of a drawing, an invoice, a handwritten message, or a letter to be sent instantaneously to the recipient, avoiding postal delays and losses.

fax header sheets
It is customary for an organisation sending fax messages to precede the actual document (or documents) being scanned with a pre-printed *header sheet*, so that the recipient will know what is being transmitted. An example is illustrated below.

FACSIMILE TRANSMISSION HEADER

From
THE NATIONAL BANK PLC
6-8 High Street
Mereford
MR3 5RJ
Telephone 0915 921524   Facsimile 0915 926644

TO...... *Kevin Roach, Accounts Supervisor*
Wyvern (Office Products) Limited

TELEPHONE NUMBER.... *0605 241851* ....FACSIMILE NUMBER.... *0605 241879*

NUMBER OF PAGES INCLUDING THIS HEADER.... *1* ....DATE *23 June 199—*

message

Thanks for your enquiry. Bank charges are as follows : 80p per credit paid in, 60p for cheques, direct debits and standing orders.
Wendy.

If you have any enquiries regarding this message please telephone the above number and ask for extension.... *25*

---

elements of a fax header

sender the sender's name, telephone number and facsimile number are present so that the recipient can get in touch if he wants to send a reply, or telephone if there are transmission problems (an extension number is also given in case of need)

page numbers the header will indicate the number of pages being transmitted, this is so that the recipient can check that the whole document has printed out - the document is normally printed out in one continuous roll

recipient the recipient's name, address, telephone number and facsimile number are present so that the recipient can be contacted in case of problems, and also so that the message can be filed correctly after transmission

message box a box is provided for brief messages or notes relating to the pages which follow

---

 # student activities - routine business communications

Performance criteria

The student activities in this section test competences in the following areas:
- *drafting of legible letters and memoranda containing all the required information within specified deadlines*
- *drafting communications in an approved format*

Exercises in the drafting of facsimile messages are also included.

simulated situation for activities

The organisation is Wyvern (Office Products) Limited. During the course of a day a number of members of staff have to draft letters, memoranda and fax messages. Students should undertake these tasks individually and if possible, type up their work, or delegate the typing to another student. The tasks should be given specific time limits by the assessor. The Catalogue and Price List for Wyvern (Office Products) Ltd are in Appendix 2 of this book. Blank stationery (letterhead, memorandum and fax header) are printed in Appendix 1.

drafting letters

1. You are Kate Maloney, clerical assistant in the Sales Department. During the course of a day you have to draft three letters for the signature of Jane Seymour, Sales Manager. The appropriate envelopes should also be prepared.

(a) A reply to Trevor Davies, Purchasing Department, Baverstock Engineering Ltd, Unit 7, Elm Industrial Estate, Mereford, MR7 9UQ. He wants details of office tables which you can supply.

(b) Pierre Lafont, Office Manager of Helmstead Insurance Brokers (76 High Street, Mereford, MR2 5TR) writes to complain that a desk recently delivered to him has a bad scratch in the veneer. It is Catalogue No. F1003.

(c) You are to draft a letter to Ms Heather Stafford, Purchasing Manager of Mereford County Council

(County Hall, Stratford Road, Mereford, MR4 ST7), as you know they are planning to re-equip their offices shortly. Jane Seymour wants to meet Ms Stafford to discuss the matter: suggest an afternoon in which they can meet, and enclose a copy of your catalogue and price list.

drafting memoranda

2.   You are to draft memoranda for the following situations

(a)   You are Asaf Patel, Administration Manager. You wish to obtain suggestions from members of staff for ways to make the running of the company more efficient. You decide to circularise the Departmental Managers with a Memorandum asking them to familiarise their staff with the scheme, and requesting that any suggestions from the staff be addressed to Mr Patel on a Memorandum. Full details of the scheme are set out on a separate sheet of paper which is attached to Mr Patel's Memorandum. Draft the Memorandum you would send to Jane Seymour, Sales Manager. You are *not* required to draft the accompanying sheet.

(b)   The Sales Department is reviewing the discounts it gives to its customers. Draft a Memorandum from Jane Seymour, Sales Manager, to Tina Brooks, Accounts Manager, asking for details of any bad payers whose discount should be reduced or stopped, and any good customers who could be given a greater discount. Jane Seymour encloses with the Memorandum an up-to-date list of the discounts given to customers. You are *not* required to draft the list.

(c)   Draft a Memorandum from Tom Blake, Managing Director, to Tim Blake, Sales Director, congratulating him and his sales team on the recent Sales figure for the financial year, which at £1,265,000 was a 15% increase on the previous year's figure.

drafting facsimile transmission messages

3.   You are John Parry, Accounts Clerk. You are to draw up fax headers and messages for the following situations (you are not required to draw up the other documents to be transmitted):

(a)   You are to send a copy of a bank statement (a single sheet) to the bank as you are querying a cheque for £1425.65 which does not tie up with any counterfoil in your company cheque book. The bank details are on the specimen header on page 81; your own company details are set out in the Appendix. Your extension number is 45. The fax follows from a telephone call you have made to the bank; their Miss Gould is expecting the fax.

(b)   You are to send 3 copy invoices (3 sheets) to Daniel Martin Trading Company, 34 Reckitt Road, Mereford, MR4 5RY, Tel 0605 567483, Fax 0605 567764. Their Accounts Assistant, Sarah Mills, has requested them, as she claims they have lost the originals.

(c)   You fax to the Sales Department of Stag Stationery plc (Unit 7, Severnside Industrial Estate, Shrewsbury, SY4 5RT, tel 0743 564732 fax 0743 564875) which supplies you with paper products, asking for an up-to-date price list.

 linking assignment

Common Skills Assignment 4
Communicating: getting the message across, pages 100 to 104

7 Communicating - supplying information

NCVQ coverage

2.3 supply information for a specific purpose

Performance criteria

- *identifying and accessing relevant sources of information*
- *abstracting, listing and classifying appropriate data correctly*
- *supplying information to the appropriate person within required deadlines*
- *reporting promptly and explaining politely difficulties in achieving targets*

introduction

You will sometimes be asked to provide information for a specific purpose - a colleague may need a telephone number, a flight time, a set of sales figures - and you will need to know *where* to obtain the information and *how* to present it within a given deadline. A customer or client may ask for information about the products or services offered by your organisation. In either situation you must deal with the enquiry promptly yourself, or pass it to a colleague who is able to provide the information.

In this Unit we will examine

- the sources of information - books, computer records, trade catalogues
- how to present information within text
- how to deal with customer enquiries

 linking assignment

Common Skills Assignment 4
Communicating: getting the message across, pages 100 to 104

importance of information

If you are to communicate information effectively you must be able to

- present information - facts and figures - in a clear and readily understood form in written business communications such as letters, memoranda, notes and reports
- know where to obtain the information
- work to deadlines
- appreciate when deadlines cannot be made, and indicate the fact to your supervisor

sources of information - reference books

You will often need to exercise initiative in finding information. Here is a list of useful sources:

Information needed	source of information
spelling	*English dictionary* - check words with which you know you have problems
word meanings	*English dictionary* - you may need this to clarify the meaning of words you are using, or to find out the meaning of words in letters received
pronounciations	*English dictionary*: there is a phonetic explanation with each word ('phonetic' means the use of special letters - for which a key is provided - which tells you exactly how a word sounds)
alternative words	*Roget's Thesaurus - a* book which gives alternative words; e.g if you are repeating a word too many times in a letter, it will suggest others with the same meaning
foreign words	*Language dictionary,* or, if the foreign words are a phrase commonly used in English, most English dictionaries have a special section at the back for foreign words and phrases
telephone numbers	Customer files, telephone directories, Yellow Pages, Kelly's directories
fax numbers	British Telecom Fax Book
travel details	• ABC Railway Guide • AA or RAC road atlases and hotel guides • ABC World Airways Guide • ABC Passenger and Shipping Guide

If your office does not possess the required reference book, try your local library, or specific sources such as travel agents or the Post Office.

sources of information - computer records

The information you are looking for may be found on computer file, either within your own organisation, or from outside sources such as viewdata.

internal records

database

Your customer's names, addresses and telephone numbers may be held on a database file which can readily be accessed on a computer terminal. The database can be used to 'sort' the data so that you can obtain exactly what you want, e.g. the details of customers who live in certain areas, have bought certain products. The use of a database is covered in full in Unit 9.

The catalogue or details of your organisations products or services may also be held on computer database file.

accounts program

If you sell to customers and buy from suppliers, details of the financial transactions may be processed and held on an accounts program file; this will provide you with instant information about
• how much you are owed and by whom
• how much you owe and to whom
• how much stock you hold
This type of information is often needed for customer queries, and also for internal reports

external records

A wide range of information - travel details, share prices, exchange rates, international news - is readily accessible on TV sets:

teletext   Ceefax (BBC), Oracle (ITV), 4-Tel (Channel 4)

viewdata   a British Telecom information service linked to a TV set via a telephone line

presenting information within text

presenting text

The styles of letter and memorandum writing have already been covered (see pages 72 -80). You should always bear in mind the importance of

• being clear and concise
• adopting the correct tone for the type of letter - apology, complaint, enquiry, giving information

presenting tables in text

If you are writing a letter and have to present information which would benefit from being set out in columns in tabular form, use your tab settings on the typewriter or word processor to achieve this.

If, for instance, you are quoting train times, do not set them out like this:

```
'Dep. London, Paddington, 9.05, 10.30, 11.45, arrive Oxford 9.55,
11.25, 12.37.'
```

It looks a muddle. Use columns instead, and highlight the headings by underlining them:

<u>Depart London Paddington</u>   <u>Arrive Oxford</u>

09.05   09.55

10.30   11.25

11.45   12.37

The result is clearer and neater; the traveller can see at a glance when indivdual trains depart and arrive.

presenting numbers

line graphs and bar charts

You may be asked to extract information in numerical form for a report, e.g. sales figures for products over a period of years. A useful skill is the ability to present these figures in visually appealing and meaningful formats:

* the line graph
* the bar chart
* the pie chart

The method of constructing these graphs and charts is explained fully in Skills Development Section 'Communicating' (pages 94 to 96).

supplying information to customers and clients

customer and client requests

Customer and client enquiries will come from a number of different sources, and you will need to know how to deal with a wide variety of requests:

* telephone requests
* face-to-face requests (when the customer calls in person)
* requests by letter

We have already dealt with communicating with customer and clients orally and in writing in Units 4, 5 and 6, and so you should be familiar with the basic techniques of speaking and writing in the 'house style' of the organisation. In this Unit we will examine:

* how to establish what the customer wants - this is often more difficult than you might think
* how to obtain the relevant information
* how to provide the information clearly and promptly
* knowing when to pass the enquiry to a colleague

establishing the customer's or client's needs

Some customers will know precisely what they want:

> *'Please let me have details of your range of "Fisley" filing cabinets.'*

Other customers will have only a general idea of what they want:

> *'My typist needs a new desk, and possibly also a new chair, and then of course she might need . . . '*

Other customers will be even less specific:

> *'I need to brighten up the office a bit, have you got any ideas about . . .?'*

It is your task to work out *exactly* what they need. The less certain they are, the more opportunity there will be for you to *sell* your organisation's products or services. It is possible that your organisation will give you specific training in selling techniques.

In order to establish the customer's or client's needs you should

listen
The customer will give you clues about what he or she needs. Listen carefully and do not interrupt, as you might hear only part of the request and then impulsively *think* you know what is needed, and recommend the wrong product or service. Listen and let the customer have his or her say.

ask
If the customer does not provide sufficient information, ask for more:

> *'What size of desk did you have in mind?'*

> *'What colour filing cabinet would you like?'*

If you are at all unclear about the requirement, *you should ask*. It is sometimes a temptation if you are unsure of yourself in a face-to-face interview to nod your head and accept what is being said because you do not want to appear ignorant. The trouble comes afterwards when you or someone else has to telephone for further details: both you and your organisation then appear incompetent.

write down
Have a pencil and pad to hand when dealing with an enquiry so that you can write down the important details. It is unlikely that you will be able to remember everything afterwards. Do not worry if it takes time to write down the details - the customer or client should not object. If you are dealing with a telephone enquiry you may need to say

> *'I will just take the details down, if I may.'* and <u>not</u>

> *'Hang on, I can't write that quickly!'*

provide information
You should have information sources at your fingertips when dealing with an enquiry: product catalogues, stock lists, price lists, computer data. If you are caught with a telephone enquiry and do not have the details to hand, ask the caller politely to hold while you obtain the appropriate information. Lastly, ensure that the information you give is accurate and up-to-date. The Sale of Goods Act 1979 states that people should be provided with goods as described in sales literature. If you give an inaccurate description or price you could be involving your organisation in legal trouble if a dispute follows.

knowing when to pass an enquiry to a colleague

There are times when you will feel out of your depth with an enquiry, and will need to pass it to a colleague or to your supervisor. This could happen for a number of reasons:

detail If you do not know what you are talking about, or *suspect* that you do not know what you are talking about, you should pass the enquiry to someone who does. Do not bluff your way through an interview: you may give out inaccurate information and waste a lot of everybody's time.

authority It may be that you do not have authority to deal with a particular level of enquiry. Your organisation may lay down guidelines for 'who' can deal with 'what'. The law, too, may restrict what you can do. The Financial Services Act 1986, for example, states that only authorised individuals in banks and building societies may give advice on savings and investment schemes.

difficulties If the customer becomes difficult and aggressive, you may need to refer the matter to your Supervisor; in fact the customer may want you to! Never get involved in a slanging match. The customer is always right.

confidential information

It is essential that you only give out information that should be disclosed. A bank or building society, for example, deals with customers' personal financial details which should not normally be revealed to an outside body. If you have worked in a bank or building society, or done work experience in one, you will know that you have to sign a 'declaration of secrecy' to stop you disclosing confidential information.

Examples of 'leaks' of confidential information would include

- telling a husband how much money his wife has in her private account
- telling a wife if her husband's salary has been paid into his private account

Some organisations will not give out certain information over the telephone. For example, banks will not normally give bank balances over the telephone to *anyone*, even to the account holder.

is your information up-to-date?

The information that you give to customers and clients can only be as good as the sources of that information. If your brochures, catalogue and price list are out of date you can waste much time and lose customers. The author remembers well a colleague who spent nearly an hour explaining a particular service to a client, not realising that the brochure was out of date and the service no longer available. In order to avoid embarrassments of this type you should ensure that your information sources are

- up-to-date
- complete
- re-ordered when they run out

a satisfied customer?

If you are able to provide accurate and up-to-date information to your customer or client, you will have a satisfied customer or client, who will come back for more. Remember that when dealing with the public you *are* your organisation. Its success depends on your competence.

meeting deadlines

Most organisations suffer their fair share of panics. Some people seem to thrive on pressure and tension. No doubt you will be familiar with situations such as

- promising to provide a customer with information and realising that there is not enough time in which to carry out the task
- trying to get a long and complex letter typed, signed and posted by 5.00 p.m.
- trying to obtain a train time when all the telephone lines to British Rail are engaged
- dealing with delays caused by computer breakdowns
- accidentally wiping data files on the computer and discovering there is no recent back-up

All these situations involve the time factor - meeting deadlines. You will from time-to-time be faced with the impossible. It is an essential skill to be able to cope with deadlines and to take action if the problem really does have no solution:

- assess the situation in hand
- do not get flustered, as you will go around in circles and achieve little!
- ensure that your priorities are correct
- 'juggle' with the order of tasks to be done if necessary
- if there is time in which to carry out the task, do so
- if you are faced with 'mission impossible', tell the Supervisor

✔ action points - dealing with deadlines

○   keep calm and assess the situation - what precisely has to be done, and by what time?

○   assess your priorities

○   rearrange your order of priorities if necessary

○   if you can deal with the situation, do so

○   if you cannot obtain information from the normal source, try other sources - other members of staff, other organisations - use your resources

○   ask for help from colleagues - they may not be as busy as they seem

○   if you cannot cope in the time given, pass the problem to your supervisor

○   if your supervisor is unhelpful (he or she may be under pressure too) patiently explain the situation until the facts sink in

○   remember that your problem is your supervisor's problem too

student activities - supplying information

Performance criteria

The student activities in this section test competences in the following areas:

- *identifying and accessing relevant sources of information*
- *abstracting, listing and classifying appropriate data correctly*
- *supplying information to the appropriate person within required deadlines*
- *reporting promptly and explaining politely difficulties in achieving targets*

simulated situation for activities

The organisation is Wyvern (Office Products) Limited. You work as a clerical assistant in the Administration Department, and are asked to carry out certain tasks for your supervisor Miss Anne Jones. Later in the day you are asked to help out in the Sales Department as they are short-staffed. You are given a number of customer queries to deal with by the Sales Supervisor, Bob Bates. The Catalogue and Price List for Wyvern (Office Products) Limited, which are required for these tasks, are printed in Appendix 2 at the back of this book.

1. Find out the following information for Miss Jones from reference books and other sources; state in each case where the information came from.

    (a) the correct spelling of 'neccesary'
    (b) the correct spelling of 'intrest'
    (c) another word for 'delay'
    (d) another word for 'payment'
    (e) the name of the best hotel in the place where you live (or near to the place where you live)
    (f) the nearest airport to where you live (and the distance to that airport)
    (g) the time of the first flight to Paris from the nearest airport to where you live
    (h) the cost of reserving a seat on a train from your nearest station to Central London (or nearest large city)

2. Miss Jones asks you to

    (a) Find out the opening hours of your local bank. She wants you to tell her in person.

    (b) Draft a letter for the signature of Jane Seymour, Sales Manager, advising customers of changes in the Price List: C1010 is to cost £57.95, C1011 £59.25 , C1012 £105.95 and C1020 £42.50.

    (c) Draw up a chart to be displayed by the telephone switchboard showing the charge rates for calls at different times of the day. The chart should suggest that the office telephone bill should be reduced.

    (d) Draft a memorandum (for Miss Jones' signature) to be sent to all Departmental Managers reminding them of all the bank holidays in the next calendar year. There is often confusion about these extra days off when staff book their holiday entitlement.

3. Miss Jones asks you to set out the following sales figures (see next page) for Wyvern (Office Products) Limited in the form of

    (a) a line graph
    (b) a bar chart

	Year 1 £000's	Year 2 £000's	Year 3 £000's
UK Sales	156	163	180
Export Sales	85	75	125

See pages 94 to 95 for an explanation of line graphs and bar charts.

4.   Miss Jones asks you to construct a pie chart to show the breakdown of office expenditure in 199-:

Salaries	£50,000
Rental	£25,000
Stationery	£12,500
Sundry Expenses	£12,500

See page 96 for an explanation of pie charts.

5.   *Later in the day you are moved to the Sales Department to help deal with customer queries. In some of the activities an outside caller is required; these activities should be carried out with the assessor or another student playing the role of the outside caller. A telephone system will be needed for the telephone enquiries. Appendix 2 contains the Catalogue and Price List.*

(a)   Helen Reeves telephones to ask the availability and price of 'drawing office' pencils.

(b)   Fred Gardner telephones to ask the availability and price of staplers.

(c)   Jim Winter telephones to ask the availability and price of ball point pens.

(d)   Joanne Lavelle telephones to ask the availability and price of typists chairs.

(e)   Tom Woodcock telephones to ask the availability and price of telephone tables. Unfortunately he has got an old Catalogue and Price List showing item F1040 priced at £49.95.

(f)   Ted Grundy calls in person to enquire about a new desk for his secretary.

(g)   John Groves calls in person - he wants the biggest table in your catalogue.

(i)   Maria Costello of the Regello Ristorante calls in person - she needs some high quality storage units for her office records.

(h)   John Northwick of Arrow Press, 46 High Street, Mereford, MR1 0JQ, writes to enquire about the availability and price of chairs that can be stacked up. You should write a reply for the signature of Jane Seymour, Sales Manager. Use your own initials for the reference and today's date.

(i)   Tom Osborne of Osborne Associates, 87 Broad Street, Mereford, MR1 7LJ, writes to enquire about the range of leather executive chairs you may be able to supply. You should write a reply for the signature of Jane Seymour, Sales Manager. Use your own initials for the reference and today's date.

 linking assignment

Common Skills Assignment 4
Communicating: getting the message across, pages 100 to 104

Common Skills development:
Communicating

Skills developed

The skills developed in this section are as follows:

- *receive and respond to a variety of given information*
- *communicate in a variety of visual forms*
- *communicate in writing*
- *participate in oral and non-verbal communication*

You will have noted that these skills have already been developed over the last five Units when we have examined oral communication with callers, telephone skills, oral and written messages, written and visual communications. In this section we will summarise these skills and their performance criteria, and draw them together in an in-tray assignment 'Getting the message across.'

1. receive and respond to a variety of given information

performance criteria

If you are on the receiving end of a communicating process you should be able to

- clarify information as necessary through questioning and enquiry
- interpret and summarise accurately information you have received
- select and use an appropriate method of response

how this relates to the communication process

When you are on the receiving end of a communication you are part of a complex process:

the sender formulates the message
an appropriate means of communication is chosen
the message is sent
the message is interpreted
the message is clarified if necessary
the message is acted upon

In Unit 5 (pages 61 to 70) we looked at how to send and receive oral and written messages. You should re-read these pages now. These types of communication include messages received by word of mouth from a colleague or over the telephone, and formal and informal written notes produced within an organisation. The important points for a person receiving a message can be summarised as follows:

receiving oral messages
* ensure that you have understood what has been said
* if you are not sure, ask for the message to be repeated or clarified
* if you are not sure of the spelling of a word, ask for it be spelt out - use the telephonist's alphabet
* write down what has been said - have a pad and pencil to hand
* repeat all important points at the end of the conversation to make sure you have 'got the message'

receiving written messages
* read the message carefully
* look and see when it was written and assess its urgency
* if there are any details which are unclear, check them with the sender

You are reponsible for interpreting the message and taking the correct action. If you are unused to taking messages it is easy to get flustered and try and write *anything* down in order not to appear foolish. It is essential in the communication process to interpret the message in a calm and efficient manner. It does not matter at all if it takes time and if the sender has to repeat details. He or she will at least then know that the message is being dealt with in an efficient manner.

response
Some messages state what type of response is required:

> *'Please mail me an up-to-date catalogue.'*
> *'Please telephone me back by the end of the day.'*

Some messages are less clear, however, and the correct response may be ascertained *either* by asking the sender for instructions *or* by asking a colleague what the normal procedure is

> *'Do you want me to ring you with the details, or do you want them mailed?'*
> *'Does Mr Sims normally have his quotations posted or faxed?'*

2.   communicate in a variety of visual forms _____

performance criteria
A picture can often tell you more about information - particularly numerical information - than any number of words. It is therefore important to be able to
* select the appropriate method of visual presentation
* present visual information in a clear and easily assimilated way

graph, bar chart and pie chart
The starting point for any visual presentation of numbers is the 'raw' information, which will often be found in the form of a table. The table below sets out the sales in money terms of two cars - the Corsair and the Tornado over a period of four years. These figures are presented in the form of a graph and a bar chart on the next page.

	Year 1 £000's	Year 2 £000's	Year 3 £000's	Year 4 £000's
Sales of Corsair	1,000	1,250	1,500	1,250
Sales of Tornado	1,500	1,000	500	250

line graph

Note that

- the graph is given a title
- the time scale is set out on the horizontal axis and a label added
- the sales figure is £000's are set out on the vertical axis and a label added
- a key is produced to distinguish between the two lines

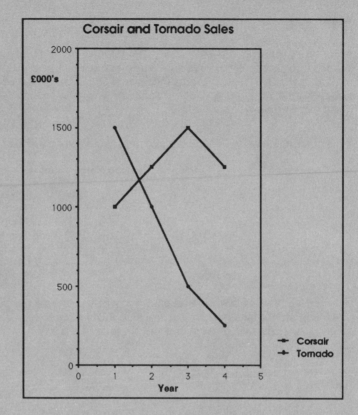

bar chart

Note that

- the chart is given a title
- the time scale is set out on the horizontal axis and labelled
- the sales figures in £000's are set out on the vertical axis and labelled
- there is a distinctively shaded bar for each type of car
- the bars are of equal width
- a key is produced to distinguish between the two types of bar

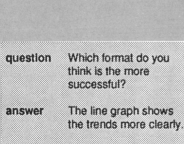

question Which format do you think is the more successful?

answer The line graph shows the trends more clearly.

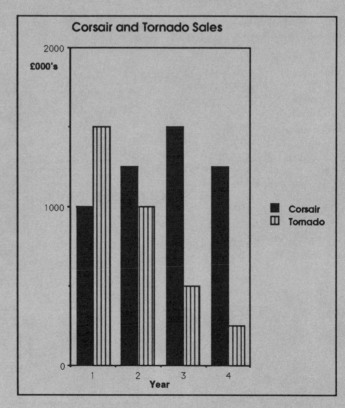

pie chart

A pie chart (illustrated below) is a circle divided into a number of parts, just as an edible 'pie' is divided into slices. Whereas the line graph and bar chart are useful in showing a *trend* over a period of time, a pie chart is used to illustrate how a single figure is made up from its constituent parts. For example total sales for an organisation for one year may be divided into sales by region, and illustrated by means of a pie chart.

A pie chart might be used, for example, to show the worldwide sales by region of Tornado Cars:

Sales of Tornado Cars by area In Year 1

Area	£000's
UK	250
Europe	500
USA	625
Japan	125
Total Sales	1 500

The total sales of £1.5M will become the whole circle of the pie divided into segments, each of which will proportionally represent a geographical sales figure. As the angle at the centre of a circle is 360° it is necessary to work out the angle for *each* segment individually before drawing in the 'slices' of the pie. The formula is as follows:

$$\frac{\text{Figure for the part of the whole}}{\text{Figure for the whole}} \times 360° = \text{the angle at the centre for the segment (°)}$$

The angle for the UK sales 'slice', for example, is therefore $\dfrac{250}{1,500} \times 360 = 60°$

The pie chart therefore appears as follows:

pie chart

Note that

- the chart is given a title
- the angles are not written in
- each segment is shaded distinctively
- a key is shown which indicates the different geographical regions

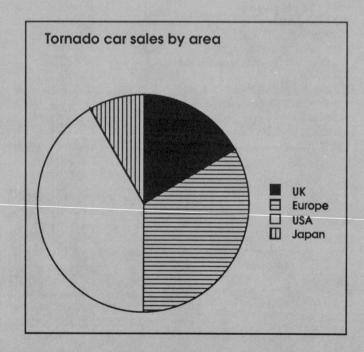

Tornado car sales by area

Key: UK, Europe, USA, Japan

3. communicate in writing ━━━━━━━━━━━━━━━━━

performance criteria

If you work in an organisation you must be familiar with the different forms of written communication, and appropriate sources of information. In particular you must be able to

- identify and consult correct sources of information
- extract relevant information from appropriate sources
- present relevant information in a manner and format that are clear, easily assimilated and appropriate for the intended use

what this means

Working in an organisation requires the ability to produce written communications in a variety of formats, normally in an accepted 'house style'. These formats, which are explained in full in Unit 6 'Communicating - routine business communications' (pages 71 to 83) include

- the letter
- the memorandum
- the facsimile message

If you are unfamiliar with these formats you should read Unit 6.

tone and style

Every written communication requires a specific tone and style which will vary according to the type of communication and the person to whom it is written. Here are some common examples of types of letter:

- *complaint* - a firm, informative and polite letter
- *enquiry* - a polite and precise letter
- *apology* - a helpful and polite letter
- *selling-* a persuasive and interesting letter

Developing tone and style is not a skill which comes easily. Practice is necessary. It is also helpful to read letters written by experienced letter writers. There may also be 'standard' letters which an organisation uses for specific purposes. e.g. for chasing up people who have not paid for goods supplied or services provided. These will be models of their kind.

sources of information

If you are writing a letter or a memorandum you may need information. This may be factual information or it may be a point of grammar or a difficult spelling. You will need to know where the information relating to travel, telephone and fax numbers is kept, and how to look up a difficult or a foreign word. These points are covered in Unit 7 (pages 84 to 86).

4. participate in oral and non-verbal communication ━━

performance criteria

When you are dealing with colleagues or callers on the telephone or personally you will need to communicate with them orally (by word of mouth) and also by using body language. In particular you should be able to

- listen to and observe others
- use appropriate vocabulary, language, tone and techniques
- use and interpret body language in sending and in interpreting messages

oral communication

Oral communication is used with colleagues and callers in two contexts:

• speaking to a person face-to-face
• speaking to a person over the telephone

Speaking to a person face-to-face also involves body language (see below) whereas speaking over the telephone relies solely on the voice. How can the voice be used effectively for communication?

tone

The tone of voice you use - the *mood* of your voice - shows your emotions and attitude very clearly. The important point is that whatever you may be thinking personally, you should not allow it to colour the communication process. For example

• if a caller is speaking for too long, you should not sound bored
• if a caller gets angry, you should not start shouting at the caller
• if the caller becomes very familiar you should not start to chat

In all cases you should adopt a calm, efficient and polite tone of voice. This is not to say that you should become inhuman - you should always react in a *controlled* way.   Like many other skills the use of *tone* comes with practice.

manner

The manner in which you speak will depend on the person to whom you are speaking. You will speak *informally* to a colleague in the same organisation, but will adopt a more *formal* manner when speaking to senior management. If you are dealing with an outside caller you will speak in a more formal manner, unless of course the caller is well known to you.

language

The words and phrases you will use will depend, of course, in the person to whom you are speaking. These are some general guidelines:

• when speaking more formally (e.g. to a senior manager or to an unknown caller) do not use slang, e.g. *'Can you hang on a sec?'*
• when speaking more formally do not use long 'posh sounding' words where short simple ones will do
• avoid workplace jargon at all times when speaking to outside callers - they will not understand what you are talking about

technique

An organisation will have a standard technique - the house style - for greeting and dealing with personal callers and telephone callers; e.g.

'National Bank, good morning, may I help you?'

Make sure you know what the house style is.

non-verbal communication - body language

Non-verbal communication involves the use of body language - gestures, facial expressions, and body posture - which confirm our links with the animal kingdom!   When you deal with a caller you should first interpret his or her body language to establish whether you have a complaint or an enquiry on your hands, and then you should respond using appropriate body signals, for example

• nod your head in encouragement and agreement
• look the caller in the eye, but do not overdo it - it may give the wrong impression!

On the next page are pictures of two callers with very different attitudes. Examine the body language - the facial expressions, the gestures and the posture. What do they tell you?

Two callers - what does their body language tell you? How would you react?

Common Skills Assignment 4
Communicating:
Getting the message across

Areas assessed

This assignment covers the following areas
- *Clerical Tasks: communicating information*
- *Common Skills: principal skill - communicating;
  other skills - applying numeracy, working with and relating to others*

Scenario

You work as a clerical assistant in the Sales Department of Wyvern (Office Products) Limited .

During the course of 14 May 199- you are required to deal with a variety of situations involving communications and are required to undertake a number of tasks. These involve

- *receiving and responding to messages*
- *visual communication - presenting figures in an appropriate format*
- *sending written communications*
- *oral and non-verbal communication*

Notes on completion of the Assignment

The tasks that follow require work to be done by individuals and by small groups. The assessor will also be involved in certain activities. Refer to the individual tasks for instructions.

Note also that Wyvern (Office Products) Limited has adopted the fully-blocked style as its house style for letters and other written communications. See Appendix 1 for photocopiable blank stationery.

Tasks

Task 1:   receiving and responding to messages

(a)   You have received the fax shown on the next page. Read it carefully, making notes if you wish, and then tell Robert Bates, your Supervisor (your assessor)

- what the message is
- what you think needs to be done
- where you will find the information

When your Supervisor has spoken with you, research the information and draft the text for a suitable fax reply in Robert Bates' name. Complete a fax header sheet with the necessary details.

---

facsimile transmission

from
HELIX INSURANCE
45 High Street
Abberton Bay
Jersey, Channel Islands, JE1 2XR

Telephone 0534 654278   Facsimile 0534 654864

---

date: **14 May 199–**

TO.... **Bob Bates, Sales**

.... **Wyvern (Office Products) Limited**

....

TELEPHONE NUMBER.... **0605 241851** ....FACSIMILE NUMBER.... **0605 241879** ....

NUMBER OF PAGES INCLUDING THIS HEADER.... **1** ....

---

message
I am flying into Heathrow next Wednesday, Flight arrives at 10.00 hrs. Can you let me know best way to get to Birmingham National Exhibition Centre? Many thanks. Max Reiner.

If you have any enquiries regarding this message please telephone the above number and ask for extension.... **45** ....

(b)　Someone has dropped a hastily written note on your desk (see illustration below). As you will see, it is far from complete. What details will you need to establish before responding to the request?

Please could you let me know the Sales figures for last month? I have got to do some budgeting, and seem to have lost the figures somewhere.   Thanks.

luv
Penny

(c)   You find this message in your in-tray. How would you respond to it? Draw up a suitable response for the signature of Robert Bates, your Sales Department Supervisor.

Note: Rivers Financial Services are normally given a 10% discount on purchases they make.

MESSAGE

while you were out

date .14 May 199- time .... 10:18 .... taken by .... Anne Jones

to .... Bob Bates

from .... John Rivers .... of .... Rivers Financial Services

phone 0605 271963

☑ telephoned   ☐ please telephone

☐ returned your call   ☐ wants to see you

☐ will telephone again   ☐ **URGENT**

☐ called in person

message
Please let Mr. Rivers have details of canteen tables
— sizes and prices — he is refitting his premises,
but is in no hurry. He wanted to know if he
gets any discount.
Address: 47 High Street, Mereford, MR1 3JR

Task 2:   *presenting figures in an appropriate format*

You are processing Wyvern (Office Products) Limited's sales figures for the last six months. The figures are as follows:
January £45,000; February £40,000; March £35,000; April £35,000; May £40,000; June £45,000.

The figures for the previous year were:
January £35,000; February £35,000; March £30,000; April £25,000; May £35,000; June £40,000.

You also note that the total sales for the last six months were split as follows:

Type of customer	£000's
Commercial	120
Professional	60
Educational	30
Other	30
Total	240

You are to:

(a) Present the sales figures for the first six months of the year so that they can be compared with the figures for last year.

(b) Show the different types of customer sales for the last six months in a visually meaningful way.

Note: you may use a computer graphics package if it is available.

Task 3:   *sending written communications*

(a) You receive a letter from Reg Coombs of Coombs Printers Ltd, 94 Oriel Court, Mereford MR3 5TG, asking for details of your 'Fisley' range of filing cabinets, as he has heard that they are very good quality. Write a letter for the signature of Jane Seymour, Sales Manager, setting out the specifications and prices for the Fisley cabinets, and enclosing your catalogue and price list. Assume that Reg Coombs does not qualify for discount.

(b) Bob Bates asks you to write a memorandum from Jane Seymour, Sales Manager, to all departmental managers (see structure chart on page 4) advising them to inform their staff that all Wyvern's employees are eligible for a 10% discount on the company's products. If any employee wishes to purchase goods they must obtain a form kept by Bob Bates, Sales Supervisor, complete it with details of the goods, and have it authorised by their departmental manager. A sample form is to be attached to each copy of Jane Seymour's memorandum. Note: you are not required to draw up the form.

(c) You receive the fax illustrated on the next page. Prepare a fax reply for transmission the same day.

---

fax from ═══════════════════

Graphic Art Studio
The Orchard
Broadway MR5 7TF

Telephone 0605 765324   Facsimile 0605 765329

date: **14 May 199–**

TO **Bob Bates, Sales**

Wyvern (Office Products) Limited

TELEPHONE NUMBER **0605 241851** FACSIMILE NUMBER **0605 241879**

NUMBER OF PAGES INCLUDING THIS HEADER **1**

message

I need some good quality automatic pencils urgently. Please fax me details and prices of what you have in stock a.s.a.p. The last ones I had from you were excellent.

John Turner

Task 4   oral and non-verbal communications

(a)   *Two students, a telephone system and a copy of Yellow Pages are needed for this simulated exercise.*
Your supervisor asks you for the names and addresses of five firms of solicitors. You cannot find the Yellow Pages, so you telephone a colleague and ask him or her to read out the names and addresses of five firms from the copy of Yellow Pages. Write down the details and then check them against the original entries in Yellow Pages.

(b)   *Two students and a telephone system are needed for this simulated exercise.*
One student is a Sales Assistant at Wyvern (Office Products) Limited, the other is a customer telephoning with a complaint about a faulty Office Table (Catalogue F1023). The customer complains that the veneer is damaged, but on enquiry it appears that the customer has been misusing the table by using it as a workbench for sawing wood.

(c)   *Two students face-to-face are needed for this simulated exercise.*
The situation is as in (b) above but the customer calls in person to complain.

(d)   The situation in (c) above should be videotaped and the interview played back with no sound so that the body language can be analysed. If no video is available, the interview could be watched by other students who will take notes (for later discussion) on the body language used by the sales assistant and the complaining customer.

8 Data processing - text processing

NCVQ coverage

3.1 produce alphanumerical information in typewritten form

Performance criteria

- *production of approximately 150 words (or numeric equivalent) in a ten minute working period with a maximum of two uncorrected errors*
- *correction of errors to be unobtrusive*
- *maintenance of security and confidentiality of information*
- *identification of faults, and action in accordance with the manufacturer's instructions, or reporting of the fault*

3.2 identify and mark errors on scripted material, for correction

Performance criteria

- *identification of all errors in text processed*
- *checking of all numerical data for accuracy, and identification of any errors or omissions*
- *marking clearly text or data for amendment*
- *ensuring that the layout conforms to specification*
- *reporting and amending - as required - any uncertain areas in the text*

introduction

Keyboarding is an essential office skill. You may already be familiar with a typewriter or a word processor, or both. This Unit aims to develop your competence in the processing of text - transcribing, checking and correcting - in the style that your organisation requires.

---

 linking assignment

Common Skills Assignment 5
Applying Technology: technology in the workplace, pages 138 to 139

the equipment

the keyboard

The object of this Unit is *not* to teach you to type - this will be dealt with elsewhere on your College course or work training. Instead, it develops your skills in processing text - transcribing, checking and correcting. It is assumed that you have at least a working knowledge of the keyboard, even if you are not a speed typist!

You should preferably at some stage learn how to touch-type (i.e type with all fingers by *touch*, and not by looking at the keyboard). It may be, however, that your work only incidentally involves keyboarding - for instance, if you are a building society cashier - and in this case you may get by with two or three finger typing.

The type of keyboard commonly used is the QWERTY keyboard, i.e a keyboard where the top row of letters spell 'QWERTY.' This is to be found on

* manual typewriters
* electric and electronic typewriters
* word processors and computers generally

The keyboard, depending on the sophistication of the machine used, combines a variety of

* alphabetic keys - the letters
* numeric keys - the numbers (computers normally have an additional numeric section to the right of the keyboard)
* function keys - electronic machines and computers often have a series of keys, normally along the top of the keyboard, which allow you to carry out certain functions (e.g. centering text)

Look at a variety of keyboards in your own workplace and see how much they correspond or differ.

maintenance by you

All equipment needs to be looked after, and your keyboard and any connected computer equipment are no exception. You should be able to carry out the following tasks:

* clean the keyboard with a recommended cleaner
* clean the VDU screen of your computer (if you have one)
* know how to change a typewriter or printer ribbon (and know where they are kept)
* know how to change a correcting ribbon on a typewriter (if you have one)

There should be a manual for the machine in question, and you should be familiar with its contents. Also remember simple tips such as

* keep the cover on the typewriter or computer when it is not in use
* do not spray correcting fluid into the typewriter
* keep your sandwiches and coffee a safe distance from your equipment

maintenance by the engineer

There will be occasions when your equipment breaks down and requires attention from an engineer. Make sure you know whom to contact in the office to arrange a call, and the procedure for recording a breakdown - some offices keep a special book for this purpose.

the desk area

We have already in Unit One looked at the importance of organising your work area efficiently. If your work involves keyboarding, it is important to set up your desk area so that you are as comfortable and as safe as possible; after all, you will spend many hours sitting and working at your keyboard.

Here are some suggestions:

- ensure that your chair is comfortable: it should be adjustable so that you can sit at the right level, with your back supported and your feet on the floor
- ensure that all loose leads are well protected - if you trip you could send both yourself and your equipment flying
- if you use a VDU (screen) for long periods, ensure you have an anti-glare filter to protect your eyes
- if you copy documents, ensure you obtain a copy-holder which will hold the document in a vertical position

processing text - the house style

If you work in an organisation, or obtain work experience in an organisation, you must be fully aware of the standard way in which letters and other written communications - which you will produce at the keyboard - are set out and processed. This standard style is known as the *house style*. In particular you should note the following:

format
You should know whether letters, memoranda and other written documents are produced in
- *fully blocked style* - i.e. all text is set to the left margin (left justified) and open punctuation is used (no punctuation, except in the body of the text)
- *semi-blocked style* - i.e. where the date is set at the right margin (right justified) and the complimentary close and name of sender start half-way across the page
- *fully displayed style* - i.e. where paragraphs are indented, the date is set to the right margin and the heading and complimentary close and name of sender are centred; standard punctuation is used (full punctuation)

These three styles are illustrated in full on pages 73 to 75.

style detail
Certain details common to most typed communications should be standard in any organisation, as house style:
- *quotation of references*, e.g. RT/HG/67, where RT are the initials of the writer, HG the initials of the typist, and 67 the number of the file in which the letter should be stored
- *the date*, e.g 30 January 1991, where the fixed order is: day - month (spelt out in full) - year
- *headings* should be standardised, e.g. normal text underlined or NORMAL TEXT IN CAPITALS
- *punctuation* and *spelling* should be standardised, for example
  - e.g. or eg, i.e. or ie
  - standardised (English style) or standardized (American style).

type-face
Ensure that you use the correct type-face for the occasion. You may need to change a daisywheel on a typewriter or a type 'font' on a word processor.

numbers
You will from time-to-time be required to set out numbers in text which you are processing; for example quotations for a job, price lists, and times of the day. You should ensure that you are familiar with the required format, e.g.
• using a decimal tab stop for figures in a column
• quoting money amounts using two decimal places for the pence - £2.00 rather than £2
• using the 24 hour clock - 09.00 and 17.30 rather than 9 a.m. and 5.30 p.m.
These figures are examples only - you should find out what *your* house style requires.

envelopes
Make sure you know how addresses are set out on any envelopes you type. If you are using a fully blocked or semi-blocked style in the letter, use the same style on the envelope:

Mr J Adams
243 The Park
St Albans
Herts
AL7 2UZ

If you are using a fully displayed style, set out the envelope in a similar way, indenting the address and using standard punctuation (except on the post code line)

Mr. J. Adams,
243, The Park,
St. Albans,
Herts.
AL7 2UZ

copies
Ensure that you know how many copies of each written communication are required, e.g. three copies of a letter - one to send, one for the file, one for circulation. If you are processing a memorandum you may need multiple copies for sending to a large number of staff - possibly even to all the staff, if it is a message from the Managing Director!

back ups
All organisations will (or should!) have 'house' guidelines for data storage. If you are using a word processor which uses a floppy disk, hard disk or other storage device, ensure that you know where a copy of your text file should be stored. Saving text, particularly as you are inputting, is very important, and the dangers of wiping out your own work - or anyone else's - do not have to be spelt out!

printing
If you are processing text, your finished work may be produced in a variety of different ways:
• on the typewriter itself
• on a computer printer - dot matrix, daisywheel, ink-jet or laser
Ensure that for each document processed you are familiar with the 'house' guidelines for the correct paper and printer to be used, particularly in terms of
• paper size and format (for instance, do you use headed paper?)
• paper colour (this may vary with the job in hand)
• paper quality (a laser printer, for instance, is fussy in this respect)
Lastly, if you are not happy with the print quality, print it again, changing the paper if necessary.

processing text

Your course may require you to type texts of 150 words, or the numeric equivalent, in ten minute working periods. As we stated earlier this book does not teach you how to type, but it does aim to instil techniques which will help you to process text accurately in the accepted house style.

The source of the text may be a handwritten sheet, a typed sheet with alterations, or a compilation from different sources. The process of typing out this material is known as *copy-typing* or *transcription*. Whatever the source, it is up to you to
- correct any spelling errors in the original
- correct any punctuation errors in the original
- rid the text of abbreviations
- clarify (tactfully) with the writer or originator of the task any problems over meaning - ambiguous words, or words which you suspect are used incorrectly

We will deal with each of these in turn

spellings
You may find that even the most senior manager may have spelling lapses, and it is up to you to detect and correct them when you are transcribing text. An important item of equipment is therefore an English Dictionary (e.g. Collins or Oxford) in which to check words. You might also like to compile a list of difficult and frequently used words. Here are some familiar stumbling blocks:

accommodate	disappear	principal (adjective)
address	embarrass	principle (noun)
advice (noun)	February	privilege
advise (verb)	fulfil	procedure
argument	harass	professional
beginning	interest	receive
benefited	interrupt	recommend
business	licence (noun	referred
committee	license (verb)	separate
comparative	necessarily	stationary (adjective)
convenient	necessary	stationery (noun)
correspondence	occurred	success
definite	omitted	supersede
dependant (noun)	parallel	transferred
dependent (adjective)	practice (noun	until
develop	practise (verb)	Wednesday

punctuation
Your house style will dictate some of the punctuation rules you observe, e.g.
- whether to use open (no) or standard (normal) punctuation in the body of letters and memoranda
- whether to use punctuations after abbreviations such as *e.g.* *i.e.* *etc.*

Otherwise you should observe the normal rules:

	paragraph	normally preceeded and followed in the text by a blank line, a paragraph is a group of sentences which together form a connected train of thought
.	**full stop**	a full stop marks the end of a sentence
;	**semi-colon**	a semi-colon marks a significant pause in the text
,	**comma**	a comma marks a slight pause in the text

'   **apostrophe**

The apostrophe indicates a possessive sense. For instance:

Your director's response to our letter

The salesman's trip

The apostrophe can also be used to indicate a missing letter. The word *it's* sometimes causes problems. It means *it is,* and is never used in a possessive sense, as in - *'its meaning'* where there is <u>no</u> apostrophe.

Note that in written communication you should not abbreviate by using apostrophes. For instance you may <u>say</u>

'I don't think so. I'm fairly sure of that.'

but you should <u>write</u>

I do not think so. I am fairly sure of that.

abbreviations

Abbreviations are commonly used in drafting text. When you come to transcribe the text and produce your typed version, it is important to set out out the abbreviated words in full. Common abbreviations include:

abbreviation	*full form*
a.s.a.p.	as soon as possible
a/c	account
chq	cheque
dept	department
hr	hour
info	information
n.b.	note that (latin: *nota bene*)
no.	number
o/s	outstanding
pls	please
wd	would

clarify meanings

There are two distinct situations in which you may suspect that the wrong word has been used:

- situations where you yourself do not know what a word means
- situations where you suspect the writer does not know what the word means, i.e. he or she has got the word completely wrong, or the word right and the spelling wrong!

If you yourself are unfamiliar with a word, you should look it up in a good dictionary, a thesaurus (a book suggesting similar words for any given word) or a reference book such as *Fowler's Modern English Usage*.

If you suspect that the person who wrote the draft you are copying has got the word or spelling wrong, tactfully query it with them. Do not try and make them look ignorant, instead make it look as if it is *you* who is asking for information. Always check the answer you are given by reference to a dictionary - the person may try and bluff his or her way out of the situation!

Some commonly confused words are listed on the next page.

words frequently confused in meaning and spelling

advice (recommendation)	*and*	advise (to give advice)
amend (to correct)	"	emend (to delete)
check (to hold back)	"	cheque (money)
complement (an addition)	"	compliment (praise)
current (existing now)	"	currant (type of fruit)
eminent (distinguished)	"	imminent (near)
ensure (to make certain)	"	insure (to protect)
impracticable (impossible)	"	impractical (not easily achieved)
principal (chief)	"	principle (a rule)
stationary (not moving)	"	stationery (envelopes etc.)
there (in that place)	"	their (belonging to them)

identification of errors

When you have typed or input your transcribed text, having carried out all the checking and correcting described so far, you the have the further task of ensuring that *your* text is correct! You yourself are probably the least well qualified to do this, because it is a well-known fact that people are often blind to their own mistakes. What then is the recommended procedure?

checking it yourself You should produce a 'hard copy' first, and check the text yourself for obvious errors. The 'hard copy' can be the piece of paper you have been typing on, or a computer print-out of the text. The checking process is known as 'proofreading.' A useful method is to compare the original with your version side-by-side on your desk. Use a ruler to keep your place in the text and compare the two, reading the text out phrase by phrase, and mark in any corrections as you go through (see the next section for the marks you use). Take care over

- punctuation (read the text out, including any paragraph breaks)
- missed words and words put in twice
- missed lines
- columns - if you use columns ensure that the information is in the correct column
- headings - it is often assumed, quite wrongly, that headings are always correct
- names, addresses and foreign words - check them very carefully
- numbers - if there are any calculations involved, check them with a calculator - twice!

asking a colleague It is useful - if not always possible - to ask a colleague to check your work,
to check your work or, better still, to read the original aloud to a colleague who has your work in front of him or her.

If there are figures and calculations involved, ask your colleague to check them with a calculator.

Case Problem
To give you an idea of the type of discipline involved in checking text that has been transcribed, look carefully at the next page. At the top is the original handwritten version, and underneath is the text that has been produced. It must have been a Friday afternoon; how many errors can you detect?

letter please to
Mr R J Davies, 45 Churchill Crescent, Mereford, MR2 7TP
his ref RJD/KL/73, our file 86

Dear Mr Davies, heading - <u>Office Furniture</u>
Thank you for yr. enquiry of 24 Jan. New para. We can supply as requested a large top single pedastal desk @ £99.95 excl. VAT. We wd also reccomend 4 metal stacking chairs @ 8.75 each, excl VAT. The total cost excl VAT would therefore be £135.95. New para. We enclose our catalogue and price list for yr. info. We hope that you will find our prices for furniture and for stationery are v. competitive.   Y.S.   R Brownridge

---

Enigma Office Supplies
54 Church Street
Mereford MR1 8YE

Tel 0605 675364 Fax 0605 675985

Our Ref RB/MF/89   Your Ref RJD/KL/73   30 January 1991

Mr R D Davies
45 Churchill Crescent
Mereford
MR2 7TP

Dear Mr Davies

<u>Office Furnture</u>

Thank you for your enquiry of 25 January.

We can can supply as requested a large top pedastal desk
at £99.95 excluding VAT.   We would also recomend 4 Metal
staking chairs at £8.75 each, including VAT. the total cost
excluding VAT would therefore be £135.99. We enclose our
catalogue and list price for your infomation. We hope that
you will find ourprices for furniture and for stationary are
very competative.

Yours sincerely

R Brownridge
Sales Manager

marking corrections

There are a number of errors in the example just given. You will want to mark changes - edit - the text so that a final and correct version can be typed out. How do you mark the changes? Set out below are the standard correction symbols which will be (or should be!) recognised in all offices.

word or letter corrections
The incorrect word or letter is ruled through neatly and the correct word or letter written above.

```
                 a                   excluding
    chairs it £8.75 each,  including VAT
```

deleting words or letters
The incorrect word or letter is neatly ruled or crossed through and a � symbol is written in the margin.

```
�    We can can supply as requested

�    We appologise for the error
```

inserting words or letters
The symbol ⋏ is inserted where the word(s) or letter(s) are to go, the inserted text is written clearly above the line, and the ⋏ symbol is written again, in the margin.

```
               i
⋏    office furniture
                single
⋏    a large top/pedestal desk
```

If there is insufficient room in the text for the inserted words, they should be written in the margin

```
single
⋏    a large top/pedestal desk
```

inserting and deleting a space
If you are inserting a space you should place a / mark between the letters concerned

If you are deleting a space you should link the letters on each side with two lines ‿

```
    we hope that you will find our/prices reason able
```

inserting a paragraph
The symbol // is placed in front of the word which is to start the new paragraph

```
    . . . £8.75 each, including VAT. // The total cost . . .
```

changing the order of letters or words
The symbol ⌒⌣ is placed around the letters or words to be changed around

```
    catalogue and/list price
```

```
    one of your freinds
```

or a balloon with an arrow can indicate the change

```
    you may order if you wish at the end of the month, ↓
```

changing capital letters to small (lower case) letters

Underline or circle the capital letter(s) and write l/c in the margin (l/c = lower case)

l/c   O̲ffice F̲urniture

changing small (lower case) letters to capital (upper case) letters

Underline or circle the lower case letter(s) and write u/c in the margin (u/c = upper case)

u/c   (o)ffice (f)urniture

indicating that a change is not required - 'stet'

It may be that you mark a change in the text, and then decide that the earlier version should stand. You should undereline the text with a dotted underline, and write stet in the margin ('stet' is latin for 'let it stand').

stet   I have decided to go on my visit on ~~Thursday~~

Now look below at the corrections marked in the text of the letter in the Case Problem on page 112 (the firm's address is omitted here).   It would seem that the typist is lacking in concentration!

Our Ref RB/MF/89   Your Ref RJD/KL/73   30 January 1991

Mr R J Davies
45 Churchill Crescent
Mereford
MR2 7TP

Dear Mr Davies

O̲ffice Furn̲iture

Thank you for your enquiry of 28 January.

We can can supply as requested a large top/pedestal desk
at £99.95 excluding VAT.   We would also recomend 4 Metal
staking chairs at £8.75 each, including VAT.   the total cost
excluding VAT would therefore be £135.99.   We enclose our
catalogue and list price for your infomation.   We hope that
you will find our prices for furniture and for stationary are
very competitive.

Yours sincerely

R Brownridge
Sales Manager

enc

final correction of errors

When your work has been checked, and correction marks made, you then have to produce the final *correct* version which can then be passed forward for signing. The method of correction used will depend on what type of machine you are using - typewriter or word processor.

typewriter corrections

The method of correcting errors used will depend on the number and type of errors, and the sophistication of the machine you are using.

eraser rubbers may be used, but they can be messy - take care that the dust produced does not clog up the typewriter mechanism

correcting fluid fluid should be used sparingly and allowed to dry before overtyping - remember that you are not plastering a wall or painting the typewriter; do not forget to fill in the gaps afterwards with the corrections!

correction paper ensure that the paper you use is fresh - worn paper is not always effective

correction ribbon if your typewriter has a correction ribbon, make sure that you erase the appropriate text

insertions ensure that you are able to insert the correct number of characters in the space available - use a halfspace facility if necessary and if your machine provides it

golden rules
- *always ensure that any corrections are also made to the copies of your text.*
- *if your typed copy has too many mistakes for you to reasonably amend it, type it again, but make sure that you get it checked*

word processor corrections

One of the conveniences of the word processor is that corrections are made to the text on the screen, and no messy fluid or other means of correction are necessary. The correcting facilities available are

- deleting text by markers or selection and inserting new text in its place
- deleting text by overtyping
- moving words, sentences, or whole blocks of text by selection and insertion

There are, however, dangers in these procedures. Take care that you do not

- delete the wrong text
- overwrite only part of the incorrect text, leaving some the incorrect text on file
- insert a block of text in the wrong place

golden rule
- *always ensure that you print out and save your corrections, and back them up - there is nothing more depressing than spending time in correcting text and then finding that the corrections have not been saved, and all you are left with is the original uncorrected text.*

security and confidentiality

dealings with outsiders

We have already seen that it is your responsibility as an employee to ensure that certain information kept within your organisation is not 'leaked' to an outside body. This type of information includes

- details of your employees
- information about the security of your premises
- financial information, such as your banking arrangements
- information about your customers

You should therefore follow the following guidelines when processing text:

- no internal documents should be sent to outside bodies, unless a senior person orders it
- always check that sensitive information is sent to the correct address and in the correct envelope
- if correspondence is to be sent to an individual, and you do not want anyone else to see it, mark the correspondence (above the heading) and also the envelope 'PRIVATE AND CONFIDENTIAL' (above the address)

dealings within your own organisation

If you are processing text you may well be dealing with information that is confidential *inside* your own organisation. You may work, for example, in a personnel or administrative department which deals with staff records, reports and promotion plans. When you are working in this type of position, confidentiality is of utmost importance.

You should follow the following guidelines:

- do not leave confidential information lying about on your desk where others can see it
- lock any confidential information in a drawer or filing cabinet when you are not using it
- ensure that all security regulations relating to computer data is observed, i.e. keep computer passwords to yourself, lock disk boxes as required, and file printouts
- take care that you do not leave confidential documents in the photocopier - a common mistake
- take care over what you throw in the waste bin - it can be a mine of information for the curious individual - use a shredder or a confidential waste sack
- take care when carrying confidential papers around the office - people have a habit of reading over your shoulder
- take care with file copies of confidential information - ensure that they do not become sorted in with the general filing

Most of these points are pure common sense. You should, however, always be on your guard. Sometimes the most innocent-seeming request for information from a colleague can lead to a serious breach of confidentiality and security, a breach which *could* lead to disciplinary proceedings! Remember that you will be *respected* for keeping confidentiality.

student activities - text processing

Performance criteria

The student activities in this section test competences in the following areas:

- *production of approximately 150 words (or numeric equivalent) in a ten minute working period with a maximum of two uncorrected errors*
- *correction of errors to be unobtrusive*
- *maintenance of security and confidentiality of information*
- *identification of faults, and action in accordance with the manufacturer's instructions, or reporting of the fault*
- *identification of all errors in text processed*
- *checking of all numerical data for accuracy, and identification of any errors or omissions*
- *marking clearly text or data for amendment*
- *ensuring that the layout conforms to specification*
- *reporting and amending - as required - any uncertain areas in the text*

text processing

1. What precautions would you take take to make sure that your work area is both safe and healthy when you are working at a keyboard? What would you do if your machine broke down?

2. What precautions would you take to ensure that confidential information is kept secure and not seen by anyone who should not see it?

3. If you are typing a letter, what aspects of *layout* and *presentation* will be dictated by your 'house style'?

4. What would you do if you were typing a text and suspected that the writer had used the wrong word in a certain context?

5. State the correct spelling in each of the following cases:
    (a) acomodate, accommodate, accomodate
    (b) addres, adress, address
    (c) benefited, bennefited, benefitted
    (d) business, buisness, businness
    (e) correspondance, correspondence, corespondence
    (f) fullfil, fulfill, fulfil
    (g) interest, intrest, interesst
    (h) neccesary, necessary, neccessary
    (i) refered, reffered, referred
    (j) seprate, separate, seperate

6. Correct the following sentences
    (a) Its my advise to you that the problem should be tackled now.
    (b) The principle problem is the shortage of stationary in the office.
    (c) Please insure that your polite to our imminent visitor.
    (d) I need to see all the currant files.
    (e) We consider that late payment is bad practise.

7   Spell out the following in full
    'Pls send me a chq a.s.a.p. for the o/s invoice. N.b. yr a/c is now 12 wks overdue.'

8   Check the following calculations, and correct as required:
    (a) 25 packs of fax roll at £33 per pack = £825.00
    (b) 12 x 150mm clear plastic rulers at 18p each = £2.06
    (c) £35.76 + £76.56 + £67.75 + £56.78 + £786.06 = £1023.01
    (d) £35.76 + £76.56 + £67.75 + £56.78 + £786.06 plus VAT at 17.5% (£179.00) = £1210.91
    (e) US$10,000 converted at a rate of $1.95 to £1 = £19,500

transcribing text

9.   Transcribe the following letter in fully blocked style, with open punctuation, for the signature of Jane Seymour, Sales Manager. Take one copy. The date is 4 February of the current year. Make any changes to the original which you are think are necessary. Type a suitable envelope.

Letter to
Dr N Spicer
Hollybush Cottage, Kiln Lane, Broadgreen, MR6 2JP

Our file 95

Dear Dr Spicer
Heading (underlined) <u>*Office Supplies*</u>

Thank you for yr letter of 28 Jan. We will be pleased to supply office furniture and stationary as requested. Para. In answer to yr spacific enquiry about tables, we can supply one each of the following three sizes.
75cm x 75cm @ £55.75, 120cm x 60 cm @ £58.50, 90 x 90 @ £61.50.
= £170.75. The prices quoted do not include VAT.
Para. The tables all have detachable legs for ease of transport and storage, and can also be fitted with draws if necessary. Our firm wd be pleased to deliver free of charge. We suggest you allow three wks for delivery. Para. We wd also be pleased to supply your needs for stationery. We offer a wide variety of office materials, including paper, envelopes, files and folders. We can also arrange printing of yr letterheads and complements slips. Perhaps if you wd like to telephone us we can quote for yr requirements. Para. We look foreward to hearing from you. Yours sincerley. Jane Saymour. Sales Manager.

---

10. Transcribe the following letter in semi-blocked style, for the signature of Tina Brooks, Accounts Manager. Take one copy. The date is 4 February of the current year. Make any changes to the original which you are think are necessary. Type a suitable envelope.

Letter to T F Pain, Accounts Department, Broadheath Electronic Supplies, Unit 8 Avon Industrial Estate, Mereford MR5 7TD. Our file 54.

Dear Mr Pain. Heading <u>Overdue Account</u>
Further to our recent statement of a/c we do still not appear to have recieved pmt. of the £5,675.78 o/s. We attach copies of the relavant invoices for your info together with a fresh statement. The original terms we granted were pmt within 30 day's of invoice up to a credit limit of £5,000. The following invoices have been o/s for 90 days: Inv. 8976 £345.67, Inv 9017 £675.87, Inv 9456 £2014.89. Total over 90 day's = £3063.43. Para. We regret that if we do not recieve pmt within 7 day's we will have no alternetive but to place the matter in the hands of our solicitors. In the meantime we regret we are unable to supply you with the goods ordered on yr Purchase Order 7645 of 1 Febraury. Para. We look forward to hearing from you.
Yours sincerly. T Brooks. Accounts Manager.

---

11. Transcribe the following memorandum in fully blocked style with open punctuation for Asaf Patel, Administration Manager. Take one copy. The date is 5 February of the currrent year. Make any changes to the orginal which you think are necessary.

Memo to Departmental Managers, Subject - Canteen opening hours.

Please note that as from Monday 11 February the canteen will be open at the following hrs:
Monday 11.00 - 2.30, Tuesday 11.15 - 2.45, Wendesday 11.00 - 2.30, Thursday 11.15 - 2.45, Friday 10.30 - 3.00. It is hoped that these extended hrs will be more convenient for the staff. Please also note that the currant system of serving hot food from opening time is to be discontinued , and hot dishes will only be avalaible from 12.00 until 1.30. .Please emend your records as appropriate, and circulate the details among your staff a.s.a.p. Para. There will also be a wider choice of food, and special new dishes for vegitarians. We have spent some money on redecorating the canteen, and we hope that staff will appriciate the changes. In order to get some feedback I have prepared a questionaire for the staff (copies attached) and wd be gratefull if you will distribute them in yr dept and arrange for their collection and return to me at this office by 4 March. Para. Many thanks and 'bon appetitt'! A.P.

checking typescript

Check the following transcriptions of text extracts and mark the corrections which you think need to be made.

12. Thank you for your letter dated 17 Febraury. We are pleased ot inform you that your contract been has accepted.

13. There is is no possibility that we can deffer this decission any longer.

14. Thank you for your order for ofice furniture. We will deliver the goods to your premises when convenient. Please telephone this office to arrange a convenient for delivery.

15. The sales representative will arrive it 11.30. After a premilinary meeting he will have lunch with the Managing Direction.

16. I amwriting to complain about your products, and I do not suppose I am a lone in doing so.

17. I shall be grateful if you will let me know if this is convenient.

     Yours sincerely

     Eric Thorne Sales Director

18. I can see no reason why we were sent a Wooden chair when we ordered a metal chair. if a replacement is not provided within seven days we will consider taking our buisness elsewhere.

19. The invoice is is one of themost impotant and
probably the most well known of trading documents.
it is sent from the seller to the buyer to advice
how much is owed for a delivery fo goods. The
Invoice states quantity of goods suplied, the price,
any vat charged, and the total ammount owned. E.g.

2 staplers @ £5.00 = £10.00 + VAT (@17.5%) £1.75
= Total £17.50.

Many businesses do not pay on reciept the invoice,
but on issue of a statement. If a buisness pays
late, some times intrest is charged on the ammount.

20. The new keyboard for the Electra word prosessor is
very user freindly, with smooth action and clearly
marked keys. A numberic keypad is provided on the
Right hand side, and function keys enable the user
to to formatt and setout text in a flexible way.
the keyboard finished in a light cream colour and
can easilly be cleaned.

21. I am writing in anwser to your advertisement in the
Evening echo, and would like to apply for the the
post of coppy typist. as you will see from the
enclosed curicculum vitae I have been working inan
office for six months and have under taken a wide
varety of jobs, including filling, dealing with the
male, and ledger work. I wish to develop my skills
as a typist, and been have studying at the local
Colledge on a RSA course. I would be pleased to
come for interview at anytime which is convenient
you.

 linking assignment

Common Skills Assignment 5
Applying Technology: technology in the workplace, pages 138 to 139

9 Data processing - updating a computer database

introduction

As well as being able to process text on a typewriter or a word processor, it is important that you develop the skills required in operating a computer database. A computer database is a program for keeping information (data) on computer file - the computer equivalent of a card index file. The information is stored in records made up of individual items of data - e.g. names and telephone numbers. A database can be accessed easily, updated, sorted and in certain circumstances used in combination with other computer programs. It is the aim of this Unit to explain how to use an existing database. It will not normally be your job to set up the system, but to operate it. As with text processing, the skills evolve with practice.

 linking assignment

Common Skills Assignment 5
Applying Technology: technology in the workplace, pages 138 to 139

the computer

Before you can operate a database program, you need to know about the computer you are using. You need to know

- the component parts of the computer - the *hardware*
- where to find the program - the software - and how to handle the disks (if you use them)
- how to set up the computer safely and so that you yourself are comfortable
- what to do in the case of faults or breakdowns

the hardware

It is presumed at this point that you have a certain familiarity with computers, but as a reminder of computing terminology, you should read through this section.

Most office computers comprise three main components

- a processing unit containing the disk drive
- a keyboard - with function keys, QWERTY keys, and navigation/numeric keys
- a screen known as a VDU (visual display unit)

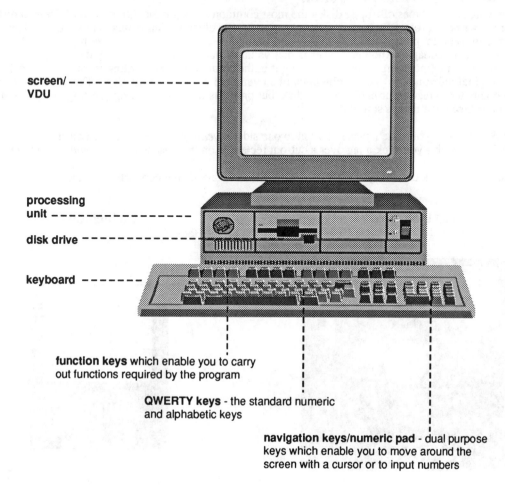

screen/ VDU

processing unit

disk drive

keyboard

function keys which enable you to carry out functions required by the program

QWERTY keys - the standard numeric and alphabetic keys

navigation keys/numeric pad - dual purpose keys which enable you to move around the screen with a cursor or to input numbers

In addition to the hardware illustrated on the previous page, there may also be

- a printer - dot matrix, daisywheel, inkjet or laser
- a mouse - a hand-held device which enables a pointer to be moved around the screen
- external data storage devices

Clearly not all systems are the same as far as the *hardware* is concerned. The *software* - the programs which run the computers - will be very similar in operation, and you should have no difficulty is relating any database program which you may use to the explanations given in this Unit.

the software

The database program and data which you use may be stored

- in a *hard disk* storage device in your computer, or housed centrally and linked to your terminal
- on *floppy disks* which you will have to insert into the computer in order to 'load' the program and record data

If the program and data are stored on hard disk, operation is simple - all you need to do is to key in a command to gain access to the database. If your program is in floppy disk format, you will need to take care with the disks; they can easily be damaged.

floppy disks - write protection

There are several types of floppy disk - the most common sizes are the 3.5 inch and 5.25 inch disks. Both types need protecting against excess heat, magnetic objects , damp, dust and bending. They are normally kept in plastic lockable cases and should never be left lying around where they are vulnerable to damage. Another danger is that valuable data stored on a floppy disk might be wiped off by someone (including yourself!) placing it in the computer and recording fresh data and deleting the original information. This problem can be overcome by *write-protecting*. This process enables the computer to read information on the disk, but prevents it from recording (writing) any data on it. Write-protecting a disk is straightforward:

- 3.5 inch disk - you slide a plastic button to one side, *revealing* a hole in the disk casing
- 5.25 inch disk - you stick a tag over a cut-out rectangle on the disk cover, thus *hiding* the hole

This procedure should always be adopted with disks containing the computer program.

5.25 inch disk   **3.5 inch disk**

write-protect tags

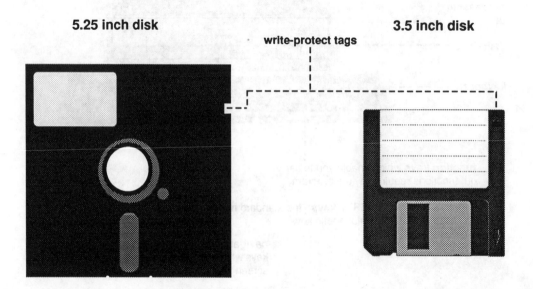

safety, comfort and maintenance

As we have already seen in the previous Unit, it is essential that your work area is made as *safe* as possible, and you yourself are made as *comfortable* as possible for the job in hand. You should also be aware of possible computer faults which can occur and know if you can fix them, or if you are not able to fix them, contact someone who can. If you are not clear about what is required, read the sections 'the equipment' and 'the desk area' on pages 106 to 107.

Of course, some faults which occur are problems with the program - the software - rather than with the hardware. If you are working with a database program, ensure that you know where the instruction manual is kept; it will often have a trouble-shooting section to help you out of difficulties. Some programs also have a 'Help' menu to which you can refer in times of need. You may also know of a supervisor who is an expert on the program and who can tell you in two minutes what a manual would reveal in fifteen.

the database program

what is a database?

Organisations *record* and *store* information - details of customers, employees, stock held, and so on. They also need to have *access* to that information. Traditionally a good filing system (see Unit 10) fulfilled that need, but in recent years the development of computers has made the task of storing, sorting and retrieving information much simpler and faster. A computer database is therefore nothing more than *a collection of related pieces of information,* for example the names, addresses and telephone numbers of your customers.

why use a computer?

You might ask why a computer is used. Why not keep all the names, addresses and telephone numbers of your customers on index cards? You could do this, but imagine the time it would take if

- you wanted the names of all the customers who lived in London
- you wanted to sort the cards in alphabetical order of the towns/cities in which the customers lived
- you dropped all the cards on the floor and had to resort them in alphabetical order!

The computer can take all the hard work out of these types of tasks and perform them almost instantaneously.

database programs

Database programs can be

- 'stand alone' programs which operate independently of other programs and may be specially written for the organisation
- part of an integrated software program which may also include a wordprocessing program and a calculation program known as a 'spreadsheet'

Whichever form the database program takes, it can usefully link up with other programs. Suppose, for instance, that you wanted to send out a standard letter to your customers. You would link up the addresses in your database with a standard letter format - with a gap for the address - in your word processing program, and the computer would print out all the letters, and possibly also address labels to match, if they were required.

database terminology

In this Unit we will be using terminology which is common to all database programs, and you will need to familiarise yourself with the various terms.

data   information

database   a collection of data organised so that the data can be added to, amended, sorted and accessed

file   a collection of records in a specified format - e.g. all the records of customer names and details

record   an individual record containing data - e.g. a customer's name and details - comparable to an index card in a manual system

field   a separate item of data contained in a record - e.g a customer's name, a customer's initials, the first line of a customer's address are all *fields* and will have
                    • a specified maximum number of characters (letters/numbers)
                    • a specified format (all numbers, or all letters)
                    The way in which fields are set up is examined in more detail in the next section

form   A form is the record (or part of the record) *as it appears on the computer screen* (see the illustration below). It is effect like a paper form, showing all the fields available, their names, and the spaces in which you can type the required information

The *organisation* of a computer database is set out in diagramatic form below.

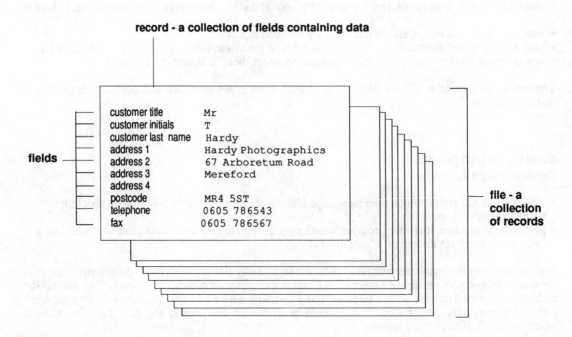

record - a collection of fields containing data

fields

customer title	Mr
customer initials	T
customer last name	Hardy
address 1	Hardy Photographics
address 2	67 Arboretum Road
address 3	Mereford
address 4	
postcode	MR4 5ST
telephone	0605 786543
fax	0605 786567

file - a collection of records

preparation of data

Data must be entered into a database in a *standard format*. If you take the example of a database containing customer details such as name, address and telephone/fax number, each field must be completed *in the same way*. This will be the 'house style' of the organisation, and will be reflected in the way in which the database will accept data. In the example below, the organisation has two new records to add to the database, but the original data (in the form of handwritten and typed notes - on the left hand side) is not in the correct format, and so amendments have been made to standardise the data for the database forms as input (illustrated on the right hand side). What differences can you detect?

original note format   **database input**

---

please add to database file CUSTOMERS -

Jim Smart
Whitchurch Supplies
Unit 7 Oak Industrial Estate Mereford
MR5 7TG
Tel 0605 765432
Fax 0605 765523

customer title	Mr
customer initials	J
customer last name	Smart
address 1	Whitchurch Supplies
address 2	Unit 7
address 3	Oak Industrial Estate
address 4	Mereford
postcode	MR5 7TG
telephone	0605 765432
fax	0605 765523

```
Laura,  pls. add to CUSTOMER.
database file. Thanks.


Phillip Jamieson,
Mercia Electrics Limited,
85, High Road,
MEREFORD.  MR1 3ED
Telephone (0605) 675432
```

customer title	Mr
customer initials	P
customer last name	Jamieson
address 1	Mercia Electrics Limited
address 2	85 High Road
address 3	Mereford
address 4	
postcode	MR1 3ED
telephone	0605 675432
fax	

The following items have been standardised in the house style of the organisation:

- the first names have been changed to initials and titles (Mr) added
- the punctuation has been removed from the second record
- the town is not input as capital (upper case) letters
- the brackets have been removed from the telephone code in the second record
- the address has in each case been split into separate lines
- the postcode is on a separate line

It must be stressed that the style suggested above is not the *only* way of dealing with customer details, it is an example of a standard house style. Your employer or College may use a different format, but it should always use the *same* format.

In the next section we will look at the actual process of accessing the database and entering data.

using the database - adding new records

Your studies assume that the database has already been set up; all you have to do is to switch on the computer, load the program, and enter the data.

accessing the file

Not all computers work in the same way, but you should find that the instructions given below relate to the way in which your College's or employer's computer operates:

- switch on the machine
- load the database program (this may be done by typing in the program name after a prompt)
- access the file that you need, e.g. CUSTOMERS (there will be a number of different files in the same database)
- a blank form is required so that you can input the information - this may be shown automatically, or you may need to move to the end of the file to find a blank form - consult the manual
- the database program may give you the option to view all the records as a list or as a series of forms - you should chose the forms option

entering the data

A blank form for the CUSTOMERS file will appear on the screen as follows

```
customer title
customer initials
customer last  name
address 1
address 2
address 3
address 4
postcode
telephone
fax
```

- the grey rectangles are the fields where you should input the information - some programs may use other means of showing the fields and their size, e.g. dots, brackets or boxes
- you can access a field by using navigation keys (on the right hand of the keyboard) or a mouse
- you can move from one field to another by pressing the Return key or using a navigation key
- you will be restricted in the number of characters (numbers or letters) you can enter in each field
- you may be restricted by the program in the type of characters used - it may for instance reject the use of letters in the 'telephone' field or the use of numbers in the 'customer last name' field
- you must check that you are using the house style of input

checking and correcting the data

On completion of a record form you must check your input very carefully. As noted above, some programs will do a certain amount of checking by limiting the *type* of characters entered and the *number* of characters in a field. There may still other errors for correction:

- typing errors which may be corrected by use of the backspace or by overtyping
- data input in the incorrect fields - use the navigation keys and re-input

A completed record on the computer screen will look like this -

customer title	Mr
customer initials	J T
customer last name	Baker
address 1	Baker & Wilson Finance
address 2	34 High Road
address 3	Mereford
address 4	
postcode	MR1 3FD
telephone	0605 876435
fax	0605 876436

accessing a new record form

Once you have completed a record form, you normally access a new record form by pressing the Return key at the end of the last field. The completed record is automatically allocated a number by the computer. If the computer does not save the completed records automatically, you should do so yourself at regular intervals.

amending and deleting database records

In the case of the CUSTOMERS file used as an example above, details on the database will have to be changed regularly as customers move premises, change telephone numbers, or even cease trading. You will therefore need both to amend and also to delete records.

amending a database record

The procedure is simple, once you are used to dealing with the database:

- switch on and load the program
- access the file, e.g. CUSTOMERS
- locate the record to be amended - normally by looking through the file 'View' option which displays one record per horizontal line and shows each field in a vertical column
- display the record as a form (i.e. as illustrated above)
- carry out the necessary amendments by overtyping or deletion and typing
- *save* the amended file and back it up!

deleting a database record

The procedure is similar to the amendment routine:

- switch on and load the program
- access the file, e.g. CUSTOMERS
- locate the record to be deleted - normally by looking through the file 'View' option which displays one record per line, or by reference to the computer-allocated record number
- select and use the delete command (you may not have to show the form on screen for this procedure)
- *save* the amended file and back it up!

using the database

One of the major advantages of a computer database is that it is a very flexible and labour-saving filing system. Once the information has been input and saved, it does not have to be sorted and filed away as would paper records. If the information, or part of it is required, it can be sorted and extracted very rapidly to produce a printed report.

sorting data

Suppose that your CUSTOMERS file used as an example earlier in this Unit contains 1,000 records. You are asked to sort out the file in two ways to produce two separate lists:

* to sort the customers into alphabetical order by last name
* to sort the town in which each customer lives into alphabetical order for a marketing exercise

If the records were kept in a paper filing system, the tasks would take a number of hours to complete and probably reduce you to a nervous wreck. The computer database can sort data almost instantaneously. We will take the first task - the alphabetic sorting of customers - as an example:

* switch on and load the program
* access the file - CUSTOMERS in this case
* select the field required - 'last name' in this case
* select the sort option
* indicate the type of sorting required - in this case from A to Z (it would also be possible, but less desirable, to sort from Z to A!)
* give the necessary command to sort
* save the sorted file

You may ask whether the database can sort the customers to take account of their *initials* as well. The answer is that it it possible by means of a *multiple sort* - last names are given the priority sort, and initials take second place. This type of sorting would be useful if you had to organise a delegates list for a conference. Sorting is also possible with most databases for *numbers* (ascending and descending order) and also for *dates* (starting with the earliest date, or the latest date). Thus if the CUSTOMERS file had included a field for the date that the record was input, it would be possible to sort the customers into *date* order.

searching for data

A database program will also carry out searches for you. It can look for words and numbers. For example a search in the CUSTOMERS file could reveal all the customers who had the last name 'Smith' or all the customers who lived in 'Leeds'. The latter search would be very useful, for instance, if your organisation was sending a salesman or representative to Leeds, and you wanted a list of customers whom he could visit.

The database can also carry out a *multiple search*, looking for more than one specified piece of information: for example all the customers living in Cardiff called 'Jones'.

reports

The end-product of a sorting or searching process in a database is normally a printed report. If the sorted data involves *all* the records of the original file, e.g. the file CUSTOMERS sorted alphabetically, the sorted file will be saved in its amended form as CUSTOMERS and printed out.

If the data is extracted as a result of a Search routine it will be saved, backed up, and then printed as a separate file. e.g. LEEDS CUSTOMERS.

back-ups and security

Organisations which use database programs are vulnerable in two respects:

- the information held on computer disk is liable to be corrupted or erased
- the information held on computer disk is often confidential, and must not normally be allowed outside the organisation

It is therefore essential that if you use a database program you are trained to back-up the information in an organised way, and also to look after it by observing security regulations.

back-ups

Floppy disks are used for two purposes

- *storing programs*, e.g. the database program, the computer operating program; these are known as program disks
- *storing data*, e.g. the database files , wordprocessing files; these are known as data disks

You should regularly back-up your database files and also have copies of your program disks (which should be write-protected). The method adopted of backing-up data files will depend on the type of computer you are using, but you will normally use floppy disks (see page 124) if you are using computers with twin floppy disk drives or computers with hard disk drives. The procedure for back-up will be explained in the computer manual; it normally involves inserting the disk in the machine and issuing an appropriate command. You should observe the points set out below when you are backing-up:

- ensure that you know how to *initialise* an unused floppy disk before using it as a back-up (refer to your supervisor if you are unsure about initialisation)
- ensure that the floppy disk is suitably labelled with the file reference and date of the copy
- store the back-up copy away from the computer - in a fire-proof safe if necessary
- if something goes wrong with the original data file or program, *back-up your back-up* before using it in the suspect machine
- back-up regularly, preferably every time you use the program
- if you use the program daily use more than one back-up data disk: you could use five - one for each working day and labelled 'Monday' & 'Tuesday' and so on . . .

security

It is essential that data held on computer file is kept confidential - particularly if it involves individuals. The Data Protection Act 1984 makes it an offence if *personal* data, for example customer files and personnel files, is leaked to an outside body.

The following safeguards should be observed:

- keep floppy disks locked up when not in use
- keep computer rooms locked when not in use - or at least restrict access to authorised personnel
- use a password to gain entry to the computer, and change the password regularly
- keep the password confidential

Some computer systems restrict access to certain files to senior members of the organisation. These members of staff have a special password to those files. That password must be guarded very carefully.

The general rule of security and confidentiality must be observed at all times. Any security breach is a major breach, and could put your job in jeopardy!

student activities - updating a computer database

Performance criteria

The student activities in this section test competences in the following areas:
- *accessing the correct field in a database*
- *transcribing data correctly and entering it into appropriate fields*
- *maintaining security and confidentiality of information*
- *reporting faults and failures promptly, and describing symptoms accurately*
- *following operating and safety procedures at all times*

1.   The database form illustrated below is the record format for a new database file CUSTOMERS. You are to input the customer details listed below, *in the same style as the data in the illustration.*

customer title	Mr
customer initials	S P
customer last name	Bulstrode
address 1	Bulstrode Engineering Limited
address 2	Unit 7B
address 3	Barnfield Industrial Estate
address 4	Mereford
postcode	MR7 2BF
telephone	0605 675453
fax	0605 675452

The list has been given to you by your filing clerk, and not everything is quite right. Note that some of the details are not set out in the house style, and some of the data is incomplete or incorrect. You will be able to work out what is incomplete and incorrect by comparison with the other details in the list. Note: if there is no fax number listed, assume there is no fax. The telephone dialling code for Mereford is 0605 and for Stourminster 0701.

Gerry Smithers, 67 Grantham Close, Mereford MR4 5TY, Tel 0605 675423

Mrs Heather Styles, 87 Lincoln Drive, Mereford MR5 6TF, Telephone Mereford 987675

John Heathcliffe, Heathcliffe Furniture 56 High Road Mereford MR6 5RF, Tel 987453 Fax 987451

Norman Perkins, Perkins Perfumerie, 7 The Arcade, Stourminster MR8 6TG, 0701 876532

Miss Annette Royal, The Style Shop, 9 The Arcade, Stourminster MR8 6TG, Tel 876501

Malcolm Eckley, Eckley & Son, 7 Station Road, Mereford MR4 8YH, Tel Mereford 675401

Martin Barnes, Barnes Bathrooms, Unit 9B Oak Industrial Estate, Mereford MR6 5RF, 524197

H T Osborne Esq., 45 The Park, St Albans, Herts AL3 4RT, Tel 0727 871685

Peter Whiteman, Whiteman Engineering Co Ltd, 78 Arboretum Mews, Mereford MR6 2TF
Tel 987342 Fax 987323

John Osborne, Heatpack International, 675 Mulberry Road, Milton Keynes MK5 9TX
Tel Milton Keynes 675432 Fax 675498

R T Sanders Esq, 56 Rochester Way, Sandridge, Mereford, MR8 7TF, Tel 0605 643256

Dr Deborah Hunt, 60 The Chimes, Stourminster, MR8 7YG Tel 098765

John Grover, Elstee Printers Limited, Unit 8 Severnside Industrial Estate, Mereford MR3 1ZE
Tel 876654 Fax 876635

Mrs Jacquie Wall, Wall Flowers, 5 The Arcade, STOURMINSTER MR8 6TG, 0701 876345

Colin Sparks, Mereford Electrics, 7 Rosemary Close, Mereford MR3 7OF, 987345

Phillip Bradfield, Bradfield Garden Centre, Stourminster Road, Mereford MR6 4LP, 0605 678425

Ms Norma Bludgeon, 78 Rectory Court, Mereford MR1 3TR, 896435

Mike Mountford, 56 Bell Lane, Broadheath, MEREFORD MR6 4AC, Tel 0605 678564

Miss Beryl Street, Vogue Photographic, 93 Jacomb Road, Mereford MR2 4RF, 908654

Bert York, Downhurst Stationers, 89 High Road, Mereford MR6 7YT, 987456

T F Pain Esq, Broadheath Electronic Supplies, Unit 8 Avon Industrial Estate, Mereford MR5 7TD
Telephone 786435 Fax 786478

Dr Nigel Spicer, Hollybush Cottage, Kiln Lane, Broadgreen MR6 2JP, 0605 566691

Terry Birmingham, 56 The Furlong, Mereford MR4 6TF, 876345

Elizabeth Oldman, White Rose Cottage, Byways, Mereford, MR8 6TR 0605 765234

Bernard Brunsdon, 67 Cemetery Street, Mereford MR7 5RT, 976452

Bob Stone, Wyvern House, Windy Ridge, Mereford MR8 5TR, 0605 765349

Mrs Tamsin Lee, Cathedral Antiques, 76 High Close, MEREFORD MR2 5TJ, 980654

Mrs A C Jones, Annie's Cookies, 78 New Street, Stourminster, MR8 9ES, Tel St. 875234

Thomas Osborne, Clocks n' Watches, 54 High Street, Mereford MR1 4SY, 876525

Jim Steel, Steel & Co, 65 High Street MEREFORD MR1 3ST, Tel 0705 876453

2.   When you have checked the data for errors, sort the records into alphabetical order by customer
last name and print out a report showing all the data. Check for errors again and amend any
records that need correcting.

3.   One of your sales representatives - Bob Bates - is visiting Stourminster next week. Search the file
for all customers who live in Stourminster and print out a report showing their details. Send this
report with a covering memorandum to Mr Bates, Sales Supervisor.

4.   You receive a number of written communications during the working day (5 March).   Amend the
     database as you think necessary, and in the case of (a) draft a suitable letter in reply.

(a)   Letter from N Perkins, Perkins Perfumerie

> *Dear Sir,*
>
> *I note from your correspondence that you are addressing me as Mr Perkins; in
> fact my name is Norma Perkins (Ms) and I shall be grateful if you will amend
> your records accordingly.*

(b)   A card from Elstee Printers Limited

Elstee Printers Limited ▬▬▬▬▬▬▬

We are moving on 5 March to new and larger premises. Our new
address will be:

Elstee Printers Limited
Unit 45 Avon Industrial Estate
Mereford MR5 7TX
Tel 0605 786123 Fax 0605 786124

(c)   A note from one of your colleagues

> *Penny,*
>
> *I see that Heatpack International have gone bust. You had better take them off
> the customer file, as Accounts Department will be the only people dealing with
> the matter from now on. Thanks.*
>
> *Steve*

 linking assignment

Common Skills Assignment 5
Applying Technology: technology in the workplace, pages 138 to 139

Common Skills development: Applying technology

Skills developed
The skill developed in this section is

- *apply a range of technological systems*

In the last two units we have looked at how two technological systems - the word processor and the computer database - have affected office procedures, producing requirements for very specific skills. We have also looked at the operation of the fax machine in Unit 6 . In this Skills section we will give an overall picture of the different technological systems that are available in the office. In the assignment which follows you will have the opportunity of putting these systems to practical use.

apply a range of technological systems ▬▬▬▬▬

performance criteria
If you operate modern technological systems in the workplace you must be able to

- identify appropriate equipment for the task
- complete the preparation procedures for the equipment
- utilise the equipment effectively
- appreciate how the equipment can help you with your task
- rectify basic errors and report more complex errors
- follow the operating safety and security procedures

knowing and using the right equipment
If you are using a piece of technological equipment - a computer, a fax machine, a photocopier - you must ensure that you *know* what you are doing. In particular you must choose the right equipment for the job. For example you would *not*

- use a photocopier for making a thousand copies of a sales leaflet - you would have it printed
- use a fax machine for sending a confidential or an important letter - you would post it

You must ensure that you know how to set up the equipment and to operate it. You should, in any event, receive formal training in its use. If you are unsure, refer to the operating instructions or to your supervisor. The procedures for dealing with computers are set out in Unit 9 (pages 122 - 125 and 131) and photocopiers are explained in Unit 11 (pages 155 to 167).

technology in the workplace ———————

If you are studying at College or working in an office you will be aware of some, if not all, of the technology that is currently available. In this section we will will look at the whole range of available systems to give you an overview of modern technology in the workplace.

word processing   We have already looked at text processing in Unit 8, and you will be aware of the different stages through which a letter or memorandum progresses before it is sent. The ability to process text on a computer, to file it and to amend it are the major advantages of word processing. If you have a standard letter or text format on file you can also *mailmerge*, i.e. automatically retrieve names and addresses from a database file and insert them in the text file to produce a batch of documents on the printer, for instance

- a letter to your customers promoting a new product
- a demand letter to customers who have not paid their bill!
- labels for addressing Christmas cards to selected customers

You will see from this that word processing is both an efficient and also a time-saving process.

DTP   DTP is short for Desk Top Publishing, a fanciful name for a sophisticated word processing program which can present and format text in combination with lines, boxes, shadings and imported pictures (graphics), all on the computer screen. The finished design is then printed out on a laser printer which gives a high quality finish. This laser printer produced copy can then be passed directly to a printer for printing. DTP is used by some publishers (this book was produced entirely on a computer DTP program) and by organisations who want to produce publicity material and in-house documents and forms cheaply and quickly.

database   We have already looked at the computer database in detail in Unit 9. As you will recall, it is essentially a computerised system for organising information and can be used for purposes such as maintaining

- customer names and addresses, and accounts
- stock records
- staff files

As noted above, the database can usefully be integrated with a word processing program in a *mailmerge* exercise.

spreadsheet   A spreadsheet is a useful and widely used computer program which enables the operator to set up simple or complex calculations on a grid on the computer screen. Once the basis of the calculation has been set up, figures can be entered and the calculations will be performed automatically. It is commonly used for

- financial forecasting - comparing future income with expenditure
- working out pricing of products and services - i.e. how much they will cost
- recording of petty cash (see Unit 14)

The advantage of a spreadsheet is that once the calculation formula is set up on the screen, you can enter and change figures, and the computer will carry out the calculations for you automatically.

integrated programs

Many software manufacturers combine the word processing, database and spreadsheet programs into one 'integrated' program. This type of program has the advantages of savings in cost, and the ease with which data can be transferred from one program to another.

accounting programs

Many organisations record their financial transactions (sales, purchases, bank payments, payroll) on specialised accounting programs. Many of the business documents described in Unit 14 (pages 204 - 223) can be generated by an accounting program and printed out on a computer printer.

fax

Fax (facsimile transmission) machines are able to transmit to another fax machine over the telephone system an exact copy (facsimile) of a document fed into the transmitting machine. They have a number of advantages:

- they are easy to operate
- transmission takes a short period of time
- they can be backed up with a telephone conversation to explain what is being sent
- they can transmit text, drawings and documents
- they can also double as photocopiers i.e. you can use them to copy documents in the office (some machines are now sold as fax/photocopiers)

electronic mail

Electronic mail (E-mail) enables you to send a text document such as a letter or a memorandum from one electronic machine to another, without the need for any paper.

• *internal E-mail*
Electronic mail can be used within the office in what is known as a local area network (LAN), i.e. a group of computer terminals linked by cable. A document can be input by one employee and sent to another.

• *external E-mail*
Electronic mail is especially useful when used between organisations. British Telecom's *Telecom Gold* system, for example, gives an electronic 'mail box' with a special number to each subscriber. If you want to send an E-mail message to a subscriber, the details and the number are sent down the telephone line and will appear on the recipient's terminal, and will be stored if the recipient is not there. This can be very useful if you want to send an E-mail letter to Australia or any destination in a different time zone when the recipient's office is likely to be empty in the middle of their night and your day!

viewdata

Viewdata is a means of obtaining information on a VDU from a central information source. It also enables the user in some cases to send information back. You will probably have seen viewdata in operation if you have been to a travel agent, and seen the agent calling up holiday details on the screen, and possibly making a booking.

Viewdata may be made available as a *public* service - in the UK a common example is Prestel, a British Telecom service giving information about a wide range of topics. It is also possible to access other databases through Prestel via computer 'gateways.' Viewdata is also available on a *private* basis, as in the travel agent example, when an organisation has a number of computer terminals linked to a central database. Each terminal will have access to the central information - e.g. of holidays available - which will be updated as items - e.g. holidays - are sold.

Common Skills Assignment 5
Applying technology:
Technology in the workplace

Areas assessed

This assignment covers the following areas

- *Clerical Tasks: data processing*
- *Common Skills: principal skill - applying technology;
  other skills - communicating, working with and relating to others*

Scenario

You work as a clerical assistant for Villas International Ltd., an independent travel agent which specialises in the rental of foreign villas and apartments to UK holidaymakers. The company, which is situated at 34 The Hop Market, Stourminster MR8 6TF, comprises the owner, a secretary and yourself.

Villas International Limited is a old-fashioned business started by Miles Ludlow twenty years ago. It has relied very much on traditional methods of selling its holidays - small advertisements in the local paper and word-of-mouth recommendations.   Recently, however, competition from other firms who advertise in the Sunday newspapers and promote a much more 'glossy' image has resulted in a substantial decline in business. Last month Miles Ludlow, who is 65, decided to retire and to sell the business to someone who was much more go-ahead and up-to-date in approach.   The buyer was Paul Robinson, a young and energetic executive in the travel business. You heard him say on his first morning when he toured the office that a lot of changes would have to be made.

The main areas of operation of the business are

- keeping in touch with owners of apartments and villas abroad in locations which stretch from Europe to Honolulu
- booking flights through the main airlines
- marketing the holidays to UK holidaymakers

The office itself is very old-fashioned, although it functions very efficiently. The records of apartment and villa owners are kept in filing cabinet drawers in alphabetical order, while the client (holidaymaker) details are kept in a card index file in a drawer.

The business relies very much on the telephone for keeping in touch with its villa and apartment owners and also for booking flights.

Marketing and advertising are very low key and are based on regular adverts in the local Stourminster Echo and an annual newsletter to regular clients, typed in the office and sent out by post. It is your job to type out the envelopes each year for the newsletter.

The only electrical equipment in the office is an elderly electric typewriter, a small desk-top photocopier, and a coffee percolator (Mr Ludlow was very particular about his coffee).

Tasks

1. What opportunities are there in this office for the introduction of new technology, particularly for

    (a) word processing
    (b) DTP
    (c) a database program
    (d) a spreadsheet program
    (e) a fax machine
    (f) electronic mail
    (g) viewdata

    Write your recommendations in the form of a memorandum to Paul Robinson stating the changes that could be made, and stressing the advantages in each case of the application of new technology.

2. Miss Preece, the secretary, has no experience of computers and states quite firmly to Mr Robinson

    'If those machines come in here, I'm off somewhere else, even if it's feet first!'

    State why you think Miss Preece is so opposed to computers. What you think you and Mr Robinson can do to try to persuade Miss Preece that new technology is not as bad as she thinks?

Notes on completion of the Assignment

It has been assumed in this Assignment that not *all* students will have access to *all* forms of new technology, and therefore Tasks 1 and 2 are theoretical, i.e. they do not involve 'hands on' experience of computers and related technology. If you do have access to computers you may be able to attempt some of the following tasks:

3. Using a database program, set up a file of thirty clients; each record should contain the client's name, address and telephone number, together with a series of fields for the dates when they booked holidays with you, and the destinations in each case. Sort the records so that you can print out reports to show which destinations are the most popular from year to year.
    Note: invent the client details.

4. Using a word processor write a letter to your clients telling them of the change of management and giving them an assurance of continued good service. If your computer system and resources permit, carry out a mailmerge exercise and print out a letter to each client on the word processor, headed with the client's name and address from the database. You can either design your letter so that window envelopes can be used, or alternatively you can use the database and word processor to print a series of address labels to stick on plain envelopes.

5. Using a DTP program design an advertisement for Villas International to place in the local newspaper. Look at other travel advertisements to give you an idea of the format required. Your advertisement should include a notice of the change of management.

10 Filing and retrieving information

NCVQ coverage:

1.1 file documents and open new files within an established filing system

Performance criteria:

- filing documents without undue delay in the correct location and sequence
- storing materials without damage in a safe and secure manner
- classifying all documents correctly
- referring classification uncertainties to an appropriate authority

1.2 identify and retrieve documents from within an established filing system

Performance criteria:

- locating, extracting and passing specified documents to the correct person or location
- notifying delays in the supply of files and/or documents, and explaining the reasons for delay politely
- recording promptly all file and document movements in a legible and accurate way

introduction

The general office will deal with a vast array of information on paper. This information will usually include letters, memoranda, reports, and financial documents. It is important that the paperwork is filed in an organised way so that it can be retrieved easily and quickly if it is required. It will not be your responsibility to set up the filing system, but it will be part of your job to acquire the skills of classifying, filing and retrieving documents from the system.

 linking assignment

Common Skills Assignment 6
Managing tasks and solving problems: Managing without the boss, pages 190 to 195

documents for filing

the documents

If you are given the task of filing you will be sorting and filing away a wide variety of documents. The precise nature of the documents will, of course, depend on the type of organisation for which you work. They might include

- letters received by your organisation
- copies of letters sent by your organisation
- memoranda written within your organisation
- sales literature - brochures, pamphlets
- magazines, press cuttings and booklets
- financial documents such as quotations, orders, invoices, and credit notes

identification and collection of documents

The office system will arrange for collection points - normally trays or wire baskets - in which your colleagues will deposit items which they want to be filed. You may also be required to circulate the desks and pick up items for filing. The document for filing may be stamped with a filing instruction, such as . . .

. . . or, the document may be crossed through. If the document is produced by your organisation it may be printed on a specific colour of paper which will indicate that it is a file copy. The important point is that you should keep up-to-date with the filing. There is nothing more depressing than an immense and growing pile of paper which needs to be put away; it is a *priority* task, even if it is not your favourite task.

file classification systems

Before explaining how and where each document is sorted and filed, we will first examine how files are *classified*. Classification is the system which dictates the order in which documents are filed, and hence how documents can be found.

Classification of documents can be

alphabetical   Documents are stored in the alphabetical order of the names of individuals, businesses and other organisations to which they relate - a very common method - look at your telephone directory or your own address book.

numerical	Each file is given a number and is filed in number order - this is a useful system for an organisation which can easily identify its customers by number, e.g. a motor insurance company which has a policy number for each customer. A numerical system normally needs an alphabetical index system as a back-up.

chronological   Documents are stored in date order with the oldest documents at the back and the newest at the front.

geographical   Documents are stored according to the geographical location of the customer - a system useful for organisations such as travel agents or electricity companies.

subject   A system useful for administration and personnel systems, whereby each document is stored according to its subject matter, e.g. tax, pensions, training, salaries - you may find that your own domestic 'filing system' is organised along the same lines.

The rules for the alphabetical and numerical classification are explained in more detail below.

alphabetical classification

Look at your telephone directory; it is a good example of the alphabetical rules in practice. In an alphabetical system, files are arranged in letter order of the title of each file. The first letter of the person or organisation concerned dictates in which letter section of the filing system the file is stored, and the subsequent letters dicate where in that letter section the file will be placed. As names of people and organisations are not entirely straightforward, certain rules must be followed:

	rule	*example*
files for individuals	files are placed in order of the first letter of the surname(last name)	COX FARDON PORTSMOUTH
	if the first letter is the same the order is determined by the next letter, and so on	FARADAY FASSON FOX
	if the surnames are the same, the order is determined by the initials	JONES, A C JONES, J E JONES, L M
	prefixes such as *de, de la, O'* *van* and *von* are treated as being the beginning of the name	DE LA MARE, W O'CASEY, S VAN BEETHOVEN, L
	names beginning with *Mc, Mac, M'* are treated as if they are all spelt *Mac*	McBETH, G MACLEAN, A
	double-barrelled names are treated as if they were one long name	FOSTER-THOMAS WILSON-SMYTHE
	file a short name before a long one	GRIFFIN GRIFFIN, J GRIFFIN, J J

	titles such as *Rev., Sir, Lady* are placed in brackets at the end of the name	FOSKETT, A J. (REV.) FOSKETT, BASIL (SIR) FOSKETT, JOSEPHINE (LADY)

files for organisations

the normal first alphabetic rule applies	BROADHEATH COMPUTERS LTD BROADHEATH VIDEO CLUB BROADWAS STORES
Saint/St. names are filed under *Saint*	ST ALBANS DISTRICT COUNCIL SAINT JAMES BOOKSHOP ST WULSTANS COLLEGE

if the name of the organisation includes a first name, file under the last name/surname

JAMES BROWN & CO. LTD. is filed as BROWN, JAMES, & CO. LTD.
ANNIE JONES CATERING is filed as JONES, ANNIE, CATERING

The words *A* or *The* in the name of an organisation are placed at the end of the name in brackets

A CUT ABOVE HAIR SALON is filed as CUT ABOVE HAIR SALON (A)
THE MEREFORD ECHO is filed as MEREFORD ECHO (THE)

organisation titles which are composed of initials are filed before names written in full	ABC LAUNDRY A-Z SUPPLIES LTD. ABADAN TOURING COMPANY

numbers in names are treated for filing as if they were written out in full

40 PLUS HEALTH FARM is filed as FORTY PLUS HEALTH FARM
4 SEASONS RESTAURANT is filed as FOUR SEASONS RESTAURANT

numerical classification

In a numerical filing system, each file is given a number, the files are stored in that numerical order, and are therefore easy to find. The main drawback is that if you want to locate a file you first have to look up the file name in an index system. For instance if you want the file for ABC LAUNDRY you will have to look up ABC LAUNDRY in the index to find its numerical reference. The index system can be organised by means of index cards, or better, on a computer database which can be referred to on a screen or on a print-out. Libraries use numerical filing systems on a decimal basis (see below).

The numerical classification can work in two ways

sequence

each file is allocated a number in sequence as it is opened - the first file will be number 0001 and if there are 4000 files, the last to be opened will be number 4000

decimal

each *type* of file is given a number, e.g. customers in geographical areas classified as South = 1, Midlands = 2, and so on, the actual file number will then follow after a decimal point, e.g.

Metal Reasearch Ltd, Brighton	=	1.005
Falcon Motors Ltd, Coventry	=	2.045

sorting the filing

presorting methods

Filing involves physical effort: walking around the office with a pile of paper to where the files are stored, looking through the files, pulling out the appropriate file wallet, leafing through documents, and placing *your* piece of paper in the correct position. You can minimise the physical effort by *presorting*, i.e. by sorting the documents for filing in the correct order at your desk. There are a number of ways of doing this

* a *desk-top sorter* - a series of hinged flaps (e.g. one for each letter of the alphabet) behind which you can place documents in alphabetical or numerical order
* a *concertina file* - a large card wallet with pockets for letters of the alphabet or ranges of numbers

which file? - filing points

We have already seen that there are a number of different ways of classifying documents for filing, the most common of which is alphabetical order. The person who has been dealing with the document should indicate where it should be filed by ringing with a pen or using a highlighter the appropriate detail - the *filing point*. Examples of filing points include:

* a letter received - the name of the person or organisation originating the document
* a letter sent - the name of the person to whom the letter is sent
* a memorandum - the name of the person who has written it, or the subject which it covers
* a financial document originated by your organisation, e.g. an invoice - the document number
* a financial document received by you, e.g. a credit note - the name of the sender

If your organisation uses a *numerical* classification system for filing, the file number will possibly already be on the document contained as a number in *Our Ref* (letters sent) or *Your Ref* (letters received). If the number cannot be found, you will need to look it up in the index system.

operating a diary system

One of the tasks which may be given to the person doing the filing is organising the necessary follow-ups. Suppose your organisation writes to a customer who has asked for details of your products. If you file the copy of your reply with no follow-up, the customer may well lose interest after a while. If, however, the file copy of your letter is marked . . .*'Diary - one month'* or *'Follow up - one month'* . . . you will need to take action to ensure that the writer of the letter gets a reminder in a month's time so that he can again contact the customer and try to achieve a sale. Follow-ups can be used for many different situations involving monitoring and control of external and internal operations of an organisation.

How does a follow-up system work? A follow-up system can be operated by using a desk diary, or alternatively by using a card index file which has two sections:

* spaces for the months of the year (at the back of the file)
* spaces for days of the month - the current month - (at the front of the file)

The usual procedure is for a *copy* (not the file copy!) of the appropriate document or a note to be inserted in the appropriate place in the follow-up file:

* if the diary date is *not* in the current month, it is placed in the *month* section (in date order)
* if the diary date *is* in the current month it is placed in the appropriate *date* section

At the beginning of each month the diary copies for that month are extracted from the back of the file (where individual months are located) and sorted into the appropriate dates at the front of the file.

cross references

When you are filing you will come across situations where you cannot file (or find) a document where you expect to. In these cases you will find a cross reference sheet (see illustrations below) guiding you to the correct place. This could happen in a number of different circumstances:

- a business may change its name and it becomes necessary to move the file because of the new classification
- a person may change his or her name (women getting married, for instance)
- a name may be difficult to classify and therefore a person may look in different places for a particular file - e.g. the stationers John Menzies may appear under 'J' or under 'M'

If there is a change of name, the reason and date are normally written on the sheet.

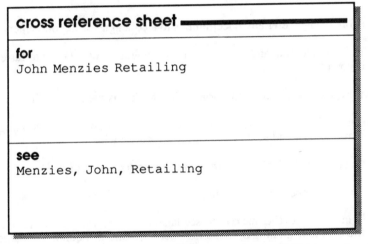

cross reference sheet - used when a name is difficult to classify

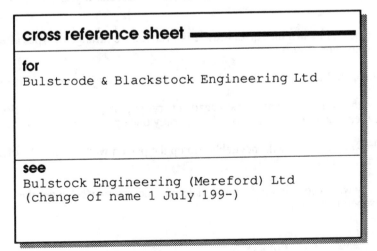

cross reference sheet - used when a name has been changed

filing method

Once you have sorted your documents and dealt with any diary notes in your diary system, you have a collection of documents ready to file.   We will now set out below as Action Points the elements of good practice in filing.

✔ action points - good practice in filing method

○   check that the documents really are for filing - ensure that they have not been placed in the filing tray by accident - they should be marked with a filing point (a stamp, a highlighted, circled or underlined word, or some other identifying mark recognised in your office)

○   sort the papers before filing - refer any uncertainties to a colleague or to your supervisor

○   remove paperclips - they can trap and conceal other documents! - use staples to fasten papers together if you need to

○   when you place the documents in the appropriate file, check it is the *correct* file

○   place the document neatly in the file so that its edges do not protrude; if it is too large, fold it neatly so that it will fit and so that you can still identify what it is

○   file the documents in chronological order - the most recent document on top

○   if there is no file currently open for the document,
either
file alphabetically in a separate file marked 'Miscellaneous' (a separate file for each letter of the alphabet, filed at the beginning of that letter section); this will contain documents for which there is no file opened
or
if you think the amount of material is sufficient, ask your supervisor if you can open a new file

○   do not cram documents in when the file or drawer is over-full, re-arrange the files after consulting with your supervisor

○   do not lean on an open drawer - you, the cabinet and its contents may end up on the floor

○   do not open more than one drawer at a time - again, everything may end up on the floor; (some cabinet systems have a safety device whereby only one drawer will open at a time)

○   do not leave a drawer open, you will inevitably trip up the person walking into the office carrying a full tray of coffee

○   lock any files away which contain confidential material - the key may be under the control of your supervisor

○   tell your supervisor
    - if there are problems with the filing system
    - if the cabinets are faulty (will not open, shut or lock)

storage methods

There are four main methods of storing filing: vertical, lateral, horizontal and rotary. We will deal with each of these in turn.

vertical system

In the vertical system, the files are stored in cardboard pockets which hang from metal guide bars which run along rails mounted at the top of deep drawers. The files are taken out by lifting them out of the drawer.

The name of each file is indicated *either* by
• a label along the top of the guide bar
or by
• a tab attached to the top of the guide bar

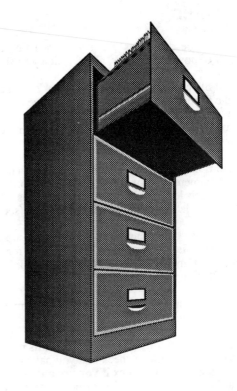

The system is known as the 'vertical suspension' system because the files are suspended vertically and are therefore kept in good order. Occasionally organisations will store files in cabinet drawers without using the suspending rails and pockets. This is not good practice because the files have a habit of sliding to the horizontal position and getting out of order. Papers may slide to the bottom of the drawer and be lost from sight!

The vertical filing system also requires considerable floor space for its operation - approximately three times the floor area of the cabinet itself. The reason for this is that the drawers need to be pulled out fully, and space is also needed for the person to gain access to the drawer which is pulled out.

lateral system

The lateral filing storage system like the vertical storage system hangs the documents in pockets from rails. The pockets are not, however, in drawers, but side-by-side in an open-fronted cabinet. The documents can be taken out and returned easily.

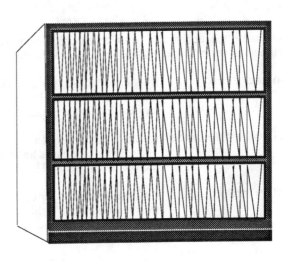

The system is also space-efficient as lateral filing does not need the drawer opening space of a vertical system. The only problem lies in identifying the files, because like the titles of books on a shelf, the file names may only be read sideways. Typed labels can help avoid a crick in the neck.

Security is made possible by the option of roller doors which pull down and can be locked shut.

horizontal and rotary methods

If your organisation needs to store large flat documents such as plans or architects' drawings, *horizontal* drawer units may be used. These shallow drawers store the documents on top of each other, and will ensure that the documents are maintained in good condition. Labels on the outside of the drawers will indicate the contents.   The *rotary* method suspends the individual files from a central pillar on rotating arms so that the files can be accessed easily.

new files

There will be occasions when you are filing a document and there is no file for it. There are a number of possible reasons, all of which you should check:

* is the file booked out in the 'Out' book? (see page 150)
* is the filing point correct, i.e. is the name or number indicated on the document correct?
* is your own classification correct - i.e. are you looking in the right place? - for instance, does the name start with *The* and are you looking in the *T* section by mistake?
* there is no file for the document

If there is *no file* for the document, your office may have a system whereby a 'miscellaneous file' will store documents, normally in alphabetical order of the filing point. Usually there is a miscellaneous file for each letter of the alphabet, and this file will be located the beginning of each alphabetic section, and labelled, for instance, 'A' or 'B' (see illustration on the next page).

There will be occasions when you or your supervisor thinks it necesary to start a new file. Perhaps there are a large number of documents for one customer in the 'Miscellaneous File' or your organisation may possibly have just signed a large contract with a new customer. If you are starting a new file you should:

* confirm with your supervisor that the file may be opened (unless your supervisor has already requested the new file)
* establish the correct file name (or number) using the classification rules (see pages 141 - 143)
* prepare a label for the filing cabinet (this may be typed on a strip for insertion in a plastic tab or on the edge of the file) - check that you have the right colour if the files are colour coded
* enter the file in the index if you use one (this may be on a card or on a computer file)
* place the file pocket in the correct place in the filing cabinet or cupboard
* file the opening documents, remembering to keep them in chronological order (newest on the top)

indexes

We have mentioned that your organisation may keep an index of files, particularly if it uses a numerical method of classification. This index may take a variety of forms:

index cards   a card will be used for each file and stored vertically and alphabetically in a drawer - much useful information can be written on the card, e.g. the file name, telephone number and contact name

visible edge cards   the cards are stored in alphabetical order in shallow drawers which slide out of a cabinet; the cards lie down flat with just the edge showing the name of the file; when you slide the drawer out you can see the name at a glance

strip index   the details required for the index are typed on a thin strip of card which is then inserted into a rigid frame which can be inserted into a ring binder file; strips can be added and taken out as the file records change

Bradshaw, T F	
Blockley, R F	
Blakley, T J	
Beckwith & Co Ltd	
Barrow Windows Ltd	
B	**MISCELLANEOUS**
Arnold, R P	
Amphlett Engineering Ltd	
Ambridge District Council	
Adler, L	
Acworth Garden Centre	
Abberley Young Farmers	
ABC Catering	
A	**MISCELLANEOUS**

A diagram of an alphabetical filing system stored in a vertical (drawer)
system, showing
* *the labelling across the top of the files*
* *the miscellaneous files for each letter of the alphabet stored at the front of*
  each alphabetical section

file security - current and dead files

As mentioned elsewhere in this book, it is the duty of the employee to ensure that security procedures are followed at all times. Filing involves the handling and storage of documents and it is therefore essential that the documents do *not* fall into the wrong hands. The dangers include the possibility of an intruder breaking into the building outside working hours and stealing sensitive documents (financial documents, plans, personnel files) or a colleague obtaining information to which access is prohibited (e.g. personnel files).

It is the duty of the person on filing duties to ensure that

* filing cabinets to which access is restricted are kept locked at all times
* other filing systems are locked at the end of the day or when the filing area is left unattended
* the keys are kept under strict control (normally by the person on filing duty and the supervisor)
* any lock failures are reported promptly to the supervisor

Some filing cabinets are fireproof and are used for the storage of valuable or confidential documents and, in some cases, computer floppy disks containing valuable back-up data.

Offices will also retain and store in a secure manner old or 'dead' files, as they are known. When papers are no longer required in a filing system because they are old or no longer used, they are taken out of the filing cabinets and either shredded (destroyed) or stored safely elsewhere in what are often known as the 'Archives.' The papers that are stored are those that may be needed in the future by the organisation's accountants or even by their lawyers, if, say a court case arises and they are needed as evidence! Most documents are retained for a period of six years.

locating and retrieving files

As well as classifying and putting away the filing you will also need to locate and take files out, either for your own reference or because someone else has asked you to do so. This may sound a simple operation, but as you will probably know from experience, you may have problems, either locating where the file is stored, or having found the location, discovering that the file is missing! To overcome these problems you need to know how your office system works.

locating the file

The location of the file will depend on the classification system that the office uses - alphabetical, numerical, geographical or subject classification. If, for instance, you are asked to find the correspondence with Mr R W Smith, and the office uses an alphabetical system, your task is relatively simple (as long as the correspondence has been filed correctly). If a numeric or other classification method is used you will need to consult a manual or computer indexing system under the entry for *Smith, R W,* and identify the appropriate number/area/subject file.

taking the file

It is important that when you take the file, you record the fact. If there is no record of the whereabouts of a file, the office becomes inefficient: people run around in circles asking for files which have gone missing and delays occur. You know the type of problem that can occur in a household if someone walks off with the train timetable!

An office will normally adopt a recording system, so that anyone taking a file will 'log' it out:

- *a book* kept by the filing cabinets in which you write the name or number of the file, your name, and the date when you took the file; when you return the file you again record the date
- *a card* (see illustration below) which is placed where the borrowed file is normally stored

			OUT
date taken	file name/ref	taken by	date returned
10.2.9-	*GREAT NORTHERN HOTEL*	*L Palmer*	

a file 'Out' card

problems and delays

We have already mentioned that one of the major frustrations in an office is not bring able to get hold of the file that you or someone else wants in a hurry. What do you do in these circumstances? There are also other problems associated with filing and retrieving documents; in this section we highlight some of these problems and suggest some solutions. When you read through this section, compare the situations and solutions with what might happen in the office where you work, or where you are on work placement.

problem	suggested solution
you are unsure about how to classify a document	• try to find a similar type of document which has already been classified • ask a colleague • ask your supervisor
you find a document in the filing tray which you suspect should not be filed	• find out who placed the document in the filing tray - look at the reference of the writer of the letter or memorandum • ask if the document should be filed or not
you cannot find a file which you yourself need	• look to see if there is any written record of it having been taken out • if there is no card or book entry, look to see if it has been filed in the wrong place, e.g. in the pocket next to the correct place • if it is urgent, ask around the office • if it still does not appear, tell your supervisor
your colleague or supervisor asks you to find a file, but someone else has booked it out	• politely tell the person who has asked you for the file that it is being used by someone else • ask whether your colleague/supervisor wants you to retrieve the file • if the matter is urgent you should ask for the file politely • do not forget to record the transfer of the file in the booking out record if it is needed for a length of time • if the person who has the file out refuses to let it go, refer the matter to the person who wants it - do not get involved in a dispute!
your colleague or supervisor asks you to find a file but it has gone missing	• carry out all the checks mentioned in the third problem set out above • if the file is still not available, tell your supervisor • do not sit on the problem and get in a stew - it is not actually your fault - it is the supervisor's job to ensure that the filing system runs smoothly
you have too much filing to do in a given time	• do not panic! • adjust your priorities - see if there are any less urgent jobs that can be delayed • ask a colleague to help • if the problem cannot be solved, refer it to your supervisor who may ask you to do overtime or give the task to someone else - remember that staffing is the supervisor's responsibility

student activities - filing and retrieving information

Performance criteria

The student activities in this section test competences in the following areas:

- *filing documents without undue delay in the correct location and sequence*
- *storing materials without damage in a safe and secure manner*
- *classifying all documents correctly*
- *referring classification uncertainties to an appropriate authority*
- *locating, extracting and passing specified documents to the correct person or location*
- *notifying delays in the supply of files and/or documents, and explaining the reasons for delay politely*
- *recording promptly all file and document movements in a legible and accurate way*

1.   What do you understand by the following terms
     (a) classification of documents
     (b) filing point
     (c) presorting
     (d) vertical suspension filing
     (e) lateral filing system
     (f) miscellaneous file

2.   You have just emptied the filing trays in the office and have twenty documents to file alphabetically. The filing points are given below. Write out the file name under which they would be filed, and then arrange them in alphabetical order.

Lady Jane Fotheringay   M Anthony
ABC Laundry   Miss A Smith
Mrs J Pendlebury   J McAllister
R Fotheringay-Smith   Sir Henry Purcell
Abbott R W   John Brown Excavating Co Ltd
The Mereford Community Centre   Rev George Blake
18 and Over Dating Agency   M Maclean
A R Smith   O'Grady Minerals Limited
De Vere Wine Bar   A R L Smith
St Asaphs Rugby Club   J Foster

3.   You find that there is no file in the system for A R Smith and ABC Laundry. What action would you take?

4.   Draw up cross reference cards for the following situations:
     (a) John Walker Engineering Ltd is filed under <u>Walker</u> rather than <u>John</u>
     (b) Mereford Dairies changed its name to Orchard Dairy Supplies Ltd on 1 September 1991
     (c) O'Grady Minerals Limited is often referred to as OGM Limited
     (d) Mrs J Pendlebury got married on 10 August 1991; her unmarried name was Mottram
     (e) The Mereford Community Centre is the commonly used name for the Mereford County Council Community and Social Recreation Centre

5. You are not sure what to do with a number of documents in your filing, either because there is no filing point, or because you suspect they have got into the tray by mistake. What would you do in the circumstances, and into what file (if any) do you think they should be sorted?

(a) a letter from your Sales Manager to Miss Helen White giving details of your products. There is no filing point, but the letter is marked *'Diary 2 weeks'*

(b) a carbon copy letter from your supplier Britton Supplies Limited, announcing a price rise in some of their products; there is no filing point but the letter is marked 'FILE' with a stamp you do not recognise.

(c) a letter of complaint from from Stafford & Co., your local solicitors, marked by your office with a date received stamp, but otherwise with no markings; it is placed inside a sales brochure from the local printing shop

(d) a memorandum written by your supervisor - it has a number of spelling and punctuation correction markings on it and is not signed or initialled

(e) a carbon copy of a staff report on one of your colleagues - there are no markings on it

6. Your organisation operates a numerical filing classification system whereby each new file created is allocated the next available number in sequence - i.e. if the last file to be created was 499, the next would be 500. It also operates an alphabetical card index system so that named files can be related to the appropriate file number. The index card for the last file to be opened is shown below. . .

Name	Loveder Software 34 Byways Road Upper Worley MR6 4TR	**File no** 499
Tel **Fax**	0605 987453	
Date opened	15 01 9-	
Contact **Salesman**	Laura Loveder Neville Gunn	

Your salesman Neville Gunn has been successful in the Rowcester area recently and has obtained four new customers for which new files are required. The files are opened in the order set out below on 15 February 199-. *Your job is to make out new index cards for the files and presort them in alphabetical order.*

Schmidt Industrie (UK) Ltd., Unit 4, Martley Industrial Estate, Rowcester RW3 4RT, Tel 0915 345654, Fax 0915 345651, Contact Klaus Middtler

John Smith Alarm Systems, 56 High Street, Rowcester, RW1 2CH, Tel 0915 564197, Contact John Smith

Kevin MacNaughton, 56 The Crescent, Rowcester, Tel Rowcester 987452

McAlistair Designs, 76 Broad Street, Rowcester, RW1 8YH, Tel 0915 986523, Contact Moira McAlistair

7.   As you have been working on the filing section of your organisation for some time, your supervisor asks you to prepare a checklist in note form to be entitled 'Good Filing Practice' as a guide to others doing the same job, e.g. temps or trainees. She asks you to mention

   • the procedures for preparing documents for filing
   • the actual process of filing
   • what to do if there is no file for the document
   • what to do if you have any queries
   • safety aspects of filing
   • security aspects of filing

   She does not expect you to explain the classification system, as it is already explained in another document available in the office.

8.   If you have access to a filing system at work, or on work experience, ask your assessor or supervisor to give you no less than twenty files to retrieve on a minimum of three occasions. Ensure each time you extract a file that you complete the necessary booking out documentation.

9.   State what you would do in each of the following situations (assume that your office uses an alphabetical classification system):

(a)   Your supervisor asks you for the file of ABC Laundry, saying that it is very urgent. You look in the filing cabinet in the 'A' section but cannot see the file anywhere.

(b)   Your Sales Manager comes into the office in a rush towards the end of the afternoon and asks you to extract all the files for customers who live in the Mereford area. This probably involves about twenty files. You are already behind with the day's work and know that you cannot carry out this task without abandoning other important work which has to be finished that afternoon. The Sales Manager is not known for being sympathetic.

(c)   Your supervisor asks you for the file for O'Grady Minerals Limited, but you find that it has been booked out to the Accounts Department supervisor. You ask her politely if you may borrow the file, but she snaps back, saying that she is busy with it.

(d)   You notice that a large number of documents placed in the filing trays, particularly by new members of staff, do not have any clear filing point marked on them. This is leading to documents being wrongly filed, and in some cases, going astray. When you talk to your colleagues who are also doing filing duties, they complain about the same thing.

(e)   You work in the Administration Department and have the key to the staff record files. A colleague from the Accounts Department asks if she can borrow it, as she has to check on some salary payments. She suspects that she may have got the banking details of one or two members of staff wrong, as the salaries are being delayed, and she knows the staff files have the banking details recorded in them.

---

 linking assignment

Common Skills Assignment 6
Managing tasks and solving problems: Managing without the boss, pages 190 to 195

11 Reprographics

NCVQ coverage

7.1 produce copies from original documents using reprographic equipment
> *Performance criteria:*
> - *producing copies to the required specification within deadlines*
> - *keeping wastage of materials to a minimum*
> - *collating documents in the correct page order*
> - *securing document pages neatly and securely*
> - *distributing the copies and original documents correctly within required deadlines*
> - *identifying faults and dealing with them according to the manufacturer's instructions*
> - *reporting delays promptly and politely explaining the reasons for delay*
> - *following the recording, operating and safety procedures at all times*

introduction

The word 'reprographics' is used to describe the process of copying documents. If you work in a large organisation you may have a special department known as 'Reprographics Department' which deals with your copying needs; if you work in a smaller organisation you are more likely to have to deal with the copying yourself. In this Unit we will examine the use of the office photocopier, which in most organisations is in common use in the general office. It is an important office skill to be able to deal with requests for photocopying, to operate the photocopier, to be able to cope when the machine breaks down, and to distribute the finished photocopying efficiently under the pressure of deadlines.

 linking assignment

Common Skills Assignment 6
Managing tasks and solving problems: Managing without the boss, pages 190 to 195

the photocopier

Modern office photocopiers are fast and efficient. They provide a good copy by producing an image of the original document in dry ink powder (toner) which is fixed into plain paper. This *electrostatic process* works by means of a revolving drum picking up the toner - in the image of the original document - onto its surface by means of static electricity (the static electricity which causes a balloon to stick to your jumper when it is rubbed against the fabric). The toner is then transferred from the drum onto the surface of the paper by means of a heat process. Your copy is then complete - and literally 'hot from the press.'

The size and sophistication of the photocopier installed by an office will depend on the amount of use it is likely to get. Types vary from small and slow desk-top copiers which are recommended for occasional one-off copies of documents, to heavy-duty floor-standing copiers which can copy documents at high speed and collate in a mechanical collator. 'Collate' means to collect together in page order a number of copies of a multi-page document. Colour copiers are also available, but because of their higher cost are used only where colour reproduction is actually needed. The illustration below shows a fairly common 'middle-of-the-range' type of office photocopier. Compare its features with those of your office or College copier.

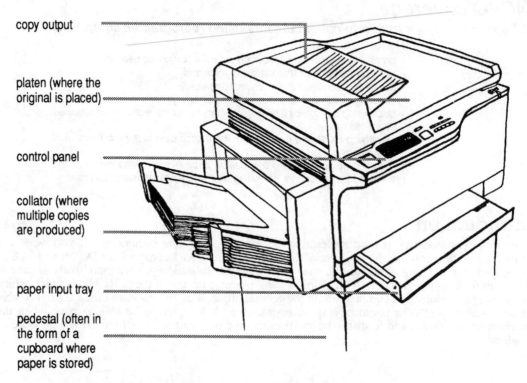

copy output

platen (where the original is placed)

control panel

collator (where multiple copies are produced)

paper input tray

pedestal (often in the form of a cupboard where paper is stored)

a typical 'middle-of-the-range' office photocopier

Whatever features your own photocopier may have - it may be more sophisticated than the machine illustrated - you should ensure that you are familiar with the way it works. The Health and Safety at Work Act requires that staff be trained in the use of equipment such as photocopiers. In the remainder of this Unit we will examine the various tasks involved in photocopying and dealing with the associated paperwork.

documents for copying

situations
You may have to photocopy material in a variety of circumstances:

- in connection with your own office tasks - e.g. a copy of a letter you are placing in a file
- an oral request from a supervisor or colleague - e.g. *'Please can I have a copy of the price change memo from Sales Department.'*
- as part of office duties when a specific member of staff is required to photocopy material for the rest of the office - in this case a written order slip (see below) may be required before the copying can be done

---

photocopy request ———————————————

name...date....................................

please supply.........copies of............sides (single side/back to back)

date required by...............................
☐ collated ☐ stapled ☐ white ☐ other colour.......................
(please tick box as appropriate)

- if a formal photocopy request form is not used members of staff may simply write instructions on a separate slip piece of paper - e.g. *'10 copies please - urgent - Laura Palmer.'*

priorities
Photocopying, like any other office task, requires decisions to be made over *priorities*. If one person is required to do the office copying they are likely to have an 'in tray' piled high with work to do. How should this pile be tackled?

- the pile should be sorted into urgent and non-urgent work
- urgent work will be indicated either by the originator writing 'URGENT!!' on it, or by the annotation of a date or time for completion of the copying
- non-urgent work will not have any specific indication on it apart from the completion date/time
- the documents/papers should be examined to make sure all the material *can* be copied (see below for an explanation of the copyright rules and unsuitable documents)
- if there is any problem over how urgent a task is, or a query over copyright or suitability, it should be referred to the originator as soon as possible

quality of documents
Certain documents will not copy well. If the copy is for internal circulation, this may not matter, as long as the document can be read and understood. If the copy is for sending out to a customer or any outside body, it may matter, and if in doubt you should refer the copy to the person sending it. A bad photocopy makes a poor impression of your organisation to the outside world. Documents that do not copy well include

- photographs
- text on brightly coloured paper - the intensity of colour reproduces as a dark mass
- faint or indistinct text - e.g. where the original is a bad photocopy!
- coloured text - e.g. light blue text on white paper

You can sometimes improve a faint original by turning up the 'darkness' setting. Similarly, if the copy comes out dark because of a colour on the original you can improve the copy by turning down the 'darkness' setting. After a while you will become skilled in 'improving' the copies you produce.

copyright

If you turn to the page following the title page in this book you will see the copyright symbol © and a sentence prohibiting copying of the book without permission. The Copyright Act sets out in law what you can and cannot photocopy without permission. The object of copyright is to protect the poor author who makes his or her living out of writing the material you wish to copy! Your internally produced material will not normally be copyright, but books and journals are. Generally speaking you are allowed under the Copyright Act to make single copies of *parts* of copyright publications, but the following are prohibited:

- copying the whole of a copyright publication
- making a number of copies of a single page

Some organisations are licensed so that they can copy copyright material. If you are in doubt about whether you can copy material, ask your supervisor. Sometimes the copyright regulations are displayed in the form of a notice by the photocopier.

size of documents
Most modern photocopiers enable you to

- *reduce* an original - produce a copy which is smaller than the original
- *enlarge* an original - produce a copy which is larger than the original
- *trim and mask* - produce a copy of part of an orginal document

The glass screen where you place the original document face downwards for photocopying will be equipped with guidance lines or arrows to tell you where to line up the document, according to its size. It therefore becomes very important that you are familiar with the different sizes of paper so that you can use these guidance marks, and also know what is required, for instance, if you are asked to 'reduce an A4 sheet to A5.' The illustration below sets out the most commonly used paper sizes.

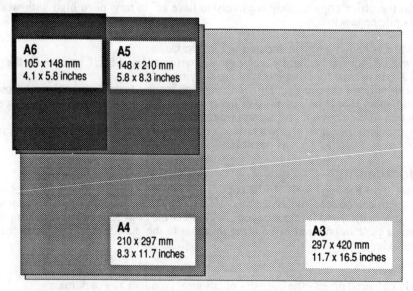

A6
105 x 148 mm
4.1 x 5.8 inches

A5
148 x 210 mm
5.8 x 8.3 inches

A4
210 x 297 mm
8.3 x 11.7 inches

A3
297 x 420 mm
11.7 x 16.5 inches

commonly used sizes of paper

use of the photocopier

Photocopiers vary in their facilities and operating procedures, and you should be familiar with the machine in your organisation or College. If in doubt, consult the manual, the operating panel on the machine, or your supervisor. Set out below are Actions Points on photocopying procedures for a typical office photocopier. Read them through and compare them with the procedures for your machine.

 action points - good practice in photocopying

- ○ sort your photocopying into urgent and non-urgent tasks

- ○ check that the documents are suitable for copying - are there copyright problems or poor originals?

- ○ refer any problems over priority, copyright or poor originals to the originator or your supervisor

- ○ ensure that the copier is set up safely and is switched on

- ○ check the settings to make sure that the machine is operating properly. The normal warning symbols on the control panel are

no paper in the tray

paper jam

toner indicator:
green = satisfactory
yellow = running out,
red = run out

- ○ check the paper tray(s) to ensure that the right amount, size and colour of paper is loaded neatly so that it will feed into the machine without any problem

- ○ place the original on the glass panel and ensure that it is correctly lined up according to its size - check against the guide lines or arrows

- ○ check whether you need to enlarge or reduce the original and set the machine accordingly

- ○ if you are doing more than one copy, do a test copy first and adjust the 'darkness' setting if you need to

- ○ if you are doing more than one copy of a document which has a number of consecutive pages and your machine has a collator - a device which will sort the pages for you - make sure the collator is switched on

- ○ as you photocopy the documents keep an eye on the quality of the copies - stop the machine if there is any problem

- ○ when you have finished take your copies *and the original* away

- ○ record your copies in the office recording system (often a book kept by the machine)

recording systems - minimising wastage

As mentioned in the last Action Point on the previous page it is common for an organisation to record

- the number of copies taken
- the name of the person who has processed the copies
- the department or section from which the request originated
- the date on which the copies were taken

The reason for this is that a photocopier is an expensive machine to run. The management of an organisation will often want to monitor the use of the machine by various departments or sections in order to cut down on wastage and inefficiency. The management may also charge the running cost of the machine to different departments or sections. Another reason for keeping a record of the copies taken is to prevent individuals carrying out unauthorised copying of private material.

record book

A book may be kept by the photocopier in which the operator of the machine will record the details mentioned above. An extract from a typical recording book is shown below.

Vector AZ109 General Office Copier

date	name	department	no. of copies
199-			
1 March	J Parry	Accounts	25
1 March	J Rosenburg	Admin	60
1 March	L Jones	Admin	5
1 March	G Moss	Admin	12

copy control cards

A number of modern photocopiers can be fitted with a device which only allows access to operators who have a special plastic card, shaped like a credit card, known as a *copy control card*. This card is inserted in the photocopier by the user and will activate the machine and indicate to the photocopier

- who is using the machine
- which department or section the user comes from

The machine then automatically records the number of copies taken and enables the appropriate department or section to be charged for the copies made. Copy control cards have many advantages:

- they replace the record book
- they enable accurate records to be made
- access to the machine is restricted to those who are authorised to use it

collating and fastening copies

If you are copying single documents, the task is straightforward - you merely take your finished copy out of the tray on the photocopier. If, however, you are asked to make five copies of a ten page document, the task is more complex: the pages of the finished copies must be collected together - *collated* - in the correct order and *fastened* in the most appropriate way.

collating copies - photocopier with a collator

Some photocopiers, as we mentioned in the Action Points on page 159, will collate copies for you. If you are making five copies of a document containing ten pages, you will need to set the collator function on the machine, and then each of the five copies will build up in separate trays (the collator) on the machine as you copy the ten original pages. You will need to take care that you copy the sheets in order and also that the sheets are copied the right way round! When you have finished copying you should take the completed sets of sheets out of the collator and stack them at right angles to each other so that the sets are kept separate.

Before copying the sheets you will need to be familar with the numbering systems of pages:

* consecutive page numbers - i.e. 1, 2, 3, 4, 5, 6, 7, 8, 9, 10
* section numbering, where each section of the document is the *first* number quoted and the page number of that section is the *second* - e.g. 1.1, 1.2, 1.3 followed by 2.1, 2.2, 2.3, 2.4. . . and so on

The golden rule of collating is to make sure the original pages are in the right order and the right way round. If you are unsure about the sequence of pages or the material to be copied, refer the matter to the originator or to your supervisor. It may save a painful half hour later, *un*stapling a set of incorrectly collated copies!

collating copies - manual method

Not all photocopiers have collators, and therefore collation may have to be done by hand. Let us assume that you want twenty copies of a ten page document. You should take twenty copies of each sheet, *in order*, and place each pile of twenty copies, *in order*, on the top of a table or desk. You can then walk around the table, picking up one copy from each pile, *in order*, until you have a complete set. The procedure is then the same as if you were using a collator - you stack the finished collated sets at right angles. If the manual collation job is too much for one person, a whole team can collect copies from piles as outlined above.

fastening copies

It will be necessary to fasten your collated copies together to keep them neat and in the correct order. The type of fastening will depend on the number of sheets involved and the type of equipment available in your office. Here are some of the more common methods:

* *stapling* - either with a hand-held stapler or with an automatic stapling machine
* *spiral binding* - a wire is wound through the edges of the sheets by a machine
* *plastic slide binders* - a simple plastic strip which grips the sheets by the edge
* *thermal binding* - the edges of the sheets are inserted into a machine and glued inside a card cover

Stapling is by far the most common and easiest of these methods, and will probably be used unless the copy is for presentation purposes, in which case your organisation will have its own method of binding. Try and find out which methods of binding are used.

Remember the golden rule of checking the page order before fastening the pages together!

distribution of copies

When you have made your photocopies according to the instructions given, you will need to ensure that the copies are distributed as soon as possible. It may be that you have been asked to make a single copy, in which case distribution will be simple - you take it to the person yourself, or use an office circulation system. It may be, however, that you are asked to make a number of copies which have to be circulated to different members of staff, or even one copy which has to be circulated to members of staff in turn.   There are different methods which may be used for ensuring that the copies reach the correct people. Some of these methods are explained below. You should find out which method your organisation has adopted.

circulating a single copy to a number of colleagues

If you are circulating a single copy to a number of colleagues, attach a typed list of names to the copy, indicating that each person should tick his or her name and pass the document on when it has been read.

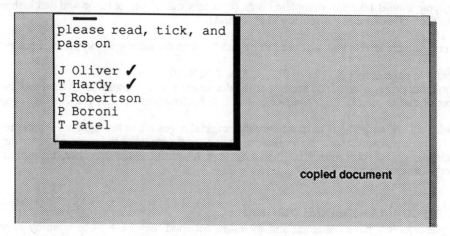

```
please read, tick, and
pass on

J Oliver     ✓
T Hardy      ✓
J Robertson
P Boroni
T Patel
```

copied document

circulating a number of copies to colleagues

If you have made copies of a document and need to circulate those copies rapidly to a number of colleagues, type a list of people who are to receive a copy and ring with your pen or highlight the appropriate name with a highlighter.

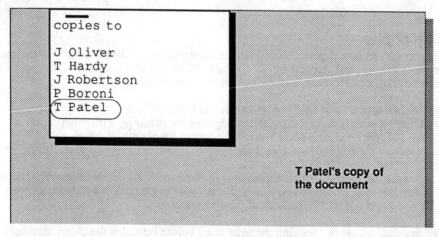

```
copies to

J Oliver
T Hardy
J Robertson
P Boroni
(T Patel)
```

T Patel's copy of the document

documents which show the name of the recipient

If the copy (such as a memorandum) shows a number of recipients, the individual's name will be ringed with a pen or highlighted with a highlighter pen (as in the illustration below).

MEMORANDUM

To J D Morsefield

From G H Jupp   **Ref.** GHJ/LP

Copies to   J Oliver   **Date** 3 March 199-
            T Hardy
            J Robertson
            P Boroni
            T Patel

Subject STAFF MEETINGS

If there are no names on the document and your organisation permits, you may write the name of the recipient clearly on the top of the copy. If in doubt, ask your supervisor.

distributing within deadlines

When you are given documents to copy there should be an indication of when the copies are required. If in doubt, ask. When you are organising your distribution, distribute the most urgent requests first, or , if an office distribution system is used, mark the urgent copies 'URGENT'. It is tempting when you have finished your copying tasks to relax and go for a coffee. Do not forget that your task is not complete until the copies reach their destination.

problems with the photocopier?

Like all sophisticated pieces of machinery - such as a car - the photocopier relies on careful treatment, regular cleaning and servicing for its efficient operation. You will be able to deal with some of the problems yourself, others will require the services of an outside engineer.

office care of the photocopier

It will be the responsibility of the supervisor to ensure that

* there is adequate paper for the machine - a system for replenishing stocks should be in operation
* the machine is cleaned regularly - there are proprietary cleaners for wiping the machine down and keeping the glass panel clean
* the machine's manual is available for use by staff - and not hidden in a drawer
* there is a system for calling the engineer if a problem cannot be solved in the office
* the photocopier is serviced regularly (a book is often kept by the machine in which faults and service visits are recorded)

dealing with machine faults yourself

You will be able to deal with a number of faults which regularly occur with photocopiers yourself

paper jam

Paper may jam inside the machine, possibly because it is the wrong type of paper, or possibly because it is damaged before it is fed in. It will be possible to open up the machine and extract the paper, *BUT TAKE CARE -*
• switch the machine off first
• parts of the copier will be very hot
• the machine will possibly be messy with toner
Do *not* attempt this unless you are trained to do so.

paper out

This symbol means that you have run out of paper, and will need to load more into the paper feed tray. It is best to check the paper tray *before* you start copying, particularly if you are making a large number of copies or are using a collator. Also check that the paper is the right colour and thickness (weight) before you start a job. If the paper does run out, there should be a fresh supply available; if there is no paper, tell someone - do not go for coffee in the hope that someone else will fill up the machine!

toner indicator

Toner is the fine - usually black - powder which sticks to the paper and gives the image of the copy. Some machines require toner to be 'poured in' from a container, and the indicator will tell you that this needs to be done. Other machines may have toner contained in a sealed cartridge which has a colour code 'window' which shows how much toner is left:

green = sufficient left
yellow = running out
red = run out

If the red colour shows, you may have to open up the machine and change the toner cartridge - follow carefully the instructions in the manual (or leaflet which accompanies the toner). Sometimes a toner cartridge will continue to work after the red colour shows; if this happens, change it when the copy quality starts to deteriorate. Note: you are not recommended to change the toner unless you have received suitable training.

calling the engineer

There will be occasions when the machine defeats you, and you will have to call an engineer. In order to prepare for situations such as these you should ensure that

• the engineer's telephone number is always to hand
• you know who is authorised to call the engineer if you cannot do so yourself
• the machine manual is to hand
• your servicing and faults record book of the machine is to hand
• the engineer completes the book when the job is completed
• any other paperwork relating to the job is filed away correctly (the engineer may hand you a servicing sheet telling you what has been done)

other reprographic methods - cost considerations

So far in this Unit we have examined copying by means of photocopiers because this form of reprographics is by far the most common. There are, however, a number of other methods of reproducing copies, and we will now look at these, pointing out the situations in which they may be more cost-effective than photocopying. You may have encountered some of these methods yourself in the workplace or at College.

stencil duplicating A stencil - known as a master - is a tough waxed sheet which can be perforated by a typewriter or by hand using a special sharp stylus. It is placed in a special duplicating machine and the ink is forced through the perforations onto special absorbent paper. Nowadays electronic scanning machines are also used to copy documents and make stencil masters for running off large numbers of copies.

cost implications *The stencil process is suitable for making between 20 to 5,000 copies. The absorbent paper is cheaper than other copy paper.*

offset litho The offset litho process involves the making of a master plate, either in paper (for shorter print runs) or in metal (for longer runs). The image to be printed is represented by a greasy coating on the plate which is itself wrapped around a revolving roller and inked continously. The greasy area on the master picks up the ink and transfers the image by way of another roller to the paper copies which are fed through the machine. The copies printed on the offset litho process are of a very high quality.

cost implications *The offset litho process is only useful for long runs of 1,000 and over. Paper plates (cheap to process) will produce up to 2,000 copies and metal plates (more expensive) up to 50,000 copies.*

The table set out below gives an indication of the most economical way of making copies. If you are in an office which has only a photocopier, you may find it worthwhile to send larger copying jobs to an outside print bureau which will be able to process the copies on an offset litho machine.

process	number of copies	quality of reproduction
photocopier	up to 100	good
stencil	100 to 1,000	good
offset litho	1,000 to 50,000	excellent

✎ student activities - reprographics

Performance criteria

The student activities in this section test competences in the following areas:

- *producing copies to the required specification within deadlines*
- *keeping wastage of materials to a minimum*
- *collating documents in the correct page order*
- *securing document pages neatly and securely*
- *distributing the copies and original documents correctly within required deadlines*
- *identifying faults and dealing with them according to the manufacturer's instructions*
- *reporting delays promptly and politely explaining the reasons for delay*
- *following the recording, operating and safety procedures at all times*

Note:
The activities set out below refer to the *photocopying* process unless indicated to the contrary.

1.   The date is 5 March and you are emptying your photocopying 'in tray'. It contains the following:

(a) a request marked 'URGENT' from a colleague Laura Palmer for 10 copies of a brochure
(b) a request marked '10 March' for 50 copies of a leaflet from a colleague Dan Bradstreet
(c) a request marked '4 March' for 2 copies of a letter from a colleague Adam Smith
(d) a request marked '8 March' for 25 copies of a memo from your supervisor
(e) a request marked '7 March' for 2 copies of a booklet from a colleague Sid Beach

In addition you receive a number of oral requests as you are emptying the tray:

(f) your Managing Director calls in to the office and asks you to copy a letter for him straightaway
(g) your supervisor asks you to make 5 copies of a notice for a forthcoming staff social
(h) one of your colleagues asks you to photocopy the crossword from the Evening Echo

You are to:
- arrange (a) to (h) into order of priority, writing down your *reasons* for your decisions
- record the jobs in priority order in a photocopying record book (you may have to rule one up yourself). A sample format is set out below. Use your own name. You work in Administration Department.

Vector AZ109 General Office Copier			
date	name	department	no. of copies

2. Identify the symbols set out below. State what action you would take if you encountered them in the course of a day's work.

(a) ©

(b)

(c)

(d)

3. What action would you take if a Manager asked you for a single copy of a ten page report urgently, and you find that the photocopier does not appear to be working?

4. Name four types of document which will not photocopy well.

5. What advice about avoiding wastage of paper would you give to a colleague who had just started work in your office?

6. *Note: attempt this activity only if you have access to a photocopier which will reduce an original document.*

   Obtain the letterhead or a compliments slip of your employer or College and a map of the locality. Mark your location prominently on the map and then reduce the document (or part of it) so that it will fit onto the letterhead or compliments slip, and can be copied to send to visitors/clients.

7. Obtain from your workplace or College a document containing four or more pages which has to be copied more than five times for internal distribution. Then . . .
   (a) copy the document
   (b) collate the pages in the correct order
   (c) fasten the pages in the method used in your organisation or College
   (d) prepare distribution slips (e.g. in the form of a list of names) to attach to the copies
   (e) ensure the copies are distributed within a given deadline

8. Assuming that you have unlimited choice of reprographic equipment, what reprographic method would you recommend for making
   (a) 2,000 copies
   (b) 20 copies
   (c) 200 copies
   (d) the best quality copies

 linking assignment

Common Skills Assignment 6
Managing tasks and solving problems: Managing without the boss, pages 190 to 195

12 Mail handling

NCVQ coverage

6.1 receive, sort and distribute incoming/internal mail

Performance criteria
- *checking mail for damaged or suspicious items, and reporting those items*
- *checking mail to ensure that all enclosures are attached, and reporting any missing items*
- *following security procedures for receipt of cash and valuables*
- *opening mail without damaging the contents*
- *sorting and delivering mail to the correct person within deadlines*
- *reporting promptly unavoidable delays in distribution to the appropriate authority*

6.2 prepare for despatch outgoing/internal mail

Performance criteria
- *checking outgoing documents for signature and any enclosures; identifying and rectifying any omissions*
- *sealing securely all outgoing items of mail in the appropriate packaging*
- *addressing all outgoing mail legibly*
- *calculating and applying the correct postal rates*
- *meeting Post Office sorting requirements, collection and postal deadlines*
- *keeping records up-to-date, legible and accurate, and filing them correctly in accordance with the procedures of the organisation*
- *following security procedures for stamps and money at all times*

introduction

If you work in an organisation you may have to deal with incoming mail and outgoing mail. If your organisation is a large one, there will be a mail room and specifically designated staff for receiving, opening and distributing mail and for preparing mail for despatch. If you work in a medium-sized concern, the mail duties may be carried out by the general staff on a rota basis, or by the office juniors. If you work in a small office, the person in charge may open the post, and his/her secretary send off the mail at the end of the day. Whatever system is used, certain factors are common: the mail must be opened promptly and distributed to the correct person as soon as possible, and before the end of the day all outgoing mail must be collected and sent off by the appropriate means.

 linking assignment

Common Skills Assignment 6
Managing tasks and solving problems: Managing without the boss, pages 190 to 195

incoming mail

how it arrives

Mail can arrive at an organisation in a variety of ways, depending on the size and location of the organisation:

- delivered through the letterbox in the morning by the Post Office
- collected from a post office box (PO Box) in the morning by a member of staff
- delivered during the day by the Post Office or by a carrier - often requiring a signature
- through the letterbox by the general public (e.g. by bank or building society customers outside opening hours)

Whatever way the mail arrives, it must be dealt with promptly so that the recipient receives it as soon as possible. We will deal with the process of *opening, sorting* and *distributing* the main mail delivery in the next sections, but will now look at procedures to be followed when items out of the ordinary are delivered.

items that have to be signed for

Certain items - letters or packages - will need to be signed for. These include:

- Datapost (Parcelforce)
- Registered Mail (Royal Mail)
- Recorded Delivery (Royal Mail)
- Trakback parcels (Parcelforce)
- Deliveries by carriers/couriers such as Parcelforce, TNT, Lynx, Securicor

If you are signing for an item, make sure that you are receiving the correct item, and that you sign in the correct place. If the form you have to sign says 'Received in good condition' and you are dubious about the condition of the parcel, you can write 'Contents not inspected' on the form to cover your organisation in case it has to claim for damaged items received. Packages sent by special delivery often contain cash, valuable items or documents, and therefore have to be taken to the recipient in the organisation without delay or loss. Some organisations will maintain a 'Special Delivery' book for recording the receipt of special deliveries. This will normally show

- the date and time of delivery
- the name of the person or organisation sending the package
- the carrier used and the reference number of the delivery (usually printed on the outside of the package and also on the delivery note given to the person taking in the package)
- the signature of the person in the organisation who receives and signs for the package

If you accept and sign for a letter or package you may also have to take the accompanying delivery note to the appropriate department, e.g. Stores, Purchasing or Accounts.

damaged items

You will no doubt from time-to-time receive a delivery that is damaged, either because it has been insufficiently packaged (the most common reason) or because it has suffered an accident in transit. Damaged packages can contain valuable items, which if they also are damaged, may result in your organisation putting in a claim to the sender for compensation. The way in which damaged packages are dealt with varies from organisation to organisation. The important point is that the damage must be recorded. This may be done by any (or all) of the following

- writing 'package damaged, contents not inspected' on the form which the carrier asks you to sign
- entering the details in a book kept in the office
- writing the details of the damage on the packet itself - otherwise the recipient in the office may think that you damaged it!

suspicious packages

If someone has a grudge against your organisation or against someone who works in your organisation, they may send an unpleasant package which you will have to deal with. In its worst form this may take the shape of a letterbomb; these fortunately are uncommon. Other suspicious packages may enclose rotten food or a dead animal sent by someone with a grudge. The author knows of a box containing a dead cat which was left at a local bank by a disgruntled customer! How do you recognise a suspicious package? Tell-tale signs include

- smell - this could indicate a dead animal, or in the case of an almond smell, explosives
- wires evident in the package
- a heavy mechanical device present in the package
- suspicious lettering and no indication of the sender

What action would you take?

- do not open, shake or prod the package, but place it gently on an open working surface
- check to see if the person to whom it is addressed is expecting it, in which case there may be no problem
- if there does seem to be a problem, calmly alert your colleagues and your supervisor, whose responsibility it will be to call the Police if it is necessary
- do not panic, or cause anyone else to panic!

opening and checking the mail

We will now look at the procedures adopted for opening the mail when it is received - normally in the morning - and checking it. Incoming mail must first be sorted into categories because some letters are more urgent than others, while some letters should not be opened at all.

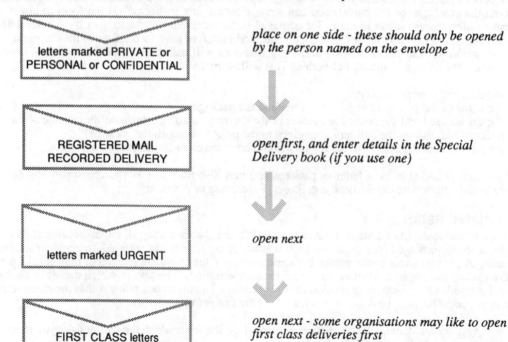

letters marked PRIVATE or PERSONAL or CONFIDENTIAL

place on one side - these should only be opened by the person named on the envelope

REGISTERED MAIL RECORDED DELIVERY

open first, and enter details in the Special Delivery book (if you use one)

letters marked URGENT

open next

FIRST CLASS letters SECOND CLASS letters

open next - some organisations may like to open first class deliveries first

opening methods

Letters may be opened either with a special letter opening knife or with an automatic letter opening machine. The automatic letter opener slices off the edge of an envelope when it is placed in the machine. If you use this machine you should ensure that the contents of each envelope are not damaged in the process. You should slit *the top* of the envelope and make sure that the contents sit at the bottom end (this can be done by tapping the envelope on a working surface). When the contents of the envelopes have been removed each envelope should be checked carefully to ensure that there is nothing left in it. This checking process is often completed by someone slitting and opening out the envelope so that it becomes a single sheet of paper.

The processing of the contents of the envelopes is dealt with in the Action Points set out below.

✔ action points - processing the incoming mail

○ remove and unfold the contents of the envelopes

○ ensure that the envelopes are placed to one side for checking

○ date stamp each item of mail (date stamp the outside of envelopes marked 'Private')

○ check to see if any letter has an enclosure ('enc' will normally be typed at the bottom of the letter) - enclosures include catalogues, documents, and cheques - these are not date stamped

○ staple any loose enclosed item to the letter (except cheques and valuable documents)

○ staple any continuation sheets to the original letter to prevent them going astray

○ if an enclosure is not present when it should be, pencil a message to that effect on the letter so that the recipient can take the necessary action (i.e. telephone the sender and tell them that they have forgotten to enclose the enclosure!)

○ if there is any money in the letter, note the amount and the form it takes on the bottom of the letter in pencil - e.g. 'Cheque for £541.45 enclosed' - initial the letter and enter the amount in the remittances book (see the next section)

○ if the item of mail forms part of a special delivery (e.g. Datapost, Registered or Recorded Mail) enter the details in the Special Delivery book (if you have one)

○ sort the letters and documents into department or individual headings - into wire baskets or pigeon holes - so that they can be distributed rapidly

○ the recipient of the letter can normally be identified from the text of the letter itself:
  - 'For the attention of . . . . .'
  - 'Dear Mr . . . . .'
  - a subject heading; e.g. 'Account No. 6757. Invoice 787545' would be for Accounts Department
  - a reference 'Your Ref. TB/LP' where 'TB' is Terry Birmingham the Finance Director

○ if the recipient cannot be identified from the letter, look at the contents of the letter itself - is it about Sales, Accounts, or an Administration matter? You will have to use your initiative on occasions!

○ if you are unavoidably delayed in sorting the mail - the office may be short-staffed, or there may be more mail than usual - ask your colleagues or your supervisor for help; a delay in distributing the mail to the office will hold up the entire organisation

processing remittances

As mentioned on the previous page, there will occasions when money - a 'remittance' - is enclosed in a letter. A remittance can take the form of cash, a cheque, or a postal order. When an organisation receives a remittance it normally records the details in a Remittances Book (see below). If you are dealing with the post and open a letter containing a remittance you should

- check the amount of the money (it may not be the amount stated in the letter!)
- write the amount and the form of remittance (cash/cheque/postal order) on the letter
- initial the letter
- enter the details of the remittance in the remittances book and sign the entry
- pass the money and the book to the organisation's cashier

A page from a Remittances Book is illustrated below

date	sender	remittance	amount	signature
12/3/9–	Microtronics Limited	chq	234.87	*L Palmer*
12/3/9–	Miss L Baylis	cash	40.00	*L Palmer*
13/3/9–	H Boyd	P.O.	5.00	*L Palmer*

circulating the mail

As we have already seen, it will be the job of the people dealing with the mail to sort it into sections for distribution. The mail staff will either distribute the mail themselves, or each section/department will collect the mail from the appropriate basket or pigeon hole. There will be occasions when a single letter will need to be seen by more than one person. This can be arranged in one of two ways:

- the single letter is circulated to a number of people by means of a circulation slip (see below), or
- photocopies are taken by the mail staff, and each person receives a copy

For circulation - please read, initial and pass on		
name	dept	initial/date
C Bamber	Sales	**C B 12 March**
J Minton	Accounts	*JM 13 March*
R Thomas	Admin	
return to	M Flanigan	**by** 20 March

processing the outgoing mail

despatching the mail within deadlines

Just as the early morning is the busy time for processing incoming mail, the late afternoon tends to be the busy time for processing the outgoing mail. It will be a measure of the efficiency of an organisation to see how it copes with this 'bottleneck' of everyone wanting to send off their correspondence. The deadlines an organisation will set itself will depend on how the mail reaches the Post Office. It may be that one member of staff is deputed to take the mail to the Post Office or Sorting Office. It is also possible in a larger organisation that the Post Office will collect the mail at certain times during the day. In either case cut-off times will be set for processing of mail for depatch; for example if the Post Office van calls at 5.30 p.m., the mail staff may want all correspondence for processing by 5.00 p.m.

To cope with these deadlines an organisation must arrange for mail to be processed as quickly and efficiently as possible. This normally involves each section of the office placing its mail in 'mail out' trays or baskets either for collection by the mail staff, or by taking the mail to the mail room.

Before the mail is despatched it must go through a rigorous process of checking. In the remainder of this Unit we will examine this checking process and see how the mail is packaged, stamped or franked, and recorded in the internal system of the organisation.

checking the outgoing mail

After a letter is dictated or written it must then be word-processed or typed and possibly be given enclosures before despatch. There is considerable margin for error here:

- there may be mistakes in the letter
- the letter may not be signed
- the enclosures may be omitted
- the enclosures may be wrong
- the letter may go in the wrong envelope

✔ action points - checking the outgoing mail

○ letter prepared - dictated or written

○ letter typed and any enclosures and copies prepared

○ letter checked and signed (or corrected and signed)

○ envelope prepared and addressed (unless window envelope used)

○ address on envelope checked - is it the same as that on the letter?

○ any enclosures checked - are they all there, and in the right order?

○ signature checked - has the letter been signed?

○ letter and any enclosures folded and placed in envelope and sealed

○ letter identified as first class, second class, or airmail

○ letter stamped or franked and despatched by the appropriate method

envelopes and packaging

If you are dealing with the outgoing mail you will need to know

- which envelopes to use - what quality and size
- how to address an envelope (if it has not already been addressed)
- what packaging to use for items other than letters

which envelope?

If you are choosing an envelope for a letter, you will need to know the policy of your organisation for use of envelopes. The choice can include the *paper quality* (e.g. the cheaper brown 'manilla' envelopes used for routine correspondence), and *type* - window envelopes (which have a transparent panel displaying the address typed on the enclosed correspondence) or plain envelopes which have to be addressed. Another factor is the *size* of envelope. There are certain envelopes specifically designed for certain sizes of paper - these are set out in the illustrations below. These sizes are internationally recognized and specified by the ISO (International Standards Organisation).

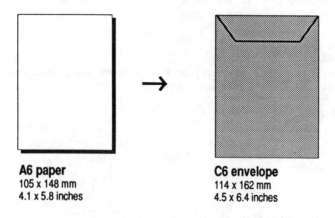

A6 paper
105 x 148 mm
4.1 x 5.8 inches

C6 envelope
114 x 162 mm
4.5 x 6.4 inches

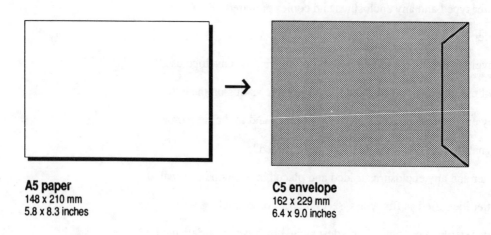

A5 paper
148 x 210 mm
5.8 x 8.3 inches

C5 envelope
162 x 229 mm
6.4 x 9.0 inches

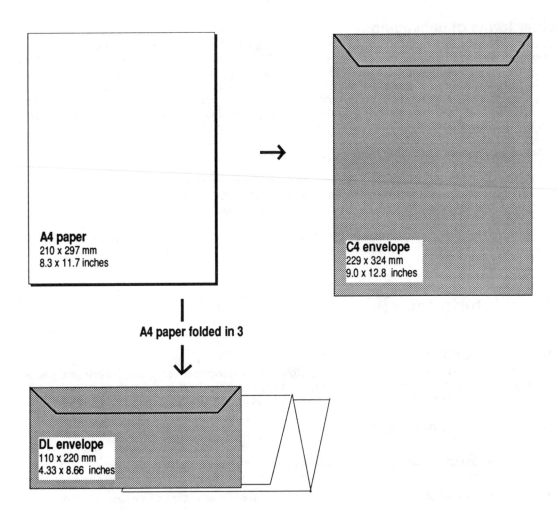

addressing the envelope

We have already examined the way in which an envelope should be addressed in Unit 6 (page 77). As a reminder look at the illustration below. Note how the letter is addressed as 'Private and Confidential' and should therefore on receipt only be opened by Mrs Cooper. The text is set out in the commonly used fully-blocked style (all lines to the left margin) and with open punctuation.

```
Private and Confidential

Mrs A D Cooper
Touchstone Enterprises Limited
Unit 14
Holworthy Industrial Estate
Mereford
MR5 4TY
```

other forms of packaging

Letters are reasonably light in weight and are normally well protected by the standard envelope. They are particularly suited by envelopes which fall into the the Post Office Preferred (POP) categories of size and weight; these include the C6 and DL envelopes illustrated on pages 174 and 175. Larger, heavier or more delicate items of mail such as bundles of documents, samples of merchandise and computer disks need more protection. Their journey through the Post Office will probably be a bumpy one, involving automatic sorting machines and being thrown manually into trolleys; they need considerable protection - particularly at the corners.

Your office may use these other forms of packaging:

• the padded envelope ('Jiffybag'or 'Mail Lite' package) for documents and computer discs
• ready-made cardboard wraparound self-seal packets for books or samples
• strong cardboard boxes with polystyrene chip filling for large items

Remember when using these forms of packaging to address them clearly - preferably with a typed label - and to mark them with the name and address of your organisation as sender.

despatching the mail

methods of despatch

There is a choice of methods offered by the Royal Mail (letter delivery) and Parcelforce (parcel delivery) for sending each item of mail, and it is one of the duties of the mail staff to ensure that the appropriate method is employed. The different methods of despatch are explained below.

sending mail within the UK

Royal Mail or Parcelforce service	what it is used for
Letterpost - second class mail	*non-urgent routine items - takes approximately 3 days*
Letterpost- first class mail	*priority items - takes approximately 1 to 3 days*
Special Delivery	*urgent letterpost items - next day delivery, and proof of posting docket (see illustration on page 178) - money back guarantee if the item does not get there on time*
Recorded Delivery	*for important items (such as documents) - an additional service for normal letterpost items providing a Certificate of Posting (see illustration on page 178) and requiring a signature on receipt*
Registered Letter Service	*for sending valuable items such as cash and jewellery through the letterpost - compensation is payable in the case of loss*
Datapost	*for urgent items - guaranteed next-day delivery (by 10.00 a.m.) to all major UK business centres, and by noon to almost everywhere else (available as Datapost EMS for foreign destinations)*
Parcelforce Standard Service	*for parcels within the UK - delivery approximately 3 to 5 days*

sending mail abroad

Royal Mail International Service	*what it is used for*
surface mail	*non-urgent letters , packets and papers - delivery normally within 2 weeks in Europe, up to 12 weeks outside Europe - slow and cheap*
airmail letters	*for letters and packets - delivery normally 2 to 4 days to cities in Europe, 2 to 7 days to cities outside Europe*
Swiftair	*faster express airmail service - a certificate of posting is available on request*

You will see that the services listed above are those available from the Royal Mail and Parcelforce, as these are the most commonly used. There are, of course, other commercial carriers and couriers in business, and you will find their local contact points in the Yellow Pages. You may already use them, or you may turn to them when your normal carrier goes on strike!

cost of depatch

The charges for the services listed above are regularly revised - normally every Autumn - and are published in leaflets produced by the Royal Mail and Parcelforce. Your office should have up-to-date copies of these leaflets:

- UK Letter Rates - A Comprehensive Guide
- Royal Mail International - A Comprehensive Mailing Guide for Business Users
- Royal Mail Parcelforce - UK Standard Service Parcel Rates
- Parcelforce Datapost UK Prices
- Parcelforce International - International Zones and Prices

You will need copies of these leaflets - or at least access to them - if you are attempting the Student Activities and Assignments which involve the calculation and application of the correct postal rates. The leaflets are available at Post Offices, and contain details of other services also available from the Royal Mail and Parcelforce.

preparing the mail for despatch

Once the mail has been sealed it will need to be sorted into categories and priorities by the mail staff. This will involve separating

- first class mail
- second class mail
- overseas mail - airmail and surface mail
- letters which require documentation - Recorded Delivery, Registered Letters, Special Delivery
- Datapost
- parcels

Items such as Datapost which are to be collected must be given priority in accordance with the time for collection. Items which require forms to be completed must also be given priority, allowing time for them to be taken to the Post Office as required.

The remaining items - letters and parcels - should then be franked or stamped, a procedure explained in the next section.

Examples of Special Delivery and Recorded Delivery forms are illustrated on the next page. The instructions for the completion of the forms are printed on the forms themselves, and you should now read them before passing on to the next section.

Certificate of Posting for Royal Mail Special Delivery

P3453

How to post:
1 Enter opposite in ink the name and full address as written on the letter/packet.
2 Peel off the adhesive service label below and affix it to the front of the letter/packet, close to the address.
3 Write the sender's name and address on the back of the letter/packet. A peel off label is provided for this purpose should you wish to use it.
4 Affix postage stamps to the letter for the first class postage and Special Delivery fee.
5 Hand this certificate together with the letter/packet to an officer of The Post Office.
6 The certificate will be validated and returned to you. Please keep it safely and produce it in the event of a claim.

The unregistered post should not be used for sending money or valuable items. You may send a Royal Mail Special Delivery letter by registered post.

Name   R. PATEL

Address

193, ORCHARD WALK
MEREFORD

Postcode   MR2 2RP

For official use

Posted after LAT (see over)	Datestamp
☐	
Accepting officers Initials	

3/ AN88862

This label is provided for your use if required. After completion affix it to the back of the letter/packet.

Sender's name   L. PALMER

Address   10, KINGSMERE ROAD
MEREFORD   Postcode   MR7 5LP

Direct posting (tick and complete LAT details)	Before LAT	After LAT (customer advised)	Item posted:	Time of Posting	Address checked	Date delivery due	Date and time received in S.O. (or timed datestamp)	Accepting officers datestamp
☐	☐	☐			☐			

3/ AN88862

Royal Mail Special Delivery

Service label for official use only

B 277585 Recorded Delivery

Certificate of Posting for Recorded Delivery
How to post

1 Enter below in ink the name and full address as written on the letter or packet.
2 Affix the numbered adhesive label in the top left-hand corner of the letter (or close to the address on a packet).
3 Affix postage stamps to the letter for the correct postage and Recorded Delivery Fee.
4 Hand this certificate, together with the letter, to an officer of The Post Office.
5 This certificate will be date-stamped and initialled as a receipt. Please keep it safely, and produce it in the event of a claim.

Name	A. R. BROWN
Address	35 CUMBERLAND RD
	MEREFORD

Postcode   MR3 2SZ

Recorded Delivery should not be used for sending money or valuable items.

For Post Office use	Date stamp
Accepting Officer's initials	

Recorded Delivery no

B   277585

P2297

franking and stamping

If your office processes a large volume of outgoing mail it will probably use a franking machine to stamp the letters, thus avoiding the laborious task of sticking stamps on manually. If your office does have a franking machine, it will also keep a stock of stamps to use on occasional items and in case of emergencies such as the franking machine breaking down. You therefore need to be familiar with the recording systems for franking machines and the control and issue of stamps.

franking machine

A franking machine prints on each envelope or on a label (for large items which will not pass through the machine)

- the value of the postage
- the date and place of posting
- the licence number of the machine

The franking machine can also print an advertising slogan for the organisation if required:

Many modern franking machines also weigh each item of mail on electronic scales incorporated into the equipment. The postage charge per item is then automatically calculated according to the rate being used (e.g. first class) and the letter or item franked with the appropriate value, which is then recorded by the machine. Some franking machines will also seal envelopes automatically.

how do you pay for franked mail?

The franking machine user normally has a contract with the franking machine manufacturer from whom the machine is purchased or, more commonly, rented. The user 'buys' the value of postage in advance, either from the manufacturer or from the Post Office. Payment is made by cheque or directly by transfer from the user's bank account (direct debit).

how do you 'top up' the franking machine?

If the user wishes to 'top up' the machine with, say, £1,000 worth of postage, the machine may either be taken to the Post Office, or more conveniently, the transaction may take place over the telephone to the manufacturer, if the equipment is fitted with a telephone 'top up' facility.

how is the postage recorded?

Every time an item of mail is franked by the organisation, the meter deducts the postage charge from the total. This meter is therefore a *descending* meter, as the total will always be going down. The franking machine also has an *ascending* meter which records the value of postage as an increasing total. The practice of recording these totals on a 'control card' has now largely been discontinued.

security and the franking machine

The use of the franking machine must be strictly controlled within the office, otherwise staff may take advantage of the machine for personal mail - sending their Christmas cards for instance. It is best that the machine is kept locked up when not in use, and the keys held by nominated staff.

postage stamps - the Postages Book

Postage stamps will be kept by the mail staff in the office. Stamps are valuable items and their issue will therefore need to be strictly controlled. Control is achieved in two ways:

- the stamps should be kept under lock and key
- only authorised members of staff should be allowed access to the stamps
- purchase and issue of stamps should be recorded on a daily basis in a *Postages Book*

A page from a Postages Book is illustrated below. Look at it carefully and then read the notes below the illustration.

date	stamps bought (£)	details of stamps issued	total issued (£)	details
199–				
18 May	15.00 ①	Balance brought forward		
18 May	20.00 ②	Stamps purchased		
		85 first class letters @ 22p	18.70	
		50 second class @ 17p	8.50	③
		2 registered letters @ £2.10	4.20	£2200 comp.
		5 airmail letters @ 26p	1.30	
		Total stamps used	32.70 ④	
		Balance carried forward	2.30 ⑤	
	35.00 ⑥		35.00 ⑥	
19 May	2.30 ⑤	Balance brought forward		

① The value of stamps in the book at the beginning of 18 May (the 'balance brought forward') is £15.00 (see second column).

② Stamps to the value of £20.00 were purchased during the day (see second column).

③ 2 registered letters with £2200 compensation cover were sent in addition to the other letters recorded in the summary in the third column.

④ The totals of stamps issued (see fourth column) are added to produce the figure of £32.70.

⑤ The stamps remaining will be counted up and their total value agreed with the difference between the total of the second column (£35.00) and the total stamps used (£32.70) - the answer being £2.30 - this is the balance of stamps 'carried forward' at the end of 18 May.

⑥ The totals of the second and fourth columns are now written in and double underlined and the £2.30 entered on the next line in the second column - 'balance brought forward' - as the opening stock of stamps for 19 May, the next day.

internal mail

So far we have examined the procedures for processing incoming and outgoing mail. Most larger organisations also have a system for the distribution of *internal mail,* a term used for items which need to be sent from one department or section of the organisation to another. These include

- memoranda
- items for circulation on circulation lists
- messages taken from telephone calls
- copies of letters
- magazines and journals

It is normal practice for the mail staff or messengers (in large organisations) to collect the internal mail from designated trays or wire baskets and to sort and distribute the items. The items of mail may either be placed in large (C4) used envelopes which are often saved from the incoming mail for this purpose; all the sender has to do is to cross out the original address and write the name of the recipient on the envelope. After a number of internal mail journeys these envelopes can become decidedly tatty, and so many organisations use instead the specially printed internal mail envelope (see illustration below). The outside of this envelope is printed with a numbered squares in which the name of the recipient is written. If you use one of these envelopes it is important to cross out the last recipient's name and to write clearly the new recipient's name, otherwise it will go to the wrong person - including possibly yourself! The flap of the envelope is usually secured by a metal tag on a piece of string threaded through a hole in the flap.

1 *Jim Rosenberg* ~~Admin~~	2 *H. Ramsey* ~~Warehouse~~
3 STEVE LAMB SALES	4
5	6
7	8
9	10
11	12
13	14
15	16
17	18
19	20

✎ student activities - mail handling

Performance criteria

The student activities in this section test competences in the following areas:

- *checking mail for damaged or suspicious items, and reporting those items*
- *checking mail to ensure that all enclosures are attached, and reporting any missing items*
- *following security procedures for receipt of cash and valuables*
- *opening mail without damaging the contents*
- *sorting and delivering mail to the correct person within deadlines*
- *reporting promptly unavoidable delays in distribution to the appropriate authority*
- *checking outgoing documents for signature and any enclosures; identifying and rectifying any omissions*
- *sealing securely all outgoing items of mail in the appropriate packaging*
- *addressing all outgoing mail legibly*
- *calculating and applying the correct postal rates*
- *meeting Post Office sorting requirements, collection and postal deadlines*
- *keeping records up-to-date, legible and accurate, and filing them correctly in accordance with the procedures of the organisation*
- *following security procedures for stamps and money at all times*

questions - incoming mail

1.   (a) What signs would make you suspicious of an item of incoming mail?
     (b) What action would you take on receipt of a package which you suspected was a letterbomb?

2.   What action would you take if a courier brings in - and asks you to sign for - a package which has split open and is spilling polystyrene chips?

3.   List the following items of incoming mail *in the order in which you would open them*: ordinary letterpost; letters marked 'Urgent'; letters marked 'Private and Confidential'; Registered and Recorded letters.

4.   What precautions would you take to avoid damaging the mail when you are opening it
     (a) with an automatic letter opener?
     (b) when you do not have an automatic letter opener?

5.   You are dealing with the incoming mail. Your office operates a 'Special Delivery Book' and a 'Remittances Book', the formats for which are illustrated below, together with specimen entries:

Special Delivery Book

date	time	sender	carrier	ref. no.	signature
199–					
12 Mar	08.45	J Smith	Lynx	7869578	L Palmer
12 Mar	09.05	Martco Ltd	Recorded	B608531	L Palmer

Remittances Book

date	sender	remittance	amount	signature
12/3/9-	*Microtronics Limited*	*chq*	234.87	*L Palmer*
12/3/9-	*Miss L Baylis*	*cash*	40.00	*L Palmer*
13/3/9-	*H Boyd*	*P.O.*	5.00	*L Palmer*

State *in detail* what action you would take with the following ten items of mail. Make entries, if required, in the Special Deliveries Book and the Remittances Book (you may have to draw up specimen pages for these books, based on the illustrations above). Use today's date, the present time and your own name, unless you are instructed otherwise.

(a) Recorded Delivery Letter from H Jenkins Ref B 277586 , which you sign for
(b) Parcelforce package from Maestro Supplies (no reference - no signature required)
(c) Securicor packet from Lorimar Hotel, Ref S34526, which you sign for
(d) Registered letter from H Daniels Ref T67252, which you sign for, containing £50 cash
(e) Letter from H Truman (ordinary letterpost) containing a cheque for £345.85
(f) Letter from L McDonald (ordinary letterpost) containing a Postal Order for £5.00
(g) Letter from Microprint Ltd indicating that a catalogue is enclosed - the catalogue is missing
(h) Datapost letter from R Patel Ref 33270102 containing £500 cash, which you sign for
(i) Parceline package from Merriman Antiques Ref P87525 - which you sign for - appears to be crushed at the corners and gives out a sound of broken glass when handled
(j) Letter from T Hick Limited containing a cheque for £85.50 - the letter states that the cheque is for £80.50

6. If a letter is addressed to 'Dear Sir' or 'Dear Madam' where else on the letter would you look to tell you to whom the letter should be passed?

7. You are one of two staff placed on incoming mail duties in the office. What action would you take - and why - if all of the following occur:
    • the post delivery to the office is delayed by an hour
    • the post, when it does arrive, is much larger than normal
    • your colleague feels sick and has to go to the staff room

questions - outgoing mail

It is recommended that students should obtain copies of (or have access to) the Post Office guides for UK and overseas postal rates before attempting this section of activities.

8. Investigate your own organisation (or your work experience organisation or your College) and write a list of the *checks* that are made by different members of staff to correspondence (and any enclosures) before it leaves the office.

9. What is wrong with the following addresses which appear on envelopes being despatched from your office:

    (a)   Private and Confidential

                  Sales Department
                  Vernons Furniture
                  56 High Street
                  Mereford MR4 8LH

(b)   Mr Lemming
                                      76 Cumberland Avenue
                                      Merford
                                      MR4 7UY.

(c)   Mr Doris Westermann
                                       Templeton Agencies
                                        49 Liecester Square
                                         W1E 7RT

(d)   R T Blackman, Manging Director,
                                      Blackman Engineering Ltd.,
                                      506, Victoria Crescent,
                                      Westminister, SW1TRY.

Note: students should also have studied Unit 6 'Communicating - Routine Business Communications' before attempting Activity 9.

10.   What envelope or packaging would you use when sending

      (a) A4 letters to customers produced on a word processor with the customer's name
           and address printed at the top of each letter
      (b) a paperback book
      (c) a stapled A4 report of ten pages together with a covering letter
      (d) a presentation set of champagne glasses
      (e) an A5 twelve page printed catalogue
      (f) an A6 invitation card to the organisation's customer party

      Choose from • jiffybag • DL window envelope • C4 envelope • C5 envelope • C6 envelope
      • strong carton

11.   What method of postal depatch would you use for sending

      (a) cash
      (b) advertising literature
      (c) statements of account
      (d) a letter which should reach its destination the following day
      (e) a business letter containing a document which must be at its destination by 10.00 am the
           following day
      (f) a demand for payment from a customer
      (g) an urgent letter to Malawi
      (h) a letter to Hamburg which must get there within a week

      Choose from • 2nd class mail • 1st class mail • Recorded Delivery • Registered Mail • Datapost
      • Special Delivery • Swiftair • Airmail

12.   Calculate the *total* cost of sending

      (a) 234 letters @ 50g by second class mail
      (b) 58 letters @ 50g by first class mail
      (c) a Registered Letter weighing 120g first class (at the highest compensation rate)
      (d) a Special Delivery letter weighing 50gm
      (e) a Recorded Delivery letter weighing 160g by first class post
      (f) an Airmail letter weighing 15g to Zurich
      (g) an Airmail letter weighing 15g to Washington USA

      Show all your workings.

13. You are entrusted with the job of managing the Postages Book (see example format below). You should draw up your own blank page in which to complete this Activity. During the course of a working day (use today's date) you handle the following transactions:

- check opening stock of stamps which totals £20.00
- purchase £15.00 new stamps
- issue 50 2nd class stamps for letters
- issue 25 1st class stamps for letters
- issue 12 stamps for Airmail letters to Germany (all the letters are 15g)
- 3 Recorded Delivery first class letters (all the letters are 100g)

You should then complete the book entries in the Postages Book

date	stamps bought (£)	details of stamps issued	total issued (£)	details

Additional Postages Book Activity
At the end of the day you check the total of the stamps and find out that you are short by three first class stamps. What action would you take? What are the normal security procedures you would adopt when looking after a Postages Book?

 linking assignment

Common Skills Assignment 6
Managing tasks and solving problems: Managing without the boss, pages 190 to 195

Common Skills development: Managing tasks and solving problems

Skills developed

The skills developed in this section are

- ***use information sources***
- ***deal with routine and non-routine tasks in combination***
- ***solve routine and non-routine problems***

The Units in this book so far have explained how to undertake clerical tasks under normal circumstances. But problems will occur in the workplace: your workload increases unexpectedly, you have to cover for a sick colleague, equipment breaks down, an unreasonable customer takes up a lot of your time with a petty complaint. In short, you are faced with the trying occurrences which frequently spoil the smooth running of the normal working day. In this section we will examine the problems that occur and suggest some approaches for solving them. The assignment which follows presents an in-tray exercise of tasks and problems caused by the sudden absence of your boss.

1. use information sources

performance criteria

If you are faced with a task which involves collecting information (e.g. prices, names, telephone numbers) it is essential that you are aware of the information sources available to you both inside and outside the office. These sources have already been examined in Unit 7 . You must be able to

- locate the appropriate sources of information
- collect the relevant information
- sort the information and use it effectively according to the requirements of the task

coping with internal sources of information

Many of your office tasks require you to use information from sources within the office, either from your own files or from the commonly used directories (telephone directory, Yellow Pages) e.g.

- the name and address of one of your customers
- the price of one of your products
- the telephone number of British Rail's passenger information service

If an outside caller or your supervisor puts you on the spot with a routine enquiry like those quoted above, you should have little difficulty in coping with the task. If, however, you are asked a *non-routine enquiry* which requires that you go out of the office to do some research, you will need a disciplined approach to the problem.

coping with external sources of information

Suppose that you work in an Administration Department of a business and your supervisor instructs you to find out about a special insurance policy which will cover the company's computers and data held on computer file, against theft, fire and loss resulting from machine breakdown. Where would you start? The questions and answers might run as follows:

Question	*What is my first source of information?*
Answer	The supervisor will recommend that you approach an insurance broker.
Question	*Which insurance broker?*
Answer	The Yellow Pages will provide you with a list of local brokers; alternatively the supervisor may tell you that the business usually uses Baker & Baker at 57 High Street.
Question	*Where next?*
Answer	Telephone the broker, or call in person after telephoning first, mentioning the type of policy required and the insurance risks to be covered.
Question	*What insurance risks?*
Answer	The supervisor has already told you that the risks are fire, theft and loss following machine breakdown. You should have written the details down.
Question	*Which insurance company should I use?*
Answer	It depends on the cost of the premium - the broker will tell you what the individual premiums are. Compare the costs, and write down for your supervisor the names of the insurance companies and the premiums they charge. The supervisor will decide which company to use.

You will see from this process that when you are faced with a non-routine task you must

- *establish exactly what the task is*, and write the details down if necessary - if you are not sure, ask!
- ask your supervisor (or whoever gave you the task) for *initial sources* of information - in the above case, the insurance broker
- *follow through* the enquiry, using your own initiative, do not continually pester your supervisor for guidance
- *analyse your findings* - in the above case the insurance premiums - do not just heap a pile of papers on your supervisor's desk and make a run for it

If you carry out a non-routine task using outside information sources of information in an efficient and self-reliant way, you will rise in your supervisor's estimation, and you will probably get more tasks to do!

2. deal with routine and non-routine tasks in combination___

performance criteria

We have already seen in Unit 1 'Work role - you and your job' (pages 13 to 16) that one of the important skills to be developed is the ability to organise one's working environment and manage one's time effectively. This means that if you are given both routine and non-routine tasks, you will have to decide which are the most important and which will have to be tackled first. You must be able to

- identify routine and non-routine tasks
- identify which tasks have priority
- place the tasks in order of priority
- complete the tasks within a deadline under supervision
- ask and use advice when it is necessary
- assess your own performance in completing tasks
- modify the way you work if you are not happy with your performance

how to be organised

In Unit 1 we explained the need for an organised desk, which will be divided into three areas:

tasks given   Incoming tasks - the morning's post to deal with, memo's and notes from colleagues, telephone messages requiring you to ring back. These are normally placed in an 'in tray' and require immediate attention, and a decision on whether they are urgent or non-urgent

tasks pending   Tasks which cannot be completed at present, either because you are too busy, or because you are waiting for further information in order to complete them. Tasks pending are often placed in a 'pending tray'.

tasks completed   The most satisfying area of the desk is the space allocated to completed tasks e.g. letters ready for signing, memo's and notes written. Completed tasks are often placed in an 'out tray'.

deciding priorities

How do you decide the order in which to complete the tasks? Some people tend to do the tasks they *like* doing first; these people normally end up in panic at the end of the day with a pile of difficult and overdue jobs to do. The order *should* depend on the *priority* of the tasks. How do you decide priority? There are a number of factors involved

- the *urgency* of the job - it may be overdue, or marked 'Urgent'
- the *importance* of the job - tasks for your customers take priority over internal routine matters
- the *originator* - are you doing the job for the Managing Director or for a colleague on the same section?

There is no precise rule which says which job will actually come first and have to be tackled at 9.00 o'clock in the morning, but the guidelines set out above indicate which jobs will be at the top of the tray. The important point is that you should always be aware of every job in hand. If messages and requests arrive during the course of the working day, do not ignore them and put them on one side because you are 'too busy', read them and place them in your order of priorities.

In the in-tray assignment which follows on page 190 - 'Managing without the boss' - you will be able to practise deciding priorities in what will turn out to be a very harrassing day. You will also be able to assess your organisational skills.

3. solve routine and non-routine problems ──────

performance criteria

When you solve a problem you normally do what you 'feel' or 'think' is right in the circumstances. You do not apply a strict formula to the situation and work out in a scientific way the 'correct solution'. Instead you often ask other people's opinions, examine a range of possible solutions, and then you use common sense. It is, however, possible to look at the problem-solving process as a *series of steps* that you take. When faced with a problem in the workplace (and outside it as well), you should be aware of the problem-solving *process*. You should be able to take the following steps:

- identify the extent and nature of the problem
- select a suitable technique for solving the problem
- devise a realistic plan of action
- apply a problem-solving technique
- select and use a realistic solution
- check and modify the solution as necessary

We will take each of these steps in turn by looking at a simple and common workplace problem - a jammed photocopier.

the problem solving process

what problem? It is essential to identify what the problem is before taking any action to rectify it. If your photocopier jams, the indicator light or symbol will show to tell you that there is a problem. What the indicator does not tell you is how serious the problem is: it may be a piece of paper stuck in the feeder tray - which you can pull out - or it may be a piece shredded to pieces in the mechanism of the copier.

which solution? The problem with problems is that there may be more than one solution. It is always worthwhile consulting other sources or asking your colleagues for their advice and experience. In the case of the jammed copier you have a number of possible solutions:
- consult the instruction manual - look at the 'troubleshooting' section
- ask your supervisor
- telephone for the mechanic

The solution you choose will depend on the nature of the problem - the nature of the jam - and the resources available for fixing it. This solution will then become the 'realistic plan of action' and the 'realistic solution' mentioned in the Performance Criteria above.

Sometimes a solution can be unexpected.   You may suspect, for instance, that your computer keyboard is broken, until you find that it has become disconnected from the CPU. You would feel fairly silly if you had called out a mechanic!

is the problem solved? It is essential once you have decided on your solution to follow it through and to ensure that the problem is solved. If the mechanic has fixed the photocopier, does it work? If it fails again, the problem may be a different one, and may require a different solution.

other problems The jammed photocopier is a fairly simple problem cured by a simple solution. Other workplace problems may be more complex: an unfair supervisor, an alcoholic colleague. Nevertheless the problem solving process remains the same: identify the problem, discuss possible solutions with others, choose the best, pursue it, and monitor its success.

Common Skills Assignment 6
Managing tasks and solving problems:
Managing without the boss

Areas assessed

This assignment covers the following areas

- *Clerical Tasks: communicating information, mail handling, liaising with callers and colleagues, filing and retrieving information, reprographics*
- *Common Skills: principal skill - managing tasks and solving problems other skills - managing and developing self, communicating, working with and relating to others, applying numeracy*

Scenario

You are the senior assistant in the Sales Department of Wyvern (Office Products) Limited. For the purposes of the assignment you may retain your own name or assume the identity of any of the three sales assistants on the structure chart set out on page 4. The date is 5 June 199-.

The Sales Director, Tim Blake, and Sales Manager, Jane Seymour, are away at a conference in Jersey, and cannot be contacted. The Sales Supervisor, Bob Bates, has been left in charge for the day. When you get to work in the morning you are met by Asaf Patel, the Adminstration Manager, who tells you that Bob Bates has been laid low by a curry and will not be in work that day. As senior assistant on the Sales Team you are in charge of the Department for the time being. Mr Patel is confident that you can cope, but adds 'If you have any problems you can't deal with, let me know, and we will sort them out.' In the Sales Department, the secretary will have sorted the post and passed to you the items which need actioning.

Tasks

Task 1: Deciding priorities and acting on them

You are to arrange in order of priority the following items which are placed in your in-tray. You should write down on a separate piece of paper for your assessor the *reasons* for your order of priority. You should then reply to the various items. Suggestions for the way in which you should reply are given with each item.

1.   A note from Tim Blake to ring in the morning Otto Schwarz, a German Sales Representative who is the company's guest at the Excelsior Hotel, Mereford, (phone number 987456) to tell him
    (a) the distance from Birmingham to Cardiff (he is driving a hired car) and the time the journey will take
    (b) how much in pounds sterling he will get for 1,000 Deutschemarks (see page 243 for an explanation of currency exchange rates)

    Research the facts in sources such as atlases and the banks. Write the details down on paper ready for the telephone call which you should make to your assessor on your training telephone system.

2. A note from Tim Blake dated yesterday asking for flight times from London Heathrow to Paris. He wants to travel out in the morning and return early the following day, having stayed overnight with a friend in Paris. He also wants details of hotels near Heathrow as he wishes to stay overnight before leaving for Paris. The note says 'let me have the details the day after tomorrow when I am back from Jersey - just type them on a sheet of paper.'

   Research the facts in hotel and air flight guides. Type the details as requested on a sheet of paper addressed to Tim Blake, Sales Director.

3. A cheque for £5,876.95 from one of your customers marked 'for the attention of the Accounts Department - settlement of invoice 615537' but addressed to Bob Bates.

   Decide on the action you are going to take with the cheque, and write down your decision on paper.

4. A fax from a firm of solicitors. *Decide on the format of your reply, and draft it as if it were being sent by Bob Bates.*

---

facsimile transmission

from
Healey, Bold and Wright, Solicitors
23B Chantry Court, Mereford MR5 6TF, Tel 0605 783626 Fax 0605 783546

---

date: 5 June 199–

TO......... Bob Bates, Sales

.... Wyvern (Office Products) Limited

....

TELEPHONE NUMBER......0605 241851......FACSIMILE NUMBER......0605 241879

NUMBER OF PAGES INCLUDING THIS HEADER...........1...........

---

message
Please let us have details, together with prices, of your canteen tables. We are opening new offices next week. URGENT! Thanks.
Betty Flowers, Office Manager,

If you have any enquiries regarding this message please telephone the above number and ask for extension...56...............

5.   The following letter is received from a firm which you know that your Department has been chasing for business for a long time. This is the first product enquiry received from them.

Draft a reply in the format which you think is most suitable. The reply should go out in the name of Jane Seymour, Sales Manager.

Wyvern Marketing
125 High Street
Mereford MR1 9SZ

Tel 0605 675412 Fax 0605 675432

Ref RT/SB/89

3 June 199-

Jane Seymour, Sales Manager
Wyvern (Office Products) Limited
12 Lower Hyde Street
Mereford MR1 2JF

Dear Jane

Office Furniture

Many thanks for the excellent lunch the other day. As we mentioned at the time we are refitting our offices in the course of the next six months and will be looking for quotations for new desks.

We already have your catalogue and will be grateful for up-to-date prices of your desks. Tim Blake mentioned we would be able to get a 20% discount, but just let us have the full prices for the present.

We look forward to hearing from you.

Yours sincerely,

Dick Tombs
Purchasing Manager

P Tombs, R Tombs, J Wasnett trading as Wyvern Marketing

---

6.   A covering letter received from Millbrook Dairies, Perry Lane, Broadwater, MR6 6LP, stating that a Purchase Order for goods is enclosed. The person who opened your post in the morning has marked *'no Purchase Order enclosed'* on the letter. You cannot find the document either.   Note: a Purchase Order is a document used for the ordering of goods (see page 208)

Decide on the action you are going to take, and carry it out in consultation with your assessor.

7. The following letter is received from a customer who is well known to you for complaining about your products, not always with justification.

    Decide on the way in which you are going to reply to this letter, and carry out the action in consultation with your assessor.

Hills & Co., Financial Consultants
76 Nether Court
Mereford MR3 5TF
Tel 0605 675423, Facsimile 0605 675231

Ref JH/RF/654

31 May 199-

The Sales Manager
Wyvern (Office Products) Limited
12 Lower Hyde Street
Mereford MR1 2JF

Dear Sir

Faulty furniture

I am writing to complain in the strongest terms about an executive chair which I recently bought from your company. The model was Catalogue No C1044, a high back leather chair on a swivel base.

The chair appears to be highly unstable. I was standing on it yesterday to open the window and it spun round and tipped right over, landing me on the floor with a badly grazed shin and a black eye where I hit the corner of the desk.

I shall be grateful if you will give me a full refund for this obviously substandard item.

Yours faithfully

John Hills
Consultant

J Hills, P Hills, FIMBRA.

8.   The following memorandum from your Accounts Department

MEMORANDUM

To R Bates, Sales Supervisor

From K Roach, Accounts Supervisor   **Ref.** KR/AC

Copies to –   **Date** 31 May 199–

Subject CUSTOMER DISCOUNTS

Please let me know the trade discount given to any customers for whom we have opened accounts since 1 January of this year. We have had one or two problems with customers querying the discounts they are allowed on invoices. Please respond by 7 June. Please list the customer names in alphabetical order. Many thanks.

K.R.

Attached to the memorandum is the following list extracted by one of the secretaries who is trying to help you out.

<u>new customers</u>

James Eliot	10%
H Barnett & Sons Ltd	20%
Jericho Winebar	10%
MacAlister Advertising Agency	15%
O'Casey & Co	20%
999 Alarm Service	10%
Naomi Scott Recruitment	15%

You should send a memorandum in reply. You should pay particular attention to the request that the names should be arranged in alphabetical order.

Task 2: Problem solving

During the course of the day a number of problems occur. How you would deal with the situations set out below? Remember that Mr Patel has promised to help you if you encounter a problem you cannot deal with. The way in which you tackle this task will depend on your assessor's requirements. It is suggested that you

- set out your solutions in writing and give a copy to your assessor
- discuss your solutions with your colleagues (fellow students or work colleagues)
- discuss your solutions with your assessor in the light of your written contribution and the group discussion

Please note that in this Task you are asked to state *how to tackle problems*; you are not asked to carry out the various jobs.

1.   Your fax machine breaks down at 9.30 a.m.

2.   You need to telephone a customer urgently but cannot seem to get through. The number given you is a Worcester number: 0906 333693.

3.   The Wyvern Marketing file (see previous Task, item 5) has gone missing from the filing cabinet and nobody has made a note in the 'file taken out' book which is normally used.

4.   At 10.00 a.m. a customer telephones asking to speak to the 'Sales Manager' and refuses to speak to you, or to tell you what the call is about.

5.   A letter arrives in the second post addressed to the Sales Department marked 'Private and Confidential'. Unfortunately the envelope, which is sealed, has no name on it.

6.   One of your colleagues falls over an opened filing cabinet drawer at 10.15 a.m. and badly grazes her shin.

7.   The Managing Director rushes into the office at 10.30 a.m., saying that his secretary has been delayed at the doctor's surgery, and could someone in your Department please word process an important report before 11.30, as he needs it for a meeting. After he has gone you discover that the report is very lengthy and there is no possibility of anyone in the Sales Department being able to tackle the job.

8.   Because you are so busy you only manage to snatch ten minutes and a sandwich at lunch time. At 2.30 p.m. you become increasingly anxious because one of your junior colleagues who normally processes incoming orders has still not come back from her lunch-hour which began at 1.00 p.m. The work is beginning to pile up in her in-tray. At 2.45 p.m. you hear some laughing down the corridor. Shortly afterwards your colleague, who has been out at the pub celebrating a birthday, arrives obviously the worse for wear, having drunk too much. In your opinion she is not really capable of working efficiently.

9.   At 3.30 p.m. two visitors arrive to see Jane Seymour, the Sales Manager, to discuss the supply of furniture. You check the diary, but there is no reference to the meeting. The visitors are sure that they have not made a mistake, and produce a letter signed by Jane Seymour confirming the appointment.

10.   At the end of the day, when you have finished processing the post, the Managing Director rings through to ask you to send a product sample to an address in London. The sample must reach its destination by 10.00 a.m. the following morning.

13 Petty cash

NCVQ coverage

4.1 process petty cash transactions

Performance criteria
- following cash handling security and safety procedures at all times
- supporting all transactions with correctly authorised petty cash vouchers
- ensuring that all transactions are recorded accurately
- reporting promptly all irregularities to an appropriate authority

introduction

A petty cash book is used to record low-value payments for various small purchases by an organisation, e.g. small items of stationery, postages, etc. It would not be appropriate for such expenses to be entered in the main account books of the organisation (which are used for the recording of larger purchases) as a large number of small payments would clutter them up. With the petty cash system an amount of cash is handed by the main cashier to a member of staff, the *petty cashier,* who will be responsible for security of the money, and will make payments as appropriate.

In order to operate a petty cash system, the petty cashier needs the following:

- a *petty cash book* in which to record transactions
- a lockable *petty cash box* in which to keep the 'float' of cash
- a stock of blank *petty cash vouchers* for claims on petty cash to be made by people who have made small purchases
- a *lockable desk drawer* in which to keep these items

 linking assignment

Common Skills Assignment 7
Applying numeracy: the Accounts Department, pages 252 to 256

the petty cash procedure

As an employee you are most likely to encounter the petty cash system when making claims for money for small purchases you have made. Before studying the form-filling procedures in detail, read the summary of a typical petty cash transaction set out below.

> *your supervisor asks you to go and buy a new jar of coffee as a business visitor is expected*

> *you go to the local stores and buy a jar of coffee; you make sure that you retain the receipt (for £2.99) which you hand to the petty cashier on your return to the office*

> *the supervisor authorises a petty cash voucher which contains details of the purchase*

> *the petty cashier gives you £2.99 in cash*

> *the petty cashier attaches the receipt to the petty cash voucher and enters the details in the petty cash book*

what items can be passed through petty cash book?

As we have already noted, petty cash is used to make small cash payments for expenses incurred by an organisation. Examples of the type of payments made from petty cash include:

- stationery items
- small items of office supplies
- casual wages
- window cleaning
- bus, rail and taxi fares (incurred on behalf of the organisation)
- meals and drinks (when the expense is incurred on behalf of the organisation)
- postages
- tips and donations

Petty cash should *not* be used to pay for private expenses of employees, unless the organisation has agreed these in advance. Usually the petty cashier will have a list of approved expenses which can be reimbursed.

A business will also decide on the maximum value of each transaction that can be paid out of petty cash: £20 is a common maximum.

case study: petty cash expenses

Situation

You are working as a clerk for Wyvern Engineering Co. Ltd. One of your duties is that of petty cashier. Which of the following expenses would you allow to be paid out of petty cash?

- envelopes for use in the office, £2.50
- postage on an urgent parcel of engineering parts, £3.75
- bus fare to work claimed by typist, £1.20
- car mileage to work of office manager called in late at night when the burglar alarm went off (false alarm!), £5.50
- tea and coffee for use in the office, £3.70
- office window cleaning, £2.80
- pot plant bought for reception area, £5.50
- floppy disks for computer, £35.00
- donation to local charity by the business, £5.00
- meal allowance paid to a member of staff required to work during the lunch hour, £3.50

Solution

For most expenses it is clear whether or not they can be drawn from petty cash. However, there are points to consider for some of the expenses.

envelopes	pay from petty cash
postage	pay from petty cash
bus fare to work	this is a personal expense and cannot be drawn from petty cash
car mileage	travel to work is a personal expense, as seen with the previous item; however, as this expense was a special journey in the middle of the night in order to resolve a business problem, it can be paid from petty cash
tea and coffee	this is a personal expense of employees and cannot normally be paid out of petty cash; however, if the ingredients were used to make drinks for official visitors and customers, it can be paid from petty cash
office window cleaning	pay from petty cash
pot plant	pay from petty cash (but plants for the general office cannot be bought with the company's money)
floppy disks	this is a business expense but, in view of the amount (too large for petty cash), it should be paid by cheque from the cash book
donation	pay from petty cash
meal allowance	pay from petty cash, provided that it is company policy to make an allowance in these circumstances

Note: before payment can be made in each case, it must be authorised by an official of the company - see Petty Cash Voucher (on the next page).

the imprest system

Most petty cash books operate on the *imprest system*. With this system the petty cashier starts each week with a certain amount of money in the petty cash tin - the imprest amount. As payments are made during the week the amount of money will go down and, at the end of the week, the cash will need topping up by the main cashier to the imprest amount. For example:

	Started week with imprest amount	£100.00
Less	Total of petty cash amounts paid out during week	£80.50
	Cash held at end of week	£19.50
Add	Amount drawn from cashier to restore imprest amount	£80.50
	Cash at start of next week, i.e. imprest amount	£100.00

In short, *the petty cash will need to be topped up by the amount spent during the week*. Some organisations may only need to top up the petty cash to the imprest amount on a monthly basis. If the petty cash runs out at any time, the imprest amount may be increased to avoid the problem.

petty cash voucher

The petty cashier, who is likely also to have other tasks within the organisation, is responsible for control of the petty cash, making cash payments when appropriate and keeping records of payments made. Payments out of petty cash are made only against correct documentation - an authorised petty cash voucher (see the illustration below). Petty cash vouchers are completed as follows:

- the date
- the details and amount of expenditure
- the signature of the person making the claim and receiving the money
- the signature of the person authorising the payment to be made - the petty cashier or supervisor
- the receipt should be attached to the petty cash voucher

Most petty cash vouchers are numbered. The number will be entered in the petty cash book by the petty cashier, and will act as a reference for that transaction. Each voucher will be filed in numerical order and can easily be located if there is any query on the transaction.

Petty Cash Voucher	No 807		
	Date *11 May 19-1*		
For what required		**AMOUNT**	£
Envelopes		1	55
Parcel tape		3	10
		4	65
Signature *T. Harris*			
Passed by *D. Adams*			

petty cash and VAT

Many purchases that you make will include Value Added Tax - or VAT as it is commonly known. VAT will therefore feature on documents relating to those purchases:

• on *receipts* for low value cash purchases
• on *invoices* for higher value items

We will look at receipts in this Unit and at invoices in the next Unit. The principles relating to VAT are common to both receipts and invoices, and we will now examine these principles, as they are important to your studies.

what is VAT?

Value Added Tax is a tax on spending. The VAT rate in 1991 is 17.5% of the price of the item sold. Most businesses which have an annual sales turnover (amount of sales in a year) exceeding £35,000 (1991 figure) must register for VAT. They are then given a registration number which must be quoted on all receipts, invoices and other business doscuments. Businesses which are VAT registered must charge VAT on items that they sell (ouput tax), but they can also reclaim VAT paid on items that they have bought (input tax). The difference between VAT on sales (output tax) and VAT on purchases (input tax) is paid to the government (through HM Customs & Excise), normally every three months, on completion of a VAT return.

VAT on petty cash transactions - dealing with receipts

If you are making petty cash purchases which involve VAT, it is important that the VAT amount is recorded because the organisation may be able to reclaim the VAT, or at least set it off against VAT which it owes on sales which it has made. It will be the job of the petty cashier to record the VAT content of a purchase in the VAT column of the petty cash book (see illustration on page 199).

There are however two problems relating to VAT and petty cash transactions:

• some receipts *do not show the VAT content* of the price of the item purchased
• some items are zero-rated, i.e. *there is no VAT charged* - e.g food, newspapers, postage stamps

An example of a receipt which does not show the VAT content is illustrated below. The receipt is for an adaptor plug purchased at Wyvern Electrics. It shows:

a till receipt

• the name of the retailer
• the VAT registration number of the retailer
• the price of the item - £4.70
• the amount of money given - a £10 note
• the amount of change given - £5.30
• the date and time of the transaction

```
Wyvern Electrics
VAT  454 7106 52

Qty 1        4.70
Total        4.70

Cash        10.00
Change       5.30

11/03/92 09.30
```

What it does not show, however, is the VAT content of the purchase price - *it only shows the price after the VAT has been added on.*

How do you calculate purchase price before the VAT is added on? The formula, with VAT at 17.5%, is:

price including VAT ÷ 1.175 = price before VAT is added on

in this case: £4.70 ÷ 1.175 = £4.00 = price before VAT is added on

The VAT content is therefore £4.70 less £4.00 = 70p

layout of a petty cash book

Receipts	Date	Details	Voucher No.	Total Payment	Analysis columns				
					VAT	Postages	Stationery	Travel	Sundry
£				£	£	£	£	£	£

When the petty cashier has completed the petty cash voucher, paid the cash, and calculated any VAT content, the details can be entered in the petty cash book . The layout of the book shows that:

- receipts from the main cashier are entered in the column on the extreme left
- there are columns for the date and details of all receipts and payments
- there is a column for the petty cash voucher number
- the total payment (i.e. the amount paid out on each petty cash voucher) is in the next column
- the VAT content (if any) is entered in the next column
- then follow the analysis columns which analyse each transaction entered in the 'total payment' column - the amounts entered in these columns will *not* include VAT

You will see that the amount of each petty cash payment is in effect entered *twice:*

- once on the left in the Total Payment column - the whole amount paid is shown here
- once on the right in the Analysis columns - showing the type of expense and the VAT content

A business or organisation will use whatever analysis columns are most suitable for it; there may well be more columns than those shown. Note that if VAT is charged, the total amount of the petty cash payment *never* goes in the Analysis column; these show the amount of the expense *before* VAT is added. As we saw in the last section, the petty cashier may have to calculate this figure by dividing the total payment by 1.175 (for a VAT rate of 17.5%).

The electrical adaptor purchased from Wyvern Electrics (see the receipt on the previous page) will be entered as shown below. Remember that the total payment was £4.70 and the VAT was 70p.

Receipts	Date	Details	Voucher No.	Total Payment	Analysis columns				
					VAT	Postages	Stationery	Travel	Sundry
£				£	£	£	£	£	£
	11 Mar	Electrical	31	4.70	0.70				4.00

case study: entries in the petty cash book

situation

You are a clerk working for Mercia Insurance Brokers. As part of your duties you are required to keep the petty cash, issue petty cash vouchers and make entries in the petty cash book. There are a number of transactions for the week to be entered in the petty cash book. All of these, unless indicated to the contrary, include VAT at 17.5%.

19-1
10 Apr. Started the week with an imprest amount of £50.00
10 Apr. Paid stationery £4.70 on voucher no. 47
10 Apr. Paid taxi fare £2.35 on voucher no. 48
11 Apr. Paid postages £0.75 on voucher no. 49 (no VAT)
12 Apr. Paid taxi fare £2.35 on voucher no. 50
12 Apr. Paid computer labels £9.40 on voucher no. 51
13 Apr. Paid postages £3.68 on voucher no. 52 (no VAT)
13 Apr. Paid postages £2.85 on voucher no. 53 (no VAT)
14 Apr. Paid window cleaner (sundry) £4.70 on voucher no. 54

solution

Receipts	Date	Details	Voucher No.	Total Payment	Analysis columns				
					VAT	Postages	Stationery	Travel	Sundry
£	199-			£	£	£	£	£	£
50.00	10 Apr.	Cash balance							
	10 Apr.	Stationery	47	4.70	0.70		4.00		
	10 Apr.	Taxi fare	48	2.35	0.35			2.00	
	11 Apr.	Postages	49	0.75		0.75			
	12 Apr.	Travel	50	2.35	0.35			2.00	
	12 Apr.	Stationery	51	9.40	1.40		8.00		
	13 Apr.	Postages	52	3.68		3.68			
	13 Apr.	Postages	53	2.85		2.85			
	14 Apr.	Window cleaner	54	4.70	0.70				4.00
				30.78	3.50	7.28	12.00	4.00	4.00

Note the following points:

- the opening balance of cash (£50) is shown in the Receipts column on the first day of the week

- the Analysis columns and Total Payment column are added up and the totals shown

- the totals of the Analysis columns (including the VAT column) add up to the total of the Total Payment column, i.e £30.78 - this is an important arithmetic check to be performed by the petty cashier

- The amount of cash received from the main cashier to restore the imprest amount will be the same as the amount paid out, i.e. £30.78 - this is not shown here

Please also note that the petty cash book is not 'balanced off' here - this is a procedure required in your studies at a higher level if you chose the 'Financial' route to qualification.

petty cash security and safety procedures

The job of petty cashier involves looking after cash and therefore the observing of security and safety procedures are of prime importance if the cash is not to go missing!

The Action Points listed below summarise these security and safety procedures.

✔ action points - control of petty cash

The main procedures for the operation and control of petty cash are:

○   ensure that you start each week with the imprest amount of cash which has been agreed with the supervisor

○   keep the petty cash in a locked cash box, and keep control of the keys

○   provide petty cash vouchers (in number order) on request

○   pay out of petty cash against correctly completed petty cash vouchers ensuring that
 -   the voucher is signed by the person authorising payment (or yourself)
 -   the voucher is signed by the person receiving the money
 -   a receipt (if possible) is attached to the petty cash voucher, and that receipt and petty cash voucher are for the same amount

○   write up the petty cash book (to include calculation of VAT amounts as appropriate)

○   store the petty cash vouchers safely - file them in numerical order

○   expect a surprise check of petty cash from the supervisor - at any one time the cash held plus amounts of petty cash vouchers should equal the imprest amount

○   at the end of each week (or month) total the columns in the petty cash book and draw an amount of cash from the cashier equal to the amount of payments made, in order to restore the imprest amount

○   present the petty cash book and cash in hand for checking by the supervisor on request

○   deal with any discrepancies promptly; these can include:

 •   a receipt and petty cash voucher total differing - raise the matter with the person who made the purchase and adjust the cash accordingly

 •   a difference between the totals of the Analysis columns and the Total Payments column in the Petty Cash Book - check the addition of the columns, check the figures against the vouchers, check your VAT calculations (does the VAT plus the Analysis column amount equal the Total Payment amount?)

 •   a difference between the cash in the Petty Cash box and the balance shown in the Petty Cash Book - if this is not an arithmetic difference it may be a case of theft, and should be reported promptly to your supervisor

student activities - petty cash

Performance criteria

The student activities in this section test competences in the following areas:
- following cash handling security and safety procedures at all times
- supporting all transactions with correctly authorised petty cash vouchers
- ensuring that all transactions are recorded accurately
- reporting promptly all irregularities to an appropriate authority

Note: photocopiable specimen petty cash vouchers and a petty cash book layout are to be found in Appendix 1 at the end of this book.

1. You work as a clerk in the office of Temeside Printers Ltd. One of your duties is that of petty cashier. Which of the following expenses will you allow to be paid out of petty cash?

(a) postage on a parcel of printing sent to a customer, £3.85
(b) a rubber date stamp bought for use in the office, £4.60
(c) rail fare to work claimed by the office manager's secretary, £2.50
(d) donation to charity, £5.00
(e) tea and coffee for use by office staff, £5.50
(f) mileage allowance claimed by works foreman who had to visit a customer, £4.80
(g) meal allowance paid to typist who had to work her lunch hour £4.00
(h) window cleaning, £3.50
(i) purchase of shelving for the office, £35.00
(j) taxi fare claimed for delivering an urgent parcel of printing to a customer, £6.25

2. As petty cashier, prepare petty cash vouchers under today's date for signature by the person making the claim. You are authorised to approve payments up to £20.00. VAT is to be ignored.
Note: photocopiable petty cash vouchers are reproduced in Appendix 1.

Voucher no. 851: £4.45 claimed by Jayne Smith for postage on an urgent parcel of spare parts sent to a customer, Evelode Supplies Ltd.
Voucher no. 852: £2.12 claimed by Tanya Howard for air-mail envelopes bought for use in the office.

3. The business for which you work is registered for VAT. The following petty cash amounts include VAT at 17.5% and you are required to calculate the amount that will be shown in the VAT column and the appropriate expense column (VAT amounts, if they do not work out exactly, should be rounded down to the nearest penny):

(a) £9.40
(b) £4.70
(c) £2.35
(d) £2.45
(e) £15.60
(f) £3.47
(g) £8.75
(h) 94p
(i) 99p
(j) £19.41

4. On returning from holiday, you are told to take over the petty cash book. This is kept on the imprest system, the float being £75 at the beginning of each month. Analysis columns are used for VAT, Travelling Expenses, Postages, Stationery, and Miscellaneous.

    Enter the following transactions (VAT is not payable on postage, donations, rail fares). You can assume that all payments have been authorized. Total the analysis columns and agree them with the total of the Total Payments column. Remember to round VAT amounts down to the nearest penny.

    199-
1 Aug.	Balance of cash £75.00
2 Aug.	Voucher no. 39: taxi fare £3.80
4 Aug.	Voucher no. 40: parcel postage £2.35
7 Aug.	Voucher no. 41: pencils £1.26
10 Aug.	Voucher no. 42: travel expenses £5.46
12 Aug.	Voucher no. 43: window cleaner £8.50 (miscellaneous)
14 Aug.	Voucher no. 44: large envelopes £2.45
17 Aug.	Voucher no. 45: donation to charity £5 (miscellaneous)
18 Aug.	Voucher no. 46: rail fare £10.60
20 Aug.	Voucher no. 47: recorded delivery postage £0.75
23 Aug.	Voucher no. 48: roll of packing tape £1.50
25 Aug.	Voucher no. 49: excess postage paid £0.55
27 Aug.	Voucher no. 50: taxi fare £5.40

5. Prepare a petty cash book with five analysis columns for VAT, Postages, Travelling Expenses, Meals, and Sundry Office Expenses. Enter the following transactions for the week (VAT is not payable on postages or on rail fares). Total the analysis columns and agree them with the total of the Total Payments column. Remember to round VAT amounts down to the nearest penny.

    199-
1 June	Balance of cash £100.00
1 June	Postages £6.35, voucher no. 123
2 June	Taxi fare £3.25, voucher no. 124
2 June	Postages £1.28, voucher no. 125
3 June	Envelopes £4.54, voucher no. 126
3 June	Window cleaning £5.87, voucher no. 127
4 June	Meal £10.85, voucher no. 128
4 June	Postages £9.50, voucher no. 129
4 June	Taxi fare £9.40, voucher no. 130
5 June	Marker pens £6.34, voucher no. 131

6. You are going on holiday and handing your job as petty cashier to a colleague who is not familiar with the security and safety aspects of the job, although she can manage the paperwork. Prepare a checklist of the security and safety aspects of the job so that she can learn them easily. Write them out as numbered points rather than as solid text - they will be more easily remembered in this format.

 linking assignment

Common Skills Assignment 7
Applying numeracy: the Accounts Department, pages 252 to 256

14 Processing incoming invoices

NCVQ coverage

4.2 process incoming invoices for payment

Performance criteria
- *identifying discrepancies between invoices and delivery notes*
- *identifying errors in invoice charges*
- *reporting discrepancies and errors promptly*
- *passing for payment correct and authorised invoices*
- *keeping records accurately, legibly and up-to-date*

introduction

When an organisation orders goods, it will eventually have to pay for them. Most goods are supplied *on credit:* the goods arrive first and payment is made later, often after thirty or even sixty days. In order that the supplier of the goods can tell the organisation buying the goods how much the goods cost, and what charges or discounts (if any) are applicable, the supplier will send to the buyer a document known as an *invoice*. This can either be sent as a paper document by post, or as an electronic message through the supplier's computer to the buyer's computer, a system known as Electronic Data Interchange (EDI). A typical paper invoice is illustrated on page 210.

If you are working in an organisation you may have to check incoming invoices sent by suppliers. The purpose of this checking procedure is to make sure that you have been charged the right amount for the right goods. Once the invoice has been checked and found to be in order, it can be passed to the person or department which makes payments for the organisation. If there are errors on the invoice, they will be queried with the supplier of the goods.

In this Unit we will look at

- the ordering process and the documentation involved
- the checking procedures
- the records you will have to complete in the office to record the invoice.

---

 linking assignment

Common Skills Assignment 7
Applying numeracy: the Accounts Department, pages 252 to 256

the buying and paying process in the organisation

If you work for an organisation you should find out what person or department deals with ordering goods and what person or department deals with paying for goods. In a larger organisation there may be a *purchasing department* which deals with ordering goods, and an *accounts department* which makes the payments. In a smaller organisation these functions may be left to individuals, e.g. the buyer and the accounts clerk. Whatever the circumstances, the purchasing and accounting functions - set out in the diagram below - remain the same.

the organisation

purchasing department
- goods ordered
- goods received
- invoice received and checked
- invoice passed to accounts department

 invoice - checked and authorised

accounts department
- authorised invoice received
- invoice held until payment due
- invoice paid on due date
- cheque sent to supplier for invoice amount

business documents

There are a number of business documents - including the invoice - with which you will need to be familiar when dealing with ordering and paying for goods. A number of documents will be introduced in this Unit, and you will encounter others later in your studies. For the purposes of this Unit we will look at the following business documents:

purchase order   the official order form which the buyer uses to order the goods required

delivery note   the document which accompanies the goods and gives details of the goods sent - it is normally signed when the goods are received

invoice   the document which is sent by the seller stating how much is owed and when it has to be paid

statement   a document sent by the seller to the buyer, normally every month, giving details of invoices issued and payments made (just as a bank sends a regular statement to its customer showing money paid in and money paid out)

purchase order

In the example shown below, Martley Machine Rental Limited are ordering from Stourford Office Supplies some paper for their laser printer. The purchasing department or buyer at Martley Machine Rental will post or fax this purchase order, which will have been typed out in the office, or produced on a computer accounting program. The details of the laser paper will have been obtained from Stourford Office Supplies' catalogue, or possibly by means of a written or telephoned enquiry.

PURCHASE ORDER
MARTLEY MACHINE RENTAL LTD
67 Broadgreen Road
Martley MR6 7TR
Tel 090655 6576 Fax 090655 6342

Stourford Office Supplies Unit 12 Avon Industrial Estate Stourford SF5 6TD	No Date Delivery	47700 13 March 199– to above address

catalogue	quantity	description	price
3564749	15 reams	100gsm white Supalaser paper	£4.00 per ream

authorised   signature... *C J Farmer* ....   date *13 March 199–*

Note the following details

- each purchase order has a specific reference number - this is useful for filing, and quotation on later documents such as delivery notes, invoices and statements - here it is 47700
- the heading 'Delivery' enables the buyer to indicate if the goods are to be delivered to an address other than the address on the letterhead, e.g. to a warehouse or to a different office
- the catalogue number of the goods required is stated - this number can be obtained from the supplier's trade catalogue
- the quantity of the goods required is stated - here it is supplied in reams (packs of 500 sheets)
- the description of the goods is set out in full
- the price will have been obtained from Stourford Office Supplies' catalogue or from an enquiry
- the purchase order is signed by the buyer in the purchasing department, and dated on the bottom - without this authorisation the supplier will not supply the goods!

delivery note

The delivery note is prepared by the supplier of the goods, and is either typed in the supplier's office or produced on a computer printer if the supplier has a computer accounting program.

The delivery note travels with the goods, normally in the care of the van driver, in which case the person receiving the goods will be asked to sign the delivery note. If the goods are *posted*, the delivery note will be packed with the goods in the carton, or possibly in a transparent envelope on the ouside of the box containing the goods. If the goods are posted by letter post or parcel post, the signature of the recipient will not be needed, unless they are sent recorded delivery, registered post or datapost.

━ DELIVERY NOTE ━

Stourford Office Supplies
Unit 12, Avon Industrial Estate, Stourford SF5 6TD
Tel 0807 765434 Fax 0807 765123

Martley Machine Rental Ltd 67 Broadgreen Road Martley MR6 7TR	Delivery Note No	26754
	Date	26 March 199–
	Your Order No	47700
	Delivery	Van Delivery

product code	quantity	description
3564749	15 reams	100 gsm white Supalaser paper

received
signature........... *G Hughes* ....name (capitals)............... *G HUGHES* ....
.... *30 March 199-*
date.................................

Note the following details

- the delivery note has a numerical reference, useful for filing and later reference if there is a query
- the delivery note quotes the purchase order number - this enables the buyer to 'tie up' the delivery with the original order
- the method of delivery is stated - here the delivery is by van
- the delivery note quotes the supplier's catalogue reference, the quantity supplied and the description of the goods - these details will be checked against
  - the goods themselves
  - the invoice when it is received
- no price is quoted on the delivery note
- the delivery note will be signed and dated by the person receiving the goods
- the person receiving the goods will also print his or her name - this is to enable the person to be identified later if there happens to be a query about the goods
- if the person receiving the goods does not have time to check them there and then - as is often the case - the phrase 'Contents not inspected' can be written on the delivery note (not shown here)

invoice

The invoice is the trading document which is sent by the seller to the buyer to advise how much is owed by the buyer for a particular delivery of goods. The invoice, like the delivery note, is prepared in the supplier's office, and is either typed or produced on a computer printer by a computer accounting program.

The subject of this Unit is the processing of incoming invoices. In order that you can be fully competent with dealing with invoices, you will need to be familiar with their layout and contents. Invoices produced by different organisations will all vary to some extent in terms of detail, but their basic layout will always be the same.

The invoice illustrated below is typical of a modern typed or computer printed document. Look at it carefully and then read the notes set out on the next page.

═══ INVOICE ═══

Stourford Office Supplies
Unit 12, Avon Industrial Estate, Stourford SF5 6TD
Tel 0807 765434 Fax 0807 765123
VAT Reg 0745 4672 76

Invoice to

Martley Machine Rental Ltd
67 Broadgreen Road
Martley
MR6 7TR

Invoice No	652771
Account	MAR435
Date/tax point	26 March 199–
Your Reference	47700

deliver to

as above

product code	description	quantity	price	unit	total	disc %	net
3564749	100 gsm white Supalaser	15	4.00	ream	60.00	0	60.00

Terms
Net monthly
Carriage paid
E & OE

GOODS TOTAL	60.00
CASH DISCOUNT	00.00
SUBTOTAL	60.00
VAT	10.50
TOTAL	70.50

invoice details and terms

addresses

The invoice shows the address
- of the seller/supplier of the goods - Stourford Office Supplies
- where the invoice should be sent - to Martley Machine Rental Ltd
- where the goods should be sent - if different from the invoice address

references

There are a number of important references on the invoice:
- the numerical reference of the invoice itself - 652771
- the account number allocated to Martley Machine Rental Ltd by the seller - MAR435 - possibly for use in the seller's computer accounting program
- the original reference number on the purchase order sent by Martley Machine Rental Ltd - 47700 - which will enable the buyer to 'tie up' the invoice with the original order

date

The date on the invoice is important because the payment date (here one month) is calculated from this date. The date is often described as the 'tax point' because it is the transaction date as far as VAT calculations are concerned, i.e. it is when the sale took place and the VAT was charged.

the goods

As the invoice is a statement of the amount owing, it must specify accurately the goods supplied. The details - set out in columns in the body of the invoice - include
- *product code* - this is the catalogue number which appeared on the original purchase order and on the delivery note
- *description* - the goods must be precisely specified
- *quantity* - this should agree with the quantity ordered
- *price* - this is the price of each unit shown in the next column
- *unit* is the way in which the unit is counted and charged for, e.g.
  - *reams* of paper (packs of 500 sheets)
  - *boxes* of ballpoint pens (100 in a box, for instance)
  - *items* of furniture (e.g. individual desks and chairs)
- *total* is the unit price multiplied by the number of units
- *discount %* is the percentage allowance (known as trade discount) given to customers who regularly deal with the supplier i.e. they receive a certain percentage (e.g. 20%) deducted from their bill
- *net* is the amount due to the seller after deduction of trade discount, and before VAT is added on

cash discount and VAT

Further calculations are made in the box at the bottom of the invoice
- *Goods* is the net amount due to the seller (the total of the *net* column)
- *Cash Discount* is a percentage of the Goods total (often a 2.5% discount) which the buyer can deduct if he or she pays straightaway rather than waiting the month allowed on the invoice - there is no Cash Discount in this example
- *Value Added Tax (VAT)*, calculated as 17.5% of the total *after* deduction of any Cash Discount is added to produce the invoice total (see page 200 for an explanation of VAT)

terms

The terms for payment are stated on the invoice. In this case these include
- *Net monthly* - this means that full payment of the invoice (without cash discount) should be made within a month of the invoice date
- *Carriage paid* means that the price of the goods includes delivery
- *E & OE* stands for 'errors and omissions excepted' which means that if there is a error or something left off the invoice by mistake, resulting in an incorrect final price, the supplier has the right to rectify the mistake and demand the correct amount

statement

A supplier will not normally expect a buyer to pay each individual invoice as soon as it is received: this could result in the buyer having to write a number of cheques during the month. Instead, a *statement of account* is sent by the supplier to the buyer at the end of the month. This statement, which can be typed out, or printed by the seller's computer accounting program, will show exactly what is owed by the buyer to the seller. It contains details of

* invoices issued for goods supplied - the full amount due, including VAT
* refunds made (on documents known as *credit notes*)
* payments received from the buyer

The statement issued by Stourford Office Supplies to Martley Machine Rental Ltd - referring to the invoice explained on the previous page - is illustrated below. You will see that it has a tear-off slip attached on the right. This is known as a *remittance advice*. The buyer can detach this, tick the invoice(s) being paid in the far right-hand column, and send it with the cheque to the supplier.

The columns on the statement show the date of the transaction, the type (here 'inv' is an abbreviation for 'invoice'), the value of the transaction, and the balance due to the supplier in the 'outstanding' column.

statement ———————————————— | remittance advice
Stourford Office Supplies
Unit 12, Avon Industrial Estate, Stourford SF5 6TD
Tel 0807 765434 Fax 0807 765123
VAT Reg 0745 4672 76

Stourford Office Supplies
Unit 12, Avon Industrial Estate, Stourford SF5 6TD

Account MAR435   Date 31 March 199–

Account MAR 435

Martley Machine Rental Ltd
67 Broadgreen Road
Martley
MR6 7TR

please indicate items you are paying (✔) and return this advice with your remittance

date	type	reference	value	outstanding	ref	outstanding	✔
26/03/–9	inv	652771	70.50	70.50	652771	70.50	
			TOTAL	70.50	TOTAL	70.50	

Please Note
You are not required at this stage of your studies to process statements or to issue cheques. The statement is explained and illustrated here because it completes the cycle of trading documents - the buyer normally pays on receipt of the statement. The statement helps you to appreciate why checking and authorising the invoice is such an important task: only authorised invoices appearing on the statement can be paid. The cycle of trading documents is illustrated at the top of the next page.

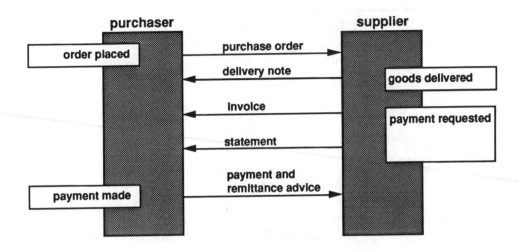

summary of the cycle of trading documents

checking the invoice , delivery note and purchase order

If you are processing a delivery of goods and the trading documents, there are two areas that have to be carefully checked. They are:

- have the correct *goods* been invoiced?
- are the *calculations* on the invoice correct?

The first of these checks is the more important. If incorrect goods have been invoiced, there is no point in checking the calculations - the invoice will have to be queried with the supplier and possibly sent back.

The three documents involved in the checking process are the purchase order, the delivery note, and the invoice (see pages 208 to 210)

check 1 - goods received and delivery note
When the goods are received they should be checked against the delivery note - the quantities should be counted and the condition of the goods checked. Any discrepancies or damage should be notified immediately to the supplier, usually on a *discrepancy note*, so that repacements can be sent or the buyer credited with the value of the missing or damaged goods (i.e. the bill reduced by the issue of a *credit note*).

check 2 - delivery note and purchase order
The delivery note should then be checked against the original purchase order. The illustration on the next page shows the details that should be checked:

- *catalogue number* (i.e. the supplier's catalogue) - has the right type of goods been delivered?
- *quantity* - has the right amount been delivered?
- *specifications* - are the goods delivered to the same specifications as those ordered
- *purchase order reference number* - do the goods relate to the purchase order being examined?

If all is in order, the delivery note will be filed with the purchase order under the purchase order reference number, ready for checking against the invoice when it arrives.

PURCHASE ORDER

MARTLEY MACHINE RENTAL LTD

67 Broadgreen Road
Martley MR6 7TR
Tel 090655 6576 Fax 090655 6342

Stourford Office Supplies
Unit 12
Avon Industrial Estate
Stourford SF5 6TD

No
Date
Delivery

47700
13 March 199-
to above address

catalogue	quantity	description	price
3564749	15 reams	100gsm white Supalaser paper	£4.00 per ream

authorised   signature....*C J Farmer*........................   date...**13 March 199-**

catalogue
number

quantity

specifications

purchase order
reference number

━ DELIVERY NOTE ━

Stourford Office Supplies

Unit 12, Avon Industrial Estate, Stourford SF5 6TD
Tel 0807 765434 Fax 0807 765123

Martley Machine Rental Ltd
67 Broadgreen Road
Martley
MR6 7TR

Delivery Note No   26754
Date   26 March 199-
Order No   47700
Delivery   Van Delivery

product code	quantity	description
3564749	15 reams	100 gsm white Supalaser paper

received
signature............*G Hughes*........................print name (capitals)....*G HUGHES*..........
                        30 March 199-
date..

details to check on the purchase order and delivery note

check 3 - invoice, delivery note and purchase order

When the invoice arrives from the supplier, it should be checked against the delivery note and the purchase order (which will probably be filed together). The specific points to look at are:

- invoice and delivery note

Are the details of the goods on the invoice and on the delivery note the same? The product code, description and quantity of the goods should agree.

- invoice and purchase order

Has the correct price been charged? The unit price quoted by the supplier or obtained from the supplier's catalogue will be stated on the purchase order, and should agree with the unit price stated on the invoice. If there is a difference, it should be queried with the supplier. The difference could be a mistake on the supplier's part, or it could be the buyer using an out-of-date catalogue, in which case the invoice price would hold.

Now look at the invoice below and the purchase order and delivery note on the previous page. Can you spot any discrepancies? The answers are set out below

---

INVOICE

Stourford Office Supplies
Unit 12, Avon Industrial Estate, Stourford SF5 6TD
Tel 0807 765434 Fax 0807 765123
VAT Reg 0745 4672 76

Invoice to

Martley Machine Rental Ltd
67 Broadgreen Road
Martley
MR6 7TR

Invoice No	652771
Account	MAR435
Date/tax point	30 March 199-
Your Reference	47780

deliver to

as above

product code	description	quantity	price	unit	total	disc %	net
3564748	80 gsm white Supalaser	15	3.50	ream	52.00	0	52.00

Terms
Net monthly
Carriage paid
E & OE

GOODS TOTAL	52.00
CASH DISCOUNT	00.00
SUBTOTAL	52.00
VAT	9.01
TOTAL	42.99

Answer: the purchase order and delivery note agree, but the invoice has a number of discrepancies: the order reference differs (47700 and 47780); the product code differs (3564749 & 3564748); the product description differs (100gsm and 80 gsm) and the price differs (£4.00 and £3.50 per ream).

check 4 - are the calculations on the invoice correct?

The invoice involves a series of calculations which must all be checked. If any *one* of these calculations is incorrect, the final total will be wrong, so accurate checking is essential. What are the checks that must be made?

quantity x unit price

The quantity of the items multiplied by the unit price must be correct. The result - the *total price* - is used for the calculation of any trade discount applicable.

trade discount

Any trade discount - an allowance given to approved customers - must be *deducted* from the total price worked out. Trade discount is calculated as a percentage of the total price, e.g. a trade discount of 20% on a total price of £150 is calculated

$$£150 \times \frac{20}{100} = £30$$

The net price charged (before VAT) is therefore

$$£150 - £30 = £120 = \text{net total}$$

cash discount

Any cash discount - an allowance sometimes given for immediate payment - is *deducted* from the net total *before* VAT is calculated. In the invoice illustrated this calculation would be shown in the box at the bottom right of the document.

VAT

Value Added Tax is charged at the rate of 17.5% (1991 figure). To calculate VAT, the total *after* the deduction of any cash discount is treated as follows

$$\text{total} \times \frac{17.5}{100} = \text{VAT amount}$$

If you are using a calculator, all you need to do is to multiply the total by 0.175 to give the VAT, which is then added to the total.

Remember that any fractions of a penny are ignored. For example if the total price is £55.75, the VAT will be

$$£55.75 \times 0.175 = £9.75625$$

£9.75625 then loses the last three digits - the fraction of a penny - to become £9.75. The figure is *not* rounded up to £9.76, although you may find some computer invoices produced do round up!

For the purpose of your studies you must assume that the calculations on all invoices must be checked. In practice, computer produced invoices perform the calculations automatically, and in principle should be correct.

Now check the calculations on the invoice on the previous page before reading the next paragraph.

You should by now have detected a large number of errors - one can only assume that the person who prepared the invoice must have had a bad day! The errors are:

- *quantity x unit price should be £52.50, not £52.00*
- *the VAT is wrongly calculated £52.00 x 0.175 = £9.10, not £9.01 (it would be £9.18 on £52.50)*
- *the VAT has been deducted instead of added: the total should be £52.50 + £9.18 = £61.68*

recording the invoices in the day book

Incoming invoices which have been checked need to be recorded in the books of the business. A business will often use a book known as a *day book* or *journal* to record documents received and issued: examples include the *sales day book* (for invoices issued) and, in this case, the *purchases day book* for invoices received. If you study book-keeping or accounts you will refer to a day book as a *book of original entry*, because the day book is where the invoice is first recorded in the books.

purchases day book

The purchases day book is a list of totals prepared from invoices received from suppliers. The original cost before adding VAT, the VAT charged, and the total invoice price, are all recorded in columns alongside the supplier's name. At an appropriate interval, which could be daily, weekly or monthly, each column of figures is totalled. A purchases day book is illustrated below. The diagram also shows what happens to the figures: they are transferred to the organisation's books of account.

Purchases Day Book

Date	Supplier	Invoice Number	Total before VAT		VAT		Total Invoice	
			£	p	£	p	£	p
199-								
1 Mar.	Electrocomponents Ltd	12486	120	00	21	00	141	00
3 Mar.	Stourford Office Supplies	526267	60	00	10	50	70	50
4 Mar.	Media Marketing	82727	160	00	28	00	188	00
5 Mar.	**Totals**		340	00	59	50	399	50

the amount (excluding VAT) of all incoming invoices is recorded in a *purchases account* which records how much the business has spent

the VAT total will be recorded in a *VAT account* which is used when the business completes its VAT return

the amount of each invoice (including VAT) will be recorded in a *personal account* for the supplier, so that the buyer can tell what is owed

computerised accounting systems

The illustration above shows a manual purchases day book, i.e. it is paper-based system which involves writing the details of each invoice in the day book by hand, and totalling up the columns using a calculator. Many organisations use computer accounting programs, and you may be familiar with the system whereby you call up a computer screen, and enter details of the purchase invoices on the keyboard. The *principle* of recording incoming invoices, however, is still the same, and it is interesting to note that the computer programs used still use the word 'day book' despite the fact that it is on a computer disk rather than in a book that the invoice is recorded.

authorising the invoice for payment

As we saw at the beginning of this Unit, checked invoices are passed to the Accounts Department, or the person who deals with Accounts, after they have been authorised. They will then be paid after the statement arrives and the due date for payment is reached.

what to do with incorrect invoices

Clearly only correct invoices can be passed forward for payment. Invoices with errors will need to be queried with the seller.   If the error relates to the goods sent, the seller's Sales Department should be contacted, if the error is in the calculation of the invoice, the seller's Accounts Department should be advised. A fax or a letter could be sent; often a telephone call will quickly sort out any problem.

authorising correct invoices

When an invoice is checked and found to be correct, the person carrying out the check will usually mark the document and authorise it for payment. This authorisation can take a number of forms:

- the checker can initial and date the invoice, and tick it or write 'pay' as an authorisation
- the organisation may have a special rubber stamp which acts as authorisation -see the illustration below

This procedure of authorisation obviously helps the efficiency of the organisation:

- only authorised invoices will be passed forward to Accounts Department for payment
- the checker's initials will be there in case of any future query on the invoice, e.g. an undetected error

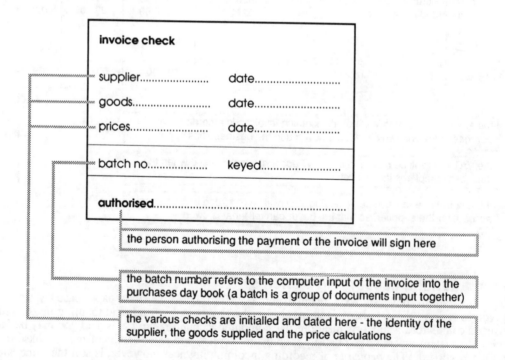

authorisation stamp placed on an invoice received for checking

student activities - processing incoming invoices

Performance criteria

The student activities in this section test competences in the following areas:

- *identifying discrepancies between invoices and delivery notes*
- *identifying errors in invoice charges*
- *reporting discrepancies and errors promptly*
- *passing for payment correct and authorised invoices*
- *keeping records accurately, legibly and up-to-date*

1. Look at the invoice reproduced below and explain what is meant by
   (a) deliver to (b) Account (c) date/tax point (d) your reference (e) product code (f) unit
   (g) disc % (h) net (i) net monthly (j) E & OE (k) cash discount (l) VAT

INVOICE

Stourford Office Supplies
Unit 12, Avon Industrial Estate, Stourford SF5 6TD
Tel 0807 765434 Fax 0807 765123
VAT Reg 0745 4672 76

invoice to

Martley Machine Rental Ltd 67 Broadgreen Road Martley MR6 7TR	Invoice No 652771 Account MAR435 Date/tax point 30 March 199- Your Reference 47700

deliver to

as above

product code	description	quantity	price	unit	total	disc %	net
3564749	100 gsm white Supalaser	15	4.00	ream	60.00	0	60.00

GOODS TOTAL	60.00
CASH DISCOUNT	00.00
SUBTOTAL	60.00
VAT	10.50
TOTAL	70.50

Terms
Net monthly
Carriage paid
E & OE

2.   Set out below is a blank invoice (which you may photocopy) from Wyvern (Office Products) Limited. Using product details and prices from the catalogue and price list to be found in Appendix 2 at the back of this book, make out invoices for the following orders:

(a)   Order No 8272 from Action Alarm Systems (Account 6912), for one Fisley 2 drawer filing cabinet (in grey) to the business at 16, High Street, Mereford MR3 1LJ. Trade discount at 10% but no cash discount. VAT at current rate, invoice No 345422, today's date. The invoice is also to be sent to the business address.

(b)   Order No PO877 from Jane's Jumpers (Account 6709), for 2 single pedestal desks (large top, light oak finish) to the shop at 34, New Street, Mereford MR3 5TF. Trade discount at 15%, but no cash discount. VAT at current rate, invoice No 345423, today's date. The invoice is to be sent to the shop.

(c)   Order No 67217 from Helpmate DIY (Account 6655), for 5 canteen tables (180 x 75cm, teak finish) to their store at 6 Broadwater Retail Park, Humberstone, HU7 6TY. Trade discount at 20% but no cash discount. VAT at current rate, invoice No 345424, today's date. The invoice is to be sent to Helpmate DIY plc, Accounts Department, Unit 1, Everoak Industrial Estate, Mereford MR5 7TG.

INVOICE

Wyvern (Office Products) Limited
12, Lower Hyde Street, Mereford, MR1 2JF
Tel 0605 241851 Fax 0605 241879
VAT Reg 841 1601 14

Invoice to

Invoice No
Account
Date/tax point
Your Reference

deliver to

product code	description	quantity	price	unit	total	disc %	net

Terms
Net monthly
Carriage paid
E & OE

GOODS TOTAL	
CASH DISCOUNT	
SUBTOTAL	
VAT	
TOTAL	

3. On this and the next page are three documents: a purchase order, a delivery note and an invoice. You are to check the documents for
   (a) discrepancies between the goods ordered and the goods supplied
   (b) discrepancies between the goods supplied and the goods charged for
   (c) calculations on the invoice (assume VAT at 17.5%)
   Set out your answer under the headings (a), (b) and (c).

PURCHASE ORDER
MARTLEY MACHINE RENTAL LTD
67 Broadgreen Road
Martley MR6 7TR
Tel 090655 6576 Fax 090655 6342

Wyvern (Office Products) Ltd 12 Lower Hyde Street Mereford MR1 2JF	No 5262 Date 13 May 199- Delivery as address

catalogue	quantity	description	price
P1040	10 packs	FR1-399 A4 Fax roll	£33.00 per pack

authorised   signature......C J Farmer............................   date..13 May 199-......

DELIVERY NOTE ━━━━━━
Wyvern (Office Products) Limited
12, Lower Hyde Street, Mereford, MR1 2JF
Tel 0605 241851 Fax 0605 241879
VAT Reg 841 1601 14

Martley Machine Rental Ltd 67 Broadgreen Road Martley MR6 7TR	Delivery Note No 26790 Date 18 May 199- Order No 5363 Delivery Van Delivery

product code	quantity	description
P1043	40 packs	FR1-396 A4 Fax roll

received
signature......G Hughes............   name (capitals)......G HUGHES............

date......20 May 199-......

INVOICE

Wyvern (Office Products) Limited
12, Lower Hyde Street, Mereford, MR1 2JF
Tel 0605 241851 Fax 0605 241879
VAT Reg 8411 1601 14

Invoice to

Martley Machine Rental Ltd	Invoice No 652876
67 Broadgreen Road	Account MAR435
Martley	Date/tax point 18 May 199-
MR6 7TR	Your Reference 5363

deliver to

as above

product code	description	quantity	price	unit	total	disc %	net
P1040	FR1-399 A4 Fax roll	10	33.00	pack	333.00	10	366.30

Terms
Net monthly
Carriage paid
E & OE

GOODS TOTAL	366.30
CASH DISCOUNT	00.00
SUBTOTAL	366.00
VAT	64.50
TOTAL	430.80

4.   You have five invoices to check for calculation errors. Set out below are the relevant extracts from the invoices (the company names have been omitted). Check the workings, using a calculator, and in each case state what the correct total should be. Assume VAT at 17.5%.

invoice (a)

product code	description	quantity	price	unit	total	disc %	net
57784	T562 Flexi-pack cups	30	27.95	pack	838.50	0	835.50

GOODS TOTAL	835.50
CASH DISCOUNT	00.00
SUBTOTAL	835.50
VAT	142.03
TOTAL	977.53

invoice (b)

product code	description	quantity	price	unit	total	disc %	net
82731	Leather executive chair	1	295.00	each	295.00	10	324.50
					GOODS TOTAL		324.50
					CASH DISCOUNT		00.00
					SUBTOTAL		324.50
					VAT		56.78
					TOTAL		267.72

invoice (c)

product code	description	quantity	price	unit	total	disc %	net
87793	Whitex Liquid paper	10	6.50	pack	650.00	20	520.00
					GOODS TOTAL		520.00
					CASH DISCOUNT		00.00
					SUBTOTAL		520.00
					VAT		91.10
					TOTAL		611.00

invoice (d)

product code	description	quantity	price	unit	total	disc %	net
56327	Wastebin - red	3	4.95	each	14.85	20	17.82
					GOODS TOTAL		17.82
					CASH DISCOUNT		00.00
					SUBTOTAL		17.82
					VAT		3.12
					TOTAL		20.94

invoice (e)

product code	description	quantity	price	unit	total	disc %	net
83737	PVC Ring Binder - black	5	9.00	pack	45.00	10	40.50
					GOODS TOTAL		40.50
					CASH DISCOUNT		00.00
					SUBTOTAL		40.50
					VAT		7.08
					TOTAL		47.58

5.   You order all your stationery and office goods from Wyvern (Office Products) Limited. Set out below are details from five delivery notes and extracts from five invoices from Wyvern (Office Products) Limited. The details are in no particular order. You are to check the delivery notes against the invoices and also against the details in the catalogue and price list set out in the Appendix to this book.

Set out any discrepancies and any recalculations of invoice totals in a Memorandum addressed to Laura Palmer, Accounts Supervisor, using today's date and your own name.

details from delivery notes:

	product code	quantity	description
(a)	E1010	5 boxes	Sherman white wove self seal envelopes
(b)	W1050	2 boxes	Fibre tip highlighters - colour yellow
(c)	D1011	20	Wippex correction fluid - white
(d)	M1012	2	Mars stapler - red
(e)	W1080	5	150mm clear plastic ruler

extracts from invoices:

product code	description	quantity	price	unit	total	disc %	net
E1010	Sherman white wove self seal envelopes	15	29.95	box	449.25	0	449.25

product code	description	quantity	price	unit	total	disc %	net
W1080	150mm clear plastic ruler	5	0.22	each	1.10	0	1.10

product code	description	quantity	price	unit	total	disc %	net
W1051	Fibre tip highlighter – wallet of 4 mixed	2	3.10	pack	6.20	0	6.20

product code	description	quantity	price	unit	total	disc %	net
M1012	Mars stapler – red	20	6.25	each	125.50	0	125.50

product code	description	quantity	price	unit	total	disc %	net
D1011	Wippex correction fluid – white	20	0.82	each	16.40	0	16.40

6.   You are asked to write up in the purchases day book a batch of invoices received from your suppliers and to total up the columns. The details of the invoices and a suggested layout for the purchases day book are set out below (you may photocopy the page if you wish). Use the current rate of VAT.

(a)   Invoice 36236 dated 1 April from K Williams Joinery for £87.50 plus VAT

(b)   Invoice 7363 dated 4 April from Musgrave Designs for £560.00 plus VAT

(c)   Invoice 6271 dated 8 April from Loveder Construction for £747.95 plus VAT

(d)   Invoice 76265 dated 9 April from Southwick Publishers for £40.00, no VAT (training manuals supplied are zero-rated goods)

(e)   Invoice T5256 dated 15 April from Express Caterers for £72.50 plus VAT

(f)   Invoice 73629 dated 16 April from Hunt Travel for £645.00 plus VAT

(g)   Invoice 4277 dated 22 April from Bishop's Car Hire for £75.00 plus VAT

(h)   Invoice 4872 dated 23 April from Evening Echo for £8.50 plus VAT

Purchases Day Book

Date	Supplier	Invoice Number	Total before VAT	VAT	Total Invoice
			£ p	£ p	£ p
	Totals				

 linking assignment

Common Skills Assignment 7
Applying numeracy: the Accounts Department, pages 252 to 256

15 Stock handling

NCVQ coverage
5.1 issue office materials on request and monitor stock levels
Performance criteria
- *responding to requisitions (orders for stock) promptly and accurately*
- *handling and storing stock safely at all times*
- *carrying out stock checks and inventory reconciliations and reporting any shortages or damage*
- *checking incoming deliveries against orders and reporting discrepancies promptly*
- *keeping records of stock movements up-to-date, legible and accurate*

introduction
When you are at work you will use items of stationery and equipment which will have to be 'topped up' or replaced from time-to-time: paper, biros, paperclips, staplers, computer disks and so on. These items are known as *stock* and will usually be controlled by a member of staff and kept under lock and key in a cupboard or a stockroom. A term you will come across when dealing with stock is 'inventory.' An inventory is a detailed list of the stock items held by an organisation.

While you will normally be a *consumer* of stock, it is important that you learn the procedures and office recording systems for

- ordering stock from the storeroom for your use in the office by means of a requisition form
- the recording of the receipt and issue of items of stock from the stockroom
- counting the stock by means of a stock check (also known as a stock take)
- agreeing (reconciling) your stock check with the stock records
- accepting incoming deliveries of stock and dealing with the paperwork involved

You should also be aware that stock can be held for two purposes: for use in the office and also for resale to your customers (if your business sells goods). In this Unit we will concentrate on the issue of stock *for office use.*

---

 linking assignment

Common Skills Assignment 7
Applying numeracy: the Accounts Department, pages 252 to 256.

requisition form - ordering stock for office use

Your first encounter with office stock will probably be the need to order an item - such as copying paper - which has either run out, or has nearly run out. The normal office procedure is for the person requiring the stock to complete a *requisition form,* an example of which is illustrated below. The person ordering the paper is Lou Jones and the organisation is Wyvern (Office Products) Ltd.

REQUISITION FORM

From ...*Lou Jones*...   No. ...*007*.........

Dept ...*Administration*...............

Quantity	Description	Ref. No.
10	*reams photocopying paper*	P1026

Signed ...*L. Jones*..................... Authorised ....Date......................

The form is completed with the following details

- the name of the person ordering the stock
- the name of the department or section in which that person works
- a reference number for the order
- the quantity of the stock required
- the stock item and reference number (the number shown in the catalogue - see Appendix 2)
- the signature of the person ordering the stock

The person requiring the stock will obtain the supervisor's authorisation (signature) and the form will then be dated and forwarded to the person handling stock issue - possibly a full time storekeeper. The stock will then be sent to the person who requested it.

The storekeeper will need to record the transaction, *either*

- by entering the details on a stock record card (if a manual recording system is used), *or*
- by entering the details onto a computer terminal (if the stock records are computerised)

We will now examine in detail the records used to record items of stock held. We will concentrate on the manual method - based on the *stock record card.* Computerised stock control works on the same principles as the manual system (see page 235).

stock records

A well organised business will have a stock control section where staff keep records of all stock held on individual *stock record cards*. The stock held may either be for resale by the business, or may be for internal issue (as discussed in this Unit). A separate card is made out for each stock item. When articles are issued (or sold), the number of items taken out of stock is deducted from the total on the stock card, and when new supplies are received, these are added to the total. A typical stock record card is shown below. The stock item is A4 photocopying paper which is used within the business, Wyvern (Office Products) Ltd., and also sold to its customers. As yet there is no stock entered on the card.

STOCK RECORD CARD

Stock Description A4 white photocopying paper

Stock units reams

Stock Ref. No. P1026

Location row A, bin 6

Minimum 1 500 reams

Maximum 10 000 reams

Re-order level 4 500 reams

Re-order quantity 5 000 reams

DATE	GOODS RECEIVED		GOODS ISSUED		BALANCE
	Reference	Quantity	Reference	Quantity	

- **stock description**   refers to the description of the stock, e.g. photocopying paper

- **stock units**   refers to how the stock is stored or packed, e.g. photocopying paper would be packed in reams (packets of 500 sheets);

- **stock reference no.**   refers to the identification number allocated to the stock by the business - it will be found on the stock inventory and on the catalogue and price list

- **location**   refers to where the stock can be found in the stores, e.g. row A, bin 6 refers to the location in the storeroom or warehouse

- **minimum**   is the minimum level of the number of items to be kept in stock

- **maximum**   is the maximum level of the number of items to be kept in stock

- **re-order level**   is the level to which the stock falls before the business reorders more items

- **re-order quantity**   is the amount which is normally reordered

- **goods received**   the two columns record the purchase order reference and the quantity of items received

- **goods issued**   the two columns record the requisition reference (see section below) and the number of items issued

- **balance**   is the number of items which remain in stock

stock levels

Businesses normally set the following stock levels, which are indicated on the stock record cards:

- minimum stock level
- maximum stock level
- re-order level

The person responsible for setting stock levels must therefore ensure that:

- the minimum level is not so low that the business runs out of that item of stock
- the maximum level is not so high that too much money is tied up in stock

minimum stock level
Stock should not be allowed to fall below this level. The setting of this level acts as a safeguard against stock falling to a dangerously low level following delays or disruptions of deliveries from suppliers.

maximum stock level
This is a 'ceiling' stock level to prevent overstocking. It will be fixed bearing in mind the cost to the company of acquiring the stock, the space available for storage, and the expected demand.

re-order level
Re-order level is the level to which stock falls before an order for further stock is placed. This level is normally higher than the minimum level and is calculated so that the replacement order will be delivered before the stock balance has reached the minimum level.

This level is normally calculated as follows:

average daily issue of stock x number of days for delivery from supplier **plus** *the minimum stock level*

for example,

```
A4, white photocopying paper
average daily issue          300 reams
normal delivery              10 days
minimum stock                1,500 reams
maximum stock                10,000 reams

Re-order level = 300 (daily issue)  x  10 (number of days delivery)  +  1,500 (minimum stock)
= 300 x 10 + 1,500
= 3,000 + 1,500
= 4,500 reams
```

incoming deliveries of stock

Suppose that the storekeeper needs to order some stock; the photocopying paper may, for instance, have reached the reorder level of 4,500 reams.   An order will have to be placed with the organisation's supplier with the normal reorder quantity - in this case 5,000 reams.   The procedure for this will vary from organisation to organisation; it will often be the responsibility of a Purchasing Department or section. When the items - e.g. reams of paper - are eventually delivered, they will be accompanied by a delivery note. The example illustrated below will accompany the delivery of photocopying paper ordered by Wyvern (Office Products) Ltd.

■ DELIVERY NOTE ■

Stourford Office Supplies
Unit 12, Avon Industrial Estate, Stourford SF5 6TD
Tel 0807 765434 Fax 0807 765123

```
Wyvern (Office Products) Ltd        Delivery Note No    27648
12, Lower Hyde Street               Date                9 April 199-
Mereford                            Your Order No       17901
MR1 2JF                             Delivery            Van Delivery
```

product code	quantity	description
3564749	5,000 reams	white photocopying paper

received
signature... name (capitals)...

date...

---

delivery note

The details on the delivery note, which the van driver will normally give to you, will include
* the *supplier's* reference number for the delivery note
* the date of issue
* *your* order number
* the method of delivery
* the description and quantity of the goods together with the *supplier's* product code
* a section for you to sign when you have checked the consignment

checking the consignment against the delivery note

You will need to check the incoming goods carefully:
* check the condition of the goods
* check that the right goods have been delivered
* check that the right quantity of goods have been delivered

Only when you are satisfied on all these points should you sign and write your name in capital leters on the delivery note. The driver will normally hand you one copy and keep one copy. If there are any discrepancies (short delivery, wrong goods) they should be noted on the delivery note *before you sign it* so that both the supplier and your organisation will know that there is a problem. Lastly - *ensure that the delivery note is passed to the person responsible for ordering the goods* - it will need to be checked against the original order and the invoice (demand for payment) when it is received.

Case Study: Wyvern (Office Products) Ltd.

In this case study we look at the stock records relating to reams of A4 white phoptocopying paper in the warehouse of Wyvern (Office Products) Ltd. This organisation, as we saw earlier, sells stationery to its customers and also issues it internally when requisition forms are issued within the organisation. The object of the Case Study is to show you how the stock cards are updated for

• requisitions
• receipt of orders

On 1 April 199-, Wyvern's stock records indicate that the company has a stock balance of 3,000 reams of A4 photocopying paper. Assuming that Wyvern has just started a new stock record card for this paper, the stock record card would appear as follows:

STOCK RECORD CARD

Stock Description A4 white photocopying paper

Stock units reams

Stock Ref. No. P1026

Location row A, bin 6

Minimum 1 500 reams

Maximum 10 000 reams

Re-order level 4 500 reams

Re-order quantity 5 000 reams

DATE	GOODS RECEIVED		GOODS ISSUED		BALANCE
	Reference	Quantity	Reference	Quantity	
199- 1 Apr.					3 000

requisitions

During the first week of April the stores have received the following requisitions for this paper

2 April	Requisition no. 101	200 reams
4 April	Requisition no. 104	300 reams
5 April	Requisition no. 116	400 reams
6 April	Requisition no. 121	250 reams

How will these requisitions be recorded on the stock record card? The stock record card is illustrated on the next page. Note that

• the Balance column on the right is the running total of the number of reams held by the business
• the Reference under 'Goods Issued' is the requisition number in each case

STOCK RECORD CARD

Stock Description ..A4.white.photocopying.paper..

Stock units ....reams.....................................

Stock Ref. No. ......P1026................................

Location ....row A, bin 6.....................

Minimum ....1 500 reams.......................
Maximum ....10 000 reams........................
Re-order level ....4 500 reams................
Re-order quantity ..5 000 reams.............

DATE	GOODS RECEIVED		GOODS ISSUED		BALANCE
	Reference	Quantity	Reference	Quantity	
199–					
1 Apr.					3 000
2 Apr.			REQ 101	200	2 800
4 Apr.			REQ 104	300	2 500
5 Apr.			REQ 116	400	2 100
6 Apr.			REQ 121	250	1 850

receipt of the stock order

Wyvern (Office Products) Ltd. have previously placed an order with their supplier, Stourford Office Supplies Ltd., for 5,000 reams of this paper (the standard re-order quantity). This order is delivered to the warehouse on 9 April. The Purchase Order Number is 17901.

The stock record card will be amended as follows:

STOCK RECORD CARD

Stock Description ..A4 white photocopying paper..

Stock units ....reams...............................

Stock Ref. No. ....P1026...............................

Location ....row A, bin 6.......................

Minimum ....1 500 reams.......................
Maximum ....10 000 reams........................
Re-order level ....4 500 reams................
Re-order quantity ...5 000 reams.............

DATE	GOODS RECEIVED		GOODS ISSUED		BALANCE
	Reference	Quantity	Reference	Quantity	
199–					
1 Apr.					3 000
2 Apr.			REQ 101	200	2 800
4 Apr.			REQ 104	300	2 500
5 Apr.			REQ 116	400	2 100
6 Apr.			REQ 121	250	1 850
9 Apr.	Purchase Order 17901	5 000			6 850

stock checks and inventory reconciliation

the stock inventory

An organisation will regularly (often twice yearly) check that the numbers of items of stock held in the storeroom or warehouse is the same as the numbers recorded on the stock record cards. The way to check the stock is to count it - this is known as a *stock check* or *stock take*. If you have worked in a shop you may well be familiar with the periodic counting of the items on the shelves. The numbers of items actually held is recorded on a *stock list* by the person doing the stock check. The stock list is also known as a *stock inventory*. An extract from a stock inventory is illustrated below; it shows the A4 paper referred to in the case study. The list will, of course, contain many items when the stock take has been completed.

stock inventory as at 31 December 199-			checker *H Ramsay*				
product code	item description	location	unit size	units counted	stock card balance	discrepancy	
P1026	*A4 white photocopying paper*	*A6*	*ream*	6,850	6,850		

the inventory reconciliation

The object of the stock check is to see if the stock record cards accurately represent the level of stock held. The two columns on the stock inventory - 'units counted' and 'stock card balance' enable this comparison to be carried out; the process is known as an *inventory reconciliation*. It is an important process because

- an accurate stock figure can then be given to the accountants so that they can value the stock
- it will highlight any discrepancies which can then be investigated

Discrepancies should be noted in the far right hand column of the stock inventory.

dealing with discrepancies

Why should there be discrepancies, and what action should you take? Differences can occur for a number of reasons:

- someone has made a mistake on the stock record card - failed to record a stock movement or failed to calculate the balance correctly
- someone has been helping themselves to the stock without authorisation
- damaged stock has been disposed of without any record having been made
- stock has been stolen

If you find a discrepancy you should

- correct the error on the stock record card - e. g. write on the next available line '31 December Stock take - amended balance 6,800 ' if, for instance, you find that there are 6,800 reams of copy paper rather than the 6,850 shown in the balance column of the stock record card
- notify your supervisor and any other people who may need to know, e.g. your storekeeper and your auditors (the accountants who will check your stock taking method and figures)

dealing with damaged and obsolete stock

When you check the stock you may find damaged stock and obsolete stock

- *damaged stock* can include broken items (e.g. torn paper) or soiled items (e.g. stained paper)
- *obsolete stock* can include computer ribbons or disks which are unusable because you may have new machines, or headed notepaper which is printed with a telephone number which has changed

Whatever the circumstances, the stock no longer has any use and will have to be thrown away or used for some other purpose (e.g. scrap paper). The important point is that you will have to amend your stock records for the damaged or obsolete stock. This will involve

- deducting the stock items from the stock inventory and making a suitable comment in the right hand comments column (see illustration below)
- amending the stock record card to show a reduced balance; the entry might read as follows:
'31 December Stock Take - 50 reams damaged - amended balance 6,800'

stock inventory as at 31 December 199–	checker H Ramsay					
product code	item description	location	unit size	units counted	stock card balance	discrepancy
P1026	A4 white photocopying paper	A6	ream	6,800	6,850	50 reams damaged

safety and security of stock

It is important to ensure that stock is stored safely and securely.

safety

Safety in the workplace is one of the employer's duties, and maintenance of safety instructions is the responsibility of the employee. You should observe the following precautions:

- no smoking!
- inflammable materials such as thinners should be stored in sealed containers and away from heat
- heavy items should be stored on the lower shelves
- use a safe stepladder or stool when taking down items from high shelves
- store the stock neatly and do not leave packing materials lying around
- issue the old stock before the new stock to avoid wear and tear - place new stock at the *back* of the shelf on receipt from the suppliers - this process is known as FIFO (first in, first out)

security

Stock may be pilfered if left unattended, and therefore security in the storeroom is essential:

- the storeroom should be kept locked and access to the keys restricted
- issue of stock should be controlled by nominated staff
- stock should only be issued on receipt of a properly authorised requisition form
- the stock record cards should be updated on each issue or receipt of stock

stock records on the computer

advantages of computer records

We have described the maintenance of stock records in terms of *manual* records - stock record cards and stock inventories. Many organisations use computers to maintain stock records. The advantages of using a computer are well known: they are accurate, they will store large amounts of information and can provide the management of an organisation with information and reports in a short space of time. Here are some of the advantages of computerised stock control:

- automatic updating of stock balance levels
- printouts and display of the current stock levels
- indication of when minimum, maximum or re-order levels are reached
- automatic production, in some cases, of a Purchase Order for re-order of stock
- valuation of stock held
- printouts of suppliers' names and addresses

how the system works

The person dealing with the receipt and issue of stock will have access to a computer terminal. All the details that would normally be written on a stock record card by hand are input into the computer. When the time comes for a stock check, the computer will print out an inventory list with the balances of all the stock items; the person counting the stock will then have to reconcile the actual quantity with the computer total. If there is a discrepancy it will have to be reported in the normal way, and the computer records adjusted, just as the stock record cards would be amended in a manual system.

bar codes

Some larger organisations operate their stock control system by means of bar codes which identify individual stock items. You will no doubt be familiar with the bar code system operated by supermarkets and other retailers: each item is 'read' with a special pen at the cash till. The pen identifies the stock item by its bar code and relays the information through the cash till to the computer which indicates what the correct selling price is. Illustrated below is the bar code for this book. If you bought the book at a larger bookshop you may have seen them read the code with a special pen at the checkout. If enough copies of the book are sold by the bookseller, and the re-order level is reached, the bookshop's computerised stock control system will automatically send out an order to Osborne Books (the publisher) for a fresh supply of books.

As far as an organisation's need for office supplies - rather than sales to the general public - are concerned, the use of barcodes for stock control is less common. Nevertheless barcoding is a very interesting and rapidly developing use of computer technology.

ISBN 1-872962-15-7

9 781872 962153 >

the bar code for this book

student activities - stock handling

Performance criteria

The student activities in this section test competences in the following areas:

- *responding to requisitions (orders for stock) promptly and accurately*
- *handling and storing stock safely at all times*
- *carrying out stock checks and inventory reconciliations and reporting any shortages or damage*
- *checking incoming deliveries against orders and reporting discrepencies promptly*
- *keeping records of stock movements up-to-date, legible and accurate*

1. (a) A form used for ordering stock for use in an office is a   ....
    (b) Stock levels and movements are recorded on a   ....
    (c)   Goods arriving at the organisation will be accompanied by a ....
    (d) A person carrying out a stock check will record the stock on an ....
    (e) The process of comparing stock on the shelves with stock in the records is known as
          ....

    Choose from: • delivery note • requisition form • stock record card • inventory list
    • inventory reconciliation

2. Design a notice to be displayed in your stock storage area setting out the safety precautions to be observed when storing and handling stock.

3. List the security precautions for the protection of stock which you would expect to find in a well-run organisation.

4. Calculate the maximum and minimum stock levels from the following information:

    - total stock should never exceed 40 days' usage
    - daily usage 4 units
    - 12 days' stock should always be held

5. Calculate the maximum and minimum stocks levels for items A and B from the following information:

    - total stock should never exceed 12 weeks' usage
    - 2 weeks' stock should always be held
    - there is space available in the stores for 80 units of each item
    - weekly usage of A = 8 units, of B = 6 units

6. Calculate the maximum, minimum and re-order stock levels from the following information:

    - total stock should never exceed 60 days' usage
    - daily usage 6 units
    - normal delivery time is 5 days
    - 10 days' stock should always be kept

7. Calculate, for stock items D and E, the re-order stock level and the re-order quantity to replenish stock levels to the maximum level, from the following information:

- total stock should never exceed 95 days' usage
- 10 days' stock should always be held
- there is space available in the store for 350 units of each item of stock
- daily usage of D = 3 units, of E = 4 units
- normal delivery time is 7 days

8. (a) Prepare a stock record card (see Appendix 1) for the following item:

• *A4 Supalaser paper*	• minimum stock 5
• stock code A4/B1	• maximum stock 60
• units = reams	• re-order level 20
• location: row 3, bin 9	• re-order quantity 50

(b) Record on the stock record card the following requisitions and purchase orders showing goods received for the month of September 199-:

1 Sep.	Balance	30 reams
2 Sep.	Requisition 41	8 reams
3 Sep.	Requisition 54	4 reams
8 Sep.	Requisition 64	12 reams
12 Sep.	Purchase Order No. 121	50 reams
13 Sep.	Requisition 71	10 reams
15 Sep.	Requisition 73	9 reams
20 Sep.	Requisition 85	15 reams
21 Sep.	Requisition 87	6 reams
25 Sep.	Requisition 91	10 reams
26 Sep.	Purchase Order No. 135	50 reams
30 Sep.	Requisition 93	11 reams

9. (a) Prepare a stock record card from the following information:

- *product:* A4 Yellow Card, code A4/Y3, location row 7, bin 5
- *units:* reams
- *maximum stock:* 35 days' usage
- *daily usage:* 3 units
- *normal delivery time:* 10 days
- *minimum stock:* 12 days' stock
- *opening balance on 1 May 19-2:* 84 reams

(b) Calculate maximum, minimum and re-order levels of stock, together with re-order quantity (to replenish stock to the maximum level)

(c) Bearing these figures in mind, enter the following requisitions on the stock record card, remembering to re-order when necessary and to show the order on the card arriving ten days later (Purchase order 126):

2 May	Requisition 184	18 reams
3 May	Requisition 187	20 reams
10 May	Requisition 188	10 reams
16 May	Requisition 394	20 reams
20 May	Requisition 401	11 reams
22 May	Requisition 422	6 reams

10.   You work for Martley Machine Rental Ltd.; you receive a delivery of stock to the storeroom. It is accompanied by a delivery note which was signed by the person receiving the goods from the van driver. You now check the delivery note (illustrated below) against the original purchase order (also illustrated below) and notice some discrepancies. You are to

(a) make a list of the discrepancies
(b) write a letter to the supplier pointing out the problems and asking for the correct stock

Note: it would be normal for faulty or incorrect goods to be returned to the supplier.

PURCHASE ORDER
MARTLEY MACHINE RENTAL LTD
67 Broadgreen Road
Martley MR6 7TR
Tel 090655 6576 Fax 090655 6342

Stourford Office Supplies
Unit 12
Avon Industrial Estate
Stourford SF5 6TD

No   47700
Date   13 March 199-
Delivery   to above address

catalogue	quantity	description
3564749	15 reams	100gsm white Supalaser paper
5366788	150	Fax roll FR1-396
5526754	100 boxes	Banmate 2000 fine point ball point pens
5423786	15	Mercury staplers, colour black

authorised   signature..... C J Farmer ....   date 13 March 19-9 ....

DELIVERY NOTE

Stourford Office Supplies
Unit 12, Avon Industrial Estate, Stourford SF5 6TD
Tel 0807 765434 Fax 0807 765123

Martley Machine Rental Ltd
67 Broadgreen Road
Martley
MR6 7TR

Delivery Note No   26754
Date   26 March 199-
Your Order No   47700
Delivery   Van Delivery

product code	quantity	description
3564749	50 reams	100 gsm white Supalaser paper
5366789	150	Fax roll FR1-399
5526754	100	Banmate 2000 fine point ball point pens
5423788	15	Mercury staplers, colour red

received
signature........ R.F.Owen ....name (capitals)........ R.F. OWEN ....

date........ 27 March 199- ....

11. You are doing a stock check of items in the office stationery store. Your stock record cards show the following balances:

item	units	location	product code
white copy paper	65 reams	A6	P4252
headed notepaper	10 reams	A7	E6272
plain DL envelopes	10 boxes of 1000	A8	E7262
window DL envelopes	7 boxes of 1000	A9	E9161
ball point pens - black	20 boxes of 50	B1	P9712
ball point pens - red	5 boxes of 50	B2	P8161
pencils HB	10 boxes of 50	B3	P6173
correction fluid	76 bottles	C1	T6694
thinner	25 bottles	C2	T6695
notepads	125	C3	P4256

You note the following on your stock count:

white copy paper	63 reams OK, 2 reams damp and wrinkled
headed notepaper	10 reams, but 2 reams out of date – with old company name
plain DL envelopes	8 boxes of 1000, 2 boxes of 800
window DL envelopes	7 boxes of 1000
ball point pens – black	18 boxes of 50 – 2 boxes missing
ball point pens – red	5 boxes of 50
pencils HB	10 boxes of 50
correction fluid	75 bottles
thinner	25 bottles
notepads	127

(a) You are to prepare an inventory list, showing any discrepancies, using the following format (use your own name as checker and today's date).

stock inventory as at .... checker						
product code	item description	location	unit size	units counted	stock card balance	discrepancy

(b) State what action you would take when you have noted any discrepancies on the stock inventory.

 linking assignment

Common Skills Assignment 7
Applying numeracy: the Accounts Department, pages 252 to 256.

Common Skills development: Applying numeracy

Skills developed

The skill developed in this section is

- *applying numerical skills and techniques*

In the last three units we have looked at the way in which numbers are handled when dealing with petty cash transactions, invoice processing and stock handling. Numeracy - the ability to handle figures - is an essential skill in many office procedures. We will now develop this skill by explaining the 'nuts and bolts' of numeracy in the context of office work. We will give practical exercises in the form of Student Activities within the text, and a full length Assignment 'The Accounts Office' at the end of the section.

apply numerical skills and techniques

performance criteria

Numeracy involves the ability to work with figures and also to draw conclusions from them. If you are skilled in numeracy you must be able to

- use and apply a variety of numerical techniques
- select and apply the appropriate technique as the situation demands
- interpret numerical information correctly
- draw valid conclusions from the interpretation

The first question must be - what are the numerical skills and techniques?

measurement The assessment of a numerical value -
- how much does a ream of copier paper cost?
- a foreign visitor is expected - how far is your office from the airport?

calculation The application of numerical values to each other -
- how much does 20 reams of copier paper cost?
- you are writing to the visitor - how do you convert miles into kilometres?

estimation The use of existing numerical values to predict future values -
- how many reams of copier paper are you likely to use in a month?
- how long is it likely to take to travel from the airport to your office?

approximation   The presentation of your results in a common sense and meaningful way -
- it is better to say that you will use 30 reams rather than 29.86 reams!
- your foreign visitor will be happy to know that you are 50 kilometres and one hour from the airport rather than 48.7 kilometres and 57 minutes!

interpretation   The ability to *read* graphs, tables and charts.

presentation   The ability to *present* numerical data in the form of graphs, tables and charts.

Numeracy also involves the use of a number of basic techniques, which we will examine in detail. These techniques include the handling of decimals, fractions, ratios, percentages, tables, charts and graphs. We will now develop these skills and techniques, applying them to the clerical tasks practised earlier in the book and also to other common office procedures.

Numeracy - tools of the trade

Before applying numeracy skills it is essential to work out what resources you are going to need and what equipment (if any) you are going to use to apply those skills.

the brain

This particular tool of the trade can often be overlooked in one's eagerness to reach for the calculator or computer. If you are presented with a numerical problem of measurement, calculation or estimation, you should adopt the following approach:

- can you work out the answer in your head?
- if you can, do so, and get someone else to check it
- if you cannot work it out in your head, attempt a rough mental estimate to compare with the result obtained from a calculator

Some hints:
- *if you are dealing with items which cost, say, £4.95 or £4.99, approximate this figure to £5 for your rough calculation*
- if you are dealing with items in 10's or 100's at a given price, move the decimal place to the right to obtain the total price, e.g. 10 items at £3.45 cost £34.50, 100 items at £3.45 cost £345.00

In short, if you are dealing with numbers, use common sense to check any figurework that you carry out. It costs nothing and can prevent 'howlers' occurring.

the calculator

Electronic calculators are an excellent aid to numerical operations. They are cheap, compact, easy to handle, and never make mistakes. You often hear people say 'this calculator got a wrong answer!' What they really mean is that the operator was at fault. The following tips should reduce the number of errors made when using a calculator:

- perform each calculation twice; if the same answer is obtained, it is more than likely to be correct
- compare this answer where possible with a rough mental estimate
- if you are adding up long lists of figures, use a calculator which prints onto a tally roll (a long paper strip); if you make a mistake, check your figures against the tally roll, or, better still, find a colleague who can call out the figures to you while you check them on the tally roll
- if you perform a series of calculations which require you to 'store' a figure, use the 'add to memory' (M+) key of the calculator, and then display the memory total when it is required by pressing the memory recall button (MR)

the computer

Computers can be used to assist in a variety of numerical functions:

* computer spreadsheet programs allow the user to perform calculations in a set format
* computer accounting programs enable organisations to issue invoices and process payroll; the user inputs the necessary numerical data and the computer does the rest - printing invoices and payslips with all the necessary calculations performed automatically
* calculators may be found as an option in utilities menus in some computer programmes - the computer numerical keyboard is used to key in the numbers and the numerical functions

the basics of numeracy - decimals and fractions ___

An understanding of decimals and fractions is basic to the skills of measurement, calculation, estimation and approximation. Even if you think you are familiar with decimals and fractions, read this section carefully, as it covers an area which is often taken for granted.

decimals

The decimal system is the conventional way of presenting figures such as money values and metric distances, weights and volumes. For example, if you say that a personal stereo costs £35.99, each of the numbers quoted in the price, because of its *position* has a specific value related to £1:

tens	units	tenths	hundredths
3	5 .	9	9

The decimal point (.) is used to locate the units column, which is to the left of it. You will also see that a figure is worth *ten times more* than the same figure in the column to its right: £100 is worth ten times more than £10. The decimal system is a very convenient way of expressing numbers. Because it is based on the number ten it makes calulation easy, either with a calculator (which accepts the decimal point) or on paper This is the reason why the continental metric system of kilometre, kilogram and litre is replacing (or has replaced) the traditional British mile (1,760 yards), pound weight (16 ounces) and gallon (8 pints) which are more complex to use in calculation.

approximation of decimal numbers: 'rounding up' and 'rounding down'

There are situations where a number expressed as a decimal becomes a nonsense because there are too many decimal figures (places) used. The average family of 2.4 children is a good example: you simply do not meet 0.4 of a child. It is common practice to *round off* one or more unnecessary numbers *after the decimal point* by removing it/them and in some cases changing the number to the left. The rules are:

* a number *less than five* may be removed - the number to its left is not changed
* a number which is *five or more* may be removed - the number to the left must be increased by one

The family of 2.4 children may be approximated by *rounding down* to 2 as follows:

* the number four is removed
* as four is less than five, the number to its left is unaffected

If the average number of children were 2.6, the figure would be *rounded up* to 3.

Please note that the reduction in the number of figures *only applies to figures to the right of the decimal point*. You should also appreciate that figures are rounded up or down for reasons of common sense. If you were in business you might say that your profit was up by 16.98769879%. You might be accurate, but it would be more sensible to say that the increase was 17%.

A common business application of the principle of rounding off is when you are calculating a money amount by applying a percentage, such as a discount, you may possibly arrive at a figure of, say, £102.188.   You clearly cannot invoice a customer for this amount and would approximate it to £102.19.

There is one exception to this rule of rounding up and rounding down. As you will have seen in your dealings with VAT on invoices and in petty cash transactions, if you calculate VAT and the calculator shows a part of a penny, that part of a penny is ignored, *i.e. you always round down in VAT calculations*.

calculations with decimals

A common example of a calculation involving decimals is the foreign currency exchange, i.e. exchanging one currency for another at a bank or a foreign exchange bureau. If you are going on holiday, or if a representative of your organisation is travelling abroad

- you will need to *buy* foreign currency before you go
- you will need to *sell* any surplus of foreign currency when you come back

If you go to your local bank or a bureau, you will find two exchange rates quoted in decimal figures on the board normally displayed in the public area. The rate is the amount of foreign currency exchanged for each £1. There will be a low rate and a high rate, e.g.

> French Franc   9.8 - 9.9

The rule is:

- the lower rate (9.8) is the rate at which you buy French Francs from the bank before you go away
- the higher rate (9.9) is the rate at which you sell French Francs back to the bank on your return

problem
You are going abroad and change £500 into French Francs. You then find that your trip is cancelled and have to change the French Francs back into pounds. What currency amounts are involved, using the rates quoted above?

solution
buying currency: *£500 x 9.8 (lower rate) = French Francs 4,900*
selling currency back: *French Francs 4,900 ÷ 9.9 (higher rate) = £494.95*

You have lost £5.05 on the deal (£500 less £494.95) - why? The bank has made a profit on the difference between the two rates!

Note that in foreign currency transactions the normal rounding up and rounding down rules apply if your calculation produces too many decimal figures.

fractions

A fraction is used to express a part of a unit. An example of a fraction is $^3/_4$. The number below the line (the denominator) is the number of equal parts into which the unit is divided, and the number above the line (the numerator) is the number of parts involved. Thus the fraction $^3/_4$ means that a unit has been divided into four parts (quarters) and three of those parts comprise the fraction. Common sense tells you that $^3/_4$ is three 'slices' of an item divided into four.

calculations with fractions

Calculations involving fractions are not uncommon. For example, a kilometre is ⁵/₈ of a mile. In other words if a mile were divided into eight parts, five of those parts would equal a kilometre. If you work in an organisation which is involved in foreign travel, you may be asked to convert miles into kilometres, and vice versa.

Question   How many miles are there in 80 kilometres? Or, put another way, what is ⁵/₈ of 80 kilometres?

Answer   80 kilometres x $\frac{5}{8}$ = $\frac{400}{8}$ = 50 miles

To arrive at this answer, the number of kilometres (80) has been multiplied by 5 (the number on the top of the fraction) and divided by 8 (the number on the bottom) to give a result of 50 miles.

You may find you have to turn miles into kilometres, perhaps for a foreign visitor to your organisation. To calculate this you must multiply the number of miles by 8 and divide by 5.

Question   How many kilometres are there in 100 miles?

Answer   100 miles x $\frac{8}{5}$ = $\frac{800}{5}$ = 160 kilometres

The rule therefore is
To calculate a fraction of a certain quantity, multiply the quantity by the figure on the top of the fraction and then divide the result by the figure on the bottom of the fraction.

 # student activities 1 - decimals and fractions

Using your calculator (and your brain!) calculate the following:

1   The cost of 99 reams of paper at £5.99 per ream
2   The cost of 15 hole punches at £3.42 per item
3   The total mileage of a sales manager attending a course for five days on a daily basis, where the single journey mileage is 59 miles
4   The total wage bill for ten employees where four work 42 hours at £6.75 per hour, four work 40 hours at £5.55 per hour and two work 18 hours at £4.50 per hour
5   The cost per staff member of a social evening out where the costs incurred are coach £50, meal £7.50 each, theatre ticket £6.00 each, total administrative costs £8.75. Calculate the answer on the basis of (a) 25 people , (b) 15 people.
6   You are expecting a German sales representative and wish to provide him with some briefing material to help him in his travels in England. Find a road atlas and work out for him in kilometres (using the fact that there are 8 kilometres to every five miles) the distances between
    (a) London and York
    (b) London and Birmingham
    (c) London and Bristol
    Next, using the exchange rate of 2.91 Deutschemarks (German currency) to the £, work out how much it will cost him in Deutschemarks to
    (d) pay a taxi fare of £6.50
    (e) pay for a meal for his wife and himself costing £12.75 per head
    (Note: Deutschemark amounts are taken to two decimal places: 1 Deutschemark = 100 pfennig)
7   If you earn £7.50 per hour on an hourly basis and only work ³/₄ of your normal 8 hour day because you are taking your driving test, how much will you earn on that day? (ignore tax)
8.   Round off to the next decimal place: (a) 234.678; (b) 1009.009; (c) 0.00987; (d) 0.00982

number relationships - ratios and percentages ————

Numbers may be used in a variety of ways to demonstrate in a meaningful way the relationship between two or more categories of items. If, for example you are asked how many men and women work in your office, you could say fifteen women and five men. It would be more meaningful to say that the *ratio* of women to men was three to one, or that the percentage of women office staff was 75%. We will now examine ratios and percentages in more detail and develop your skills in calculating and using them.

ratios

a ratio is a group of numbers (each representing a specific category of item) which illustrates the comparative size of those categories

To continue the example given above, if there are fifteen women and five men in your office, the ratio of women to men is

$$15:5$$

or, if you divide both figures by five

$$3:1$$

Note:
- the two numbers are separated by a colon (:)
- if it is possible to divide the two numbers involved by a common factor (5 in the example above), then this will be done - always choose the *highest* common factor to simplify the ratio
- it is possible for a ratio to contain more than one number, e.g. 12 : 7 : 1 could be the ratio of people with dark, blonde and ginger hair in your office

The 3 : 1 ratio in the example of office staff makes it clear at a glance that for every man in the office there are three women. Whether this is an advantage or a disadvantage is a separate matter entirely, and no doubt you will have your own views!

percentages

a percentage is a number which indicates the size of a part of a whole by equating the whole to 100

In the example given above, the number of people in the office (twenty) will be equated to 100, and the percentage of women becomes 75% and the percentage of men 25% (as 75 + 25 = 100). The percentage figure (here 75% or 25%) is sometimes referred to as the 'percentage rate.'

calculation of percentages
The figures produced so far may seem straightforward in theory, but how are percentages calculated? We will take as an example the five men in the office of twenty.

Step 1 - calculate the total number of 'items' (here people in the office)

$$5 + 15 = 20$$

Step 2 - divide the part (number of men) by the whole (number of people in the office) and multiply by 100

$$\frac{5}{20} \times 100 = 25\%$$

The same calculation may be applied to the 15 women in the office

$$\frac{15}{20} \times 100 = 75\%$$

The formula for these calculations is

$$\frac{part}{whole} \times 100 = percentage$$

calculation of a figure from a given percentage rate

If you know the percentage rate (e.g. 25%), but don't know the number which makes up the percentage, the calculation is simple. Suppose you are told that your firm's sales in the Midlands are 25% of a total of £1,000,000. What is the figure for sales in the Midlands?

The formula applied here is

$$\frac{percentage\ rate}{100} \times total\ sales$$

i.e.

$$\frac{25}{100} \times £1,000,000 = £250,000$$

The sales figure for the Midlands is therefore £250,000

common uses of percentages

profit percentages

If a trader is to survive in business he or she will buy at cost price and sell at a higher selling price. The difference between these two prices is the trader's profit:

selling price less cost price = profit

This profit can be expressed as a percentage in two distinct ways:

margin   the profit expressed as a percentage of the *selling* price, i.e.

$$margin\ \% = \frac{profit}{selling\ price} \times 100$$

mark up   the profit expressed as a percentage of the *cost* price, i.e.

$$mark\ up\ \% = \frac{profit}{cost\ price} \times 100$$

A trader can use these percentages
• to examine how successful he or she is from year-to-year
• to compare the profitability of the business with that of *other* businesses

discounts

A trader will often obtain goods from a supplier at less than the advertised selling price. This happens if a bulk order is placed, or if a number of orders are placed over a period of time. This reduction in price is known as a *trade discount,* and you will already have encountered it in dealing with invoices. It is normally expressed as a percentage:

discount % = $\dfrac{\textit{reduction in price per item}}{\textit{full selling price per item}}$ x *100*

Question: if a trader is sold goods which cost £100 at full price, and is given 5% trade discount, how much does he pay?

Answer: full amount (£100) x $\dfrac{\textit{discount rate (5)}}{100}$ = £5 trade discount

He therefore pays £100 (full selling price) less £5 (trade discount) = £95

taxation - income tax and VAT

Taxation is normally calculated by applying a percentage rate to a taxable amount. If you are earning you will know the percentage rate at which you pay income tax. Most organisations buying and selling goods and supplies will be accountable for VAT (Value Added Tax). Elsewhere in your studies you will have encountered VAT in the issue and receipt of invoices, and also in the operation of a petty cash system.

Calculation of VAT on a given price of goods is straightforward. If goods cost £200 and VAT is 17.5 %, the VAT will be

$$\frac{17.5}{100} \text{ x } £200 = \frac{£3,500}{100} = £35$$

If you are operating a petty cash system you may be faced with the situation of being given a receipt for an amount paid which contains VAT, but find that the VAT amount (which you need to record in your VAT column in the petty cash account) is not shown.

The formula for working out the VAT already included in a total amount is calculated by means of a fraction:

$$\textit{Total amount x } \frac{17.5}{117.5} = \textit{VAT amount}$$

If you are given a total of £4.70 and know that it includes VAT, the VAT amount will be calculated as follows

$$£4.70 \text{ (amount paid) x } \frac{17.5}{117.5} = \frac{£8.25}{117.5} = £0.70p$$

The VAT is therefore 70p, and can be entered in your petty cash book as required.

interest

If you invest money or borrow money you will receive or pay interest at a given percentage rate. The terminology used is

• *principal* - the amount of money invested or borrowed
• *interest rate* - the percentage interest rate applied
• *term* - the number of years (or parts of years) for which the money is invested or borrowed

The formula used for calculating an interest amount is

$$\frac{\textit{principal x interest rate x term (in years)}}{100}$$

examples of interest calculations

investing

If you invest £1,000 for 1 year at an interest rate of 10%, the interest received will be

$$\frac{£1,000 \text{ (principal)} \times 10 \text{ (interest rate)} \times 1 \text{ (term)}}{100} = £100$$

If you invest £1,000 for 2 years at an interest rate of 10%, the interest received will be

$$\frac{£1,000 \text{ (principal)} \times 10 \text{ (interest rate)} \times 2 \text{ (term)}}{100} = £200$$

borrowing

If you borrow £1,000 for 1 year at an interest rate of 20%, the interest paid will be

$$\frac{£1,000 \text{ (principal)} \times 20 \text{ (interest rate)} \times 1 \text{ (term)}}{100} = £200$$

If you borrow £1,000 for 2 years at an interest rate of 20%, the interest paid will be

$$\frac{£1,000 \text{ (principal)} \times 20 \text{ (interest rate)} \times 2 \text{ (term)}}{100} = £400$$

 # student activities 2 - ratios and percentages

---

1.   You belong to a swimming club and are organising a social event for 50 members. You make enquiries and find that 40 want a party at the local Sports and Leisure Centre and 10 would prefer a visit to the local brewery. The club accepts the majority decision and you then enquire what they will want to drink: 25 prefer soft drinks, 15 would like lager and 10 would like wine.
  (a)   What is the ratio of members who preferred the brewery visit to those who preferred the Sports and Lesiure Centre?
  (b)   What percentage of members preferred to go to the brewery?
  (c)   What is the ratio of members who preferred soft drinks to those who preferred lager?
  (d)   Express the members' preference for soft drinks, lager and wine as percentages.

2.   If a trader buys goods for £100 and then sells them for £150, what is
  (a)   his profit margin?
  (b)   his mark-up?

3.   If the trader allows a discount of 10% on the same goods (see question 2)
  (a)   what will he receive for them?
  (b)   what will be his profit margin after deduction of the 10% discount?
  (c)   what will be his mark-up after the deduction of the 10% discount?

4.   If income tax is 25%, how much tax (to the nearest £) would you pay if your taxable pay is
  (a) £3,576.75   (b) £5,635.95   (c) £8,762.87   (d) £6,514.79   (e) £5,426.54?

5.   You have £500 to invest for a year, how much interest would you receive if you invest at
  (a) 6%   (b) 7.5%   (c) 10%   (d) 6.78%   (e) 7.05%

6.   You want to borrow £5000 to help you start up a business. What is the interest charged over <u>five</u> years if the interest rates average   (a) 12%   (b) 15%   (c) 17%   (d) 20%   (e) 25%?

8.   With VAT at 17.5% what is the VAT content of (a) £470 (b) £56.95 (c) £98.70 (d) £9,400.00?

interpretation and presentation of numbers ━━━━━━━

It is a commonly accepted fact that the human brain reacts more readily when a concept is presented in visual form.   In the Skills Development Section 'Communicating' we have examined how information may be presented in the form of

* graphs
* bar charts
* pie charts

If you have not covered this topic, or cannot remember what these formats involve, you should read the appropriate pages before proceeding further with this Unit.   If you wish to develop numeracy skills you should learn to be able to

* *interpret* tables, graphs, bar charts, and pie charts, and also
* be able to *choose the most appropriate format* when you are presenting numerical data

interpretation and presentation of numerical data - a case problem

interpretation of numerical data

You are asked by a supervisor to look at the sales figures for your organisation on a regional basis. You extract the following information from the files:

	£000's
South East	1,500
West Country	1,000
Midlands	1,200
North	1,250
Total	4,950

The figures as presented tell you the different sales figures for each area, and the total sales figure. It is, however, difficult to visualise at a glance the comparative size of each region's sales. What is the best format for presenting these figures?

format	advantages and disadvantages	use in present case
table	useful for presentation of 'raw' data, but not visually effective	*not appropriate here*
graph	useful for demonstrating a long term trend, but not where many variables (here-sales regions) are involved	*not appropriate here*
bar chart	visually effective in showing many variables	*useful in this case*
pie chart	visually effective in showing the proportional make-up of a specific subject - not appropriate where a long-term trend is involved	*useful in this case*

The bar chart and the pie chart for the regional sales are set out on the next page. Which do you consider to be the more successful in showing the breakdown of sales by region?

bar chart

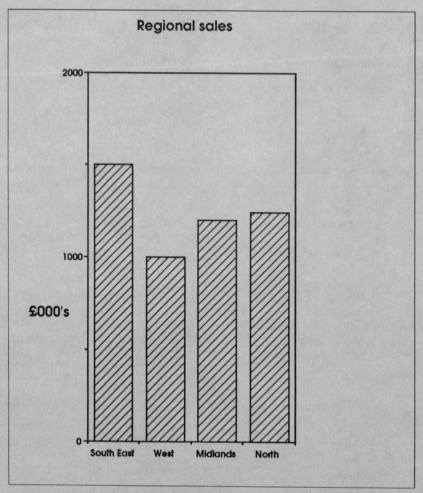

pie chart

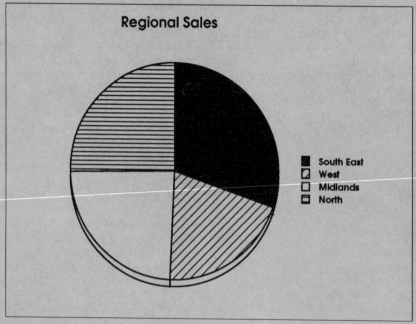

There can be little doubt that the bar chart is more successful in showing the comparative sales of the four regions.

* the proportions of sales by region are clearly visible as the columns of the bar chart - the eye does not have to work as hard as it does when looking at the pie chart
* the bar chart shows clearly the money amounts of the regional sales; these are not shown on the pie chart

This is not, of course, to say that a bar chart is *better* than a pie chart; it is better *in this case*.

 # student activities 3 - interpretation and presentation

1.   You work for Laycocks Nurseries, a garden centre chain operating garden centres in four towns in the area: Mereford, Martley, Broadwood and Pencroft. You have recently received from your Sales Department an analysis of the sales of each garden centre over the last two years.

Garden Centre	Year 1 £000's	Year 2 £000's
Mereford	250	250
Martley	157	235
Broadwood	225	168
Pencroft	105	110
Total Sales	737	763

(a)   What trends are evident, and what questions might you ask your Sales Department?
(b)   Choose a suitable presentation method from: graph, bar chart, pie chart, and set out the figures contained in the table in your chosen method.

2.   You work in the public relations department of H Schmidt Limited, the UK subsidiary of the German electronics company which has made substantial inroads into the UK market with its revolutionary Laserpunkt battery CD player.

Market Share: UK Market for CD Players

	19-1 £M	19-2 £M	19-3 £M
Japanese CD players	295	280	275
H Schmidt CD players	150	195	250
Others	140	130	115

(a) present this data in the form of a line graph
(b) comment on the trends exhibited.

Common Skills Assignment 7
Applying numeracy:
The Accounts Office

Areas assessed
This assignment covers the following areas
- **Clerical Tasks: processing petty cash and invoices**
- **Common Skills: principal skill - applying numeracy**
  other skills - communicating

Scenario
You work as a clerical assistant in the Accounts Department of Wyvern (Office Products) Limited .

During the course of a day you are to deal with a variety of tasks requiring numeracy skills. These involve

- dealing with invoices, petty cash and stock records
- calculating payroll and taxation
- dealing with matters involving the bank account
- calculating insurance premiums
- presenting and interpreting performance figures for the business

Notes on completion of the Assignment
The tasks should be completed on an individual basis - no group activity is required. There is no particular priority for the tasks given; they should all be completed accurately and within a specific deadline given by the assessor. The tasks in each case should be completed in writing.

Tasks

Task 1: calculating the payroll

(a) You are asked to calculate the pay due to Rod McKellan who worked 40 hours last week at the standard rate of pay and 2 hours of overtime. He is paid £7.50 per hour at standard rate and 'time and a half' (i.e. 1.5 times standard rate) for overtime. Ignore income tax and National Insurance.

(b) You are asked to calculate the pay due to Henry Ramsay who worked 40 hours last week at the standard rate of pay and 3 hours of overtime. He is paid £9.00 per hour at standard rate and 'time and a half' (i.e. 1.5 times standard rate) for overtime. Ignore income tax and National Insurance.

(c) Three new members of staff want to know approximately how much they are going to receive each month after deduction of tax. The rate of income tax is 25%. Ignore National Insurance. Their *taxable* pay per year is as follows: Carole £6,000; Denise £5,800; Mohammed £7,000.

Task 2:   checking incoming invoices

You are asked to check the calculations on three invoices which have come in from one of your suppliers for payment. Once they have been checked you will pass them forward for authorisation and for payment when the statement arrives.

Note: extracts from the invoices are shown. You can assume that all other details on the documents are correct. The discount in the column between 'total' and 'net' is trade discount; cash discount (if any) is deducted in the line below 'Goods Total'. Assume VAT at 17.5% - remember to round down any fractions of pence in VAT amounts calculated.

invoice (a)

product code	description	quantity	price	unit	total	disc %	net
6548	Zenith Laser Toner	10	61.50	each	615.00	20	592.00
					GOODS TOTAL		592.00
					CASH DISCOUNT		00.00
					SUBTOTAL		592.00
					VAT		103.60
					TOTAL		488.40

invoice (b)

product code	description	quantity	price	unit	total	disc %	net
6538	A4 printer paper 70gsm 2000 sheet pack	10	13.00	pack	130.00	10	143.00
					GOODS TOTAL		143.00
					CASH DISCOUNT		00.00
					SUBTOTAL		143.00
					VAT		25.03
					TOTAL		168.03

invoice (c)

product code	description	quantity	price	unit	total	disc %	net
6521	3.5" computer disks DS/DD, box of 10	5	7.25	box	72.50	10	65.25
					GOODS TOTAL		65.25
					CASH DISCOUNT		01.63
					SUBTOTAL		63.62
					VAT		11.13
					TOTAL		84.75

Task 3   checking petty cash and stock records

(a)   You have been asked by the petty cashier to check the petty cash book, as she cannot get the column totals to agree (i.e the total of all the analysis columns does not equal the total of the Total Payment column). What errors can you detect? Correct the errors and draw up a fresh page for the week. See Appendix 1 for a blank petty cash book page.

Receipts	Date	Details	Voucher No.	Total Payment	Analysis columns				
					VAT	Postages	Stationery	Travel	Sundry
£	199-			£	£	£	£	£	£
50.00	10 Apr.	Cash balance							
	10 Apr.	Stationery	47	4.70			4.00		
	10 Apr.	Taxi fare	48	2.35	0.35			2.00	
	11 Apr.	Postages	49	5.00		5.00			
	12 Apr.	Travel	50	2.35	0.35			2.00	
	12 Apr.	Stationery	51	9.40			8.00		
	13 Apr.	Postages	52	3.68		3.68			
	13 Apr.	Postages	53	15.00		15.00			
	14 Apr.	Computer ribbon	54	4.70	0.70				4.70
				47.18	1.40	23.86	12.00	4.00	4.70

(b)   You have been asked by the storekeeper to check the stock record card for the Banmate 2000 ball point pens (black). A balance of 600 boxes is shown on the card but the storeman has counted 1,000 boxes in the store. Locate the errors and draw up a new card for the storekeeper. See Appendix 1 for a blank stock record card.

STOCK RECORD CARD

Stock Description ..Banmate 2000 ball point pens (black, fine point)..........

Stock units ....boxes of 12...............

Stock Ref. No. ....W1030............................

Location ....row F, bin 3...................

Minimum ....100 boxes..........

Maximum ....1 200 boxes.........

Re-order level ....400 boxes...........

Re-order quantity ....750 boxes...........

DATE	GOODS RECEIVED		GOODS ISSUED		BALANCE
	Reference	Quantity	Reference	Quantity	
199-					
1 Jul.					1 000
2 Jul.			REQ 201	200	800
4 Jul.			REQ 204	100	400
5 Jul.			REQ 215	100	300
6 Jul.			REQ 221	150	150
9 Jul.	Purchase Order 18321	750			850
10 Jul.			REQ 228	50	800
11 Jul.			REQ 233	50	700
12 Jul.			REQ 235	100	600

Task 4 dealing with the banking

One of the functions of the Accounts Office is to deal with the company bank account. Your tasks in this respect include preparing cash and cheques for paying in, writing out cheques for expenses incurred, and dealing with other queries relating to the running of the bank account. In the course of the day you have three tasks to complete.

(a) You have just received the bank statement for the last month. Your supervisor is anxious to know the bank charges that you are likely to have to pay. Your bank has recently advised you of the following charges per item passed through the bank account:

* cheques written out - 50p each
* credits paid in - 80p each

What are the bank charges for the month?

MidWest Bank plc

branch Mereford

account Wyvern (Office Products) Limited

account number 34527625   **statement no** 67

date	description	payments	receipts	balance
		£	£	£
199–				
01 May	Balance brought forward			245.56
01 May	Cheque 345120	65.78		179.78
02 May	Cheque 345121	40.00		139.78
03 May	Credit		100.00	239.78
08 May	Credit		345.87	585.65
09 May	Cheque 345123	25.00		560.65
10 May	Cheque 345122	23.45		537.20
15 May	Cheque 345124	156.70		380.50
16 May	Cheque 345125	280.45		100.05
22 May	Credit		567.87	667.92
23 May	Credit		100.00	767.92
24 May	Cheque 345127	50.00		717.92
25 May	Cheque 345126	674.45		43.47
28 May	Credit		890.76	934.23
29 May	Cheque 345128	6.50		927.73

(b) Your company has £50,000 which it wishes to place on deposit with the bank. There are two possible accounts:
- Branch Deposit Account paying 5% per year which is simple to operate
- Money Market Deposit paying 7% per year which requires you to give notice when taking money out

Your supervisor asks you to work out the interest you will receive if the £50,000 is deposited for
(i) a year
(ii) a month
(iii) a week
Work out the interest for *both* accounts, presenting your results in a table.

(c)   You are asked to check the cash being paid into the bank. You have to count and add up the money value of the following:

25 x £20 notes, 100 x £10 notes, 36 x £5 notes,
17 x £1 coins, 12 x 50p coins, 56 x 10p coins.

What is the total money value? If you wish, obtain a bank paying in slip and use the appropriate boxes to do the addition; otherwise set out the calculation neatly on paper.

Task 5: calculating insurance premiums

Your employer is considering giving senior staff health insurance as a perk. The company will pay for health insurance which will enable the staff to have private health and hospital treatment should the need arise. The cost of health insurance depends on age: the older you are the more likely you are to need treatment, and the older you are the more expensive the premiums become.

There are three age ranges used for calculation of premiums: 16-21; 22-40; 41-65

The ratio of the age ranges among the fourteen senior staff is   2   :   3   :   2

The average rates for the three age ranges is as follows

age range	premium rate
16-21	£25 per month per employee
22-40	£40 per month per employee
41-65	£60 per month per employee

You are asked to calculate the total cost per year of providing health insurance for the fourteen senior staff.

Task 6: assessing the profit figures

You are given the following figures for the company sales over the last three years

	Year 1 £	Year 2 £	Year 3 £
Sales	1,250,000	1,500,000	2,000,000
Total expenses	1,000,000	1,250,000	1,500,000

You are asked for the following information

(a)   What is the profit for each of the three years?

(b)   What is the profit as a percentage of the sales figure for each year? Note: round off your result, where appropriate, to the nearest percentage figure - do not take the percentages into decimal figures.

(c)   Construct a line graph which shows both the sales and the profit for the three years

(d)   Construct a bar chart which shows the profit for the three years

(e)   What comments would you make about the performance of the company over the three years in respect of sales and profitability?

16 Health and safety

NCVQ coverage

9.1 operate safely in the workplace
Performance criteria
- *keeping your work area free from hazards*
- *using equipment according to the operating instructions*
- *recognising, rectifying or reporting potential hazards*
- *reporting accidents promptly and accurately in accordance with legal and/or organisational guidelines*

introduction

Health and safety in the workplace is an important factor - it can sometimes mean the difference between life and death. Your employer is obliged by law to ensure that the workplace is safe and complies with certain minimum standards of heating, ventilation and lighting.

But you the employee also have responsibilities. Health and safety in the workplace is often taken for granted: if you work for an organisation or have done work experience you should be familiar with the fire drill and the posters that warn you of accidents that can happen. It is human nature to *assume* that it will 'never happen to me' but it is also one of your duties as an employee to *ensure* that it will not! You also have a duty in law to observe safety regulations.

In this Unit we will look at

- the legal obligations of employers to maintain health and safety in the workplace
- recognising hazards in the workplace
- dealing with hazards in the workplace
- observing the basic safety procedures, including the reporting of accidents and carrying out of fire drills

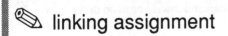 linking assignment

Common Skills Assignment 8
Applying design and creativity: Solving problems creatively, pages 271 to 272

health and safety and the law

There are two Acts of Parliament which lay down most of the regulations which employers - and in some cases employees - must observe:

* Health and Safety at Work Act 1974
* Offices, Shops and Railway Premises Act 1963

Health and Safety at Work Act 1974

The Health and Safety at Work Act 1974 - often abbreviated to HASAWA - states that it is the duty of every employer to ensure the health and safety of his (or her) employees. It is a criminal offence for the employer to ignore this law.

employer's duties under HASAWA

The law states specifically that the employer must provide

* safe machinery and equipment - and maintenance of that machinery and equipment
* safe operating systems for the machinery and equipment
* safe and healthy methods of using, handling, storing and transporting of items and substances: these can include solids, liquids and gases which may be harmful to health
* information, instruction and training in safety procedures
* supervision of employees
* safe and healthy premises - adequate toilets, canteen facilities, heating, lighting and ventilation
* safe access to the premises (offices and oil rigs are equally subject to this point of law!)
* a safe environment for visitors to the premises, e.g. maintenance contractors, sales representatives

If the employer employs more than five employees, he or she should issue a written *Statement of Policy* to the employees, giving details of the safety procedures in force on the premises. This policy may be given to the employees personally, or it may be placed where it can be read - on the notice board, for instance.

employee's duties under HASAWA

The law states that an employee must

* take care for the health and safety of himself (or herself)
* take care for the health and safety of others in the workplace
* use safety devices where they are provided
* cooperate with the employer in observing safety requirements (this can include safety training)

Offices, Shops and Railway Premises Act 1963

This Act covers railway premises, offices, shops, wholesale warehouses, canteens, toilets, storerooms and similar types of facility. The Act requires the employer to provide

* clean and uncrowded premises
* a minimum temperature (after one hour) of 16°C for employees who are not doing strenuous work
* an uncrowded working area
* suitable fresh or purified air ventilation and sufficient natural or artificial lighting
* adequate toilets (separate toilets for male and female employees)
* suitable washing facilities - hot and cold running water, soap and towels or hand dryer
* fresh drinking water!
* seats in a rest area
* unobstructed stairways with handrails
* protection around dangerous machinery
* first aid facilities and a means of escape in the event of a fire

hazards to health and safety in the workplace

Set out below are some of the health and safety hazards you might encounter in the workplace, together with some suggested solutions.

hazards	solutions
backache	*adjust the height of the chair so that you can work comfortably with a straight back, or check the height and angle of your VDU, if you use one*
eye strain	*is the light sufficient? if you use a VDU, are you a comfortable distance from the screen? do you use a VDU anti-glare screen? rectify these points if you can; speak to your supervisor if you cannot*
headache	*is the light sufficient? is the ventilation sufficient? do you work for long periods at a time at a VDU? rectify these points if you can; speak to your supervisor if you cannot*
a desk which you and others keep crashing into	*reposition it after consulting with your supervisor*
filing cabinets which topple when the top drawer is opened	*there is too much heavy material in the top drawer - reorganise the filing so that lighter and less frequently used material is stored in the top*
filing cabinet drawers which obstruct working areas	*reposition the cabinet if possible - but consult your supervisor first*
not being able to reach a book or file down from a high shelf, and possibly dislodging a pot plant in the process	*use a step ladder or stool*
trailing telephone wires or electrical leads	*reposition the equipment, or if the leads cross the floor, speak to your supervisor - it may be necessary for the leads to be taken under the carpet or floor in a special duct*
slipping on wet or shiny floors	*tell your supervisor - mats may have to be put down*
falling over boxes of stationery	*put the boxes away - all passages and stairways should be kept free of obstructions*
tripping over stairs because the light is bad	*tell your supervisor - passages and stairways should be well lit*

using equipment in the workplace

safety guidelines - electrical equipment

Most offices will have electrical equipment as standard issue: typewriters, computers, printers, fax machines, photocopiers, franking machines, and so on. A safe office is an office in which certain staff are trained in the use of that equipment, and know what to do or whom to contact if the equipment goes wrong. A safe office is an office which follows these guidelines in the use of electrical equipment:

* keep food and drink away from the equipment - biscuit crumbs and coffee can cause havoc to delicate electronics
* avoid trailing flexes
* if you see exposed wires or frayed flexes call an electrician to replace the flex
* if you see a cracked or scorched plug, replace it, or get someone to replace it
* switch off the machine when it is not in use
* know where the operating instructions are kept
* follow the operating instructions if you are not sure of what you are doing - *do not* take short cuts
* if there is a fault, follow first any troubleshooting guide in the operating instructions
* if there is a fault which you cannot fix, report it and record it (if there is a faults book) and call the maintenance engineer - do not take a screwdriver to the machine in the hope that you may be able to mend it!
* keep the telephone number of maintenance engineers to hand in case of breakdown

safety guidelines - non-electrical equipment

Certain items of equipment may not use electricity. Some of these can cause horrendous injuries if not used with care; for instance

* a stapler gun, which can fire staples into wads of paper and unsuspecting fingers with great ease
* a guillotine, which can cut paper and card and anything else which falls below the blade
* a letter opening machine
* a pair of sharp scissors

Staff using this equipment must receive proper instruction and be aware of the dangers involved.

safety guidelines - liquids and gases

Offices may use liquids which are potentially dangerous, either because they give off gases, or because they are toxic, for example the thinner used for mixing with liquid paper. These products normally have a warning on the packaging, and this should be read carefully, and due care taken in the storage and use of the product. In particular these products should not be stored where there are extremes of temperature, on a sunny windowsill for example.

moving equipment

There may be occasions when you have to move equipment. Remember that some items of equipment are extremely heavy and can cause a slipped disc in the unwary but enthusiastic employee. If you have to move an item of equipment, ensure first that you *can* lift it; if you are unable to move the item, find a strong colleague (male or female!) who can. If you do decide that you can lift a heavy item, always keep your back straight and upright, using your knees to perform the vertical movements. If you use your back to lift a photocopier, i.e by bending your spine, you could end up with an injured back, and be confined to the horizontal position for some weeks.

warning against danger of electric shock

 no smoking!

a danger warning sign meaning 'Look out!'

 naked flames prohibited (e.g. lighted matches)

warning against a substance which is dangerous if inhaled or swallowed - look on the side of your liquid paper bottle

 fire extinguisher

First Aid facilities

 Assembly Point for fire drills

a selection of workplace warning and safety symbols

dealing with accidents in the workplace

Accidents happen in the best regulated of workplaces, and can vary from the relatively minor cut or sprain to the major or even fatal accident. In this section we will look at

- the administrative procedures to be followed in the case of an accident
- how to deal with the situation if an accident occurs

administrative procedures in the case of an accident

By law the organisation should have

- at least one member of staff who is trained in first aid
- an accident reporting system - normally in the form of an Accident Book

The member of staff trained in First Aid should be known as such to the rest of the organisation: staff should be informed, either in writing or by a notice on the Notice Board, or preferably both, so that the 'first aider' can be contacted easily if he or she is needed.

The organisation should also have a system for recording the accident in writing. This can either be in the form of an Accident Book (see illustration below) or in the form of an Accident Report Form which will record similar details. The recording of accidents is important because it will warn the organisation of hazards in the building (e.g. slippery floors, unstable filing cabinets) and also be written evidence in the case of an insurance claim, or even a law suit from the employee!

What health and safety hazards can you identify in the following page from an Accident Book? There are three accidents reported. In how many cases is the accident the employee's fault, and why? (See the bottom of the page for suggested solution).

date	name/department	accident details	action
199-			
3 May	O Hardy Accounts	slipped on wet patch on toilet floor resulting in a bad sprain to the left ankle	taken to hospital by First Aider
30 June	S Laurel Sales	fell on stairway to stationery store while carrying five boxes of envelopes - broke right leg	taken to hospital by ambulance
10 July	C Lumsy Mail Room	gashed hand with knife while slitting open envelopes in Mail Room	hand bandaged by First Aider - sent home

Suggested solution: O Hardy's first accident was probably the result of a badly maintained toilet floor, and would be the employer's responsibility. The other two accidents involve the recklessness (S Laurel) and the carelessness (C Lumsy) of an employee.

dealing with an accident

If an accident occurs in the office, you may be the only person immediately to hand to deal with it. What should you do?

identify the problem

Try to see exactly what has happened. This may be obvious, of course, if a person has blood gushing from a cut, in which case you will be able to deal with the problem yourself, and obtain the necessary bandages and plasters from the First Aid cupboard. The situation will be less clear if the person has collapsed or appears immobile. A collapse could indicate electrocution, a faint, a diabetic coma, a heart attack, a stroke; immobility could mean a broken bone. All this may sound alarmist, but it could be the problem, in which case

- you should not move the patient
- you should get expert medical help - quickly

get medical help

If the accident is not serious and you are not yourself trained in first aid, contact the organisation's first aider. If the accident is serious, call an ambulance immediately. Normally your switchboard operator will do this for you. If you yourself have to telephone, dial 999, ask for the ambulance service and answer their questions. Remember also to tell your supervisor what has happened. You will feel foolish if an ambulance arrives and nobody in authority knows what is going on.

You will see that in dealing with an accident you must *stay calm* and *act decisively*. This is more easily said than done! If you do remain level-headed in an emergency, you will gain the respect of your colleagues and superiors.

dealing with fires in the workplace

Fire is probably the most feared threat to health and safety: it can cause immense damage and it can kill. The most common causes of fire in the workplace are electrical faults, careless smokers, and incorrectly stored flammable materials.

fire drills

Your organisation should have set procedures for

- activating the fire alarm
- testing the fire alarm
- using fire-fighting equipment if it is necessary
- evacuating the building so that each employee has a specific choice of routes
- assembling the employees at specific points outside the building

These procedures should be circularised to staff and practised regularly in the form of 'fire drills'.

what to do if a fire breaks out

If you discover a fire, you should only deal with it yourself if it is a *small* fire - use a fire blanket or a fire extinguisher (of the correct type) to smother the flames. If it is a major fire -

- check that there is no-one overcome by the fire
- shut the windows if possible and then the door of the room
- raise the alarm
- calmly get out of the building by the usual escape route and proceed to the assembly point
- if there is thick smoke in the corridors of the building, crawl along the floor - *never* run

fire precautions

Every organisation should observe certain regulations and precautions in order to reduce the likelihood of fire, and to impede its progress should it break out.

These include

- installation of fire exits which can be used if the main access doors are blocked by a fire
- installation of fire doors inside the building - on corridors and stairways - to prevent fire spreading if it should break out
- installation of smoke detectors which will activate the fire alarm in the event of a fire
- prohibiting smoking in areas where flammable materials are stored
- storage of flammable materials according to safety regulations (e.g. solvents and thinners)

The Fire Precautions Act 1971 states that a workplace which employs more than twenty people must be inspected by the fire authorities. If the premises are found to comply with fire regulations, the employer will be issued with a fire certificate. If the premises are not up to standard, the employer must make improvements accordingly.

When a fire certificate has been issued, it is the responsibility of the employer to ensure that the fire precautions are adequately maintained. For example

- internal fire doors should not be propped or wedged open
- internal fire doors should not be obstructed, or worse still, locked
- external fire exits should not be locked (they can normally only be opened from the inside)
- arranging for the regular disposal of flammable waste materials, e.g. waste paper
- arranging for fire alarms and fire extinguishers to be checked regularly
- arranging for regular fire drills to be held

 student activities - health and safety

Performance criteria

The student activities in this section test competences in the following areas:

- *keeping your work area free from hazards*
- *using equipment according to the operating instructions*
- *recognising, rectifying or reporting potential hazards*
- *reporting accidents promptly and accurately in accordance with legal and/or organisational guidelines*

1.   Study closely the picture on the next page.   State (either in writing or in discussion)
      (a)   the hazards you can spot
      (b)   whether it is the employer or the employee that is responsible for the hazard
      (c)   what corrective action (if any) can be taken to prevent the hazard in the future

2. What do the following symbols mean?

(a)

(b)

(c)

(d)

3. What would you do in the following situations? State in writing or in discussion the reasons for your actions.

   (a) Penny Smith, an accounts clerk, cuts her finger on a pair of scissors. She is bleeding profusely and obviously very upset. She asks you for help

   (b) You find Henry Ramsay, a warehouse assistant, in a heap at the bottom of a stairway clutching his arm. He is moaning gently, and you cannot get a lot of sense out of him.

   (c) You find Bob Bates, a Sales Supervisor, lying on the floor of his office. He appears to be unconscious. On his desk is his VDU screen with the back taken off. A screwdriver lies nearby.

   Now write up what has happened in an Accident Book. See page 262 for an example format.

4. What would you do in these situations? State in writing or in discussion the reasons for your actions.

   (a) You see a senior colleague throwing cigarette ends in the waste bin. You are sure that the cigarette ends are still alight.

   (b) You find a waste bin on fire.

   (c) Your computer terminal starts sparking and you see flames at the back of your desk.

   (d) You smell burning along the corridor. You investigate and see wisps of smoke coming from the Managing Director's office - the door to the office is shut.

   (e) You are taking part in a fire practice, and it is your responsibility to clear your office. A senior colleague refuses to take part in the exercise, saying that she is 'far to busy to be playing at fire drills, and anyway everybody knew it was going to take place, so the whole thing is pointless.'

 linking assignment

Common Skills Assignment 8
Applying design and creativity: Solving problems creatively, pages 271 to 272

Common Skills development:
Applying design and creativity

Skills developed
The skill developed in this section is

> *• apply skills and techniques to develop varied ideas in the creation of new or modified products, services or situations*

When you speak about 'design and creativity' people often conjure up pictures of painting and pottery, art students and way-out fashion. They are right, but they ignore the fact that design and creativity also affect everyday life, including the office environment. In this book we have already looked at a number of aspects of office work which involve design and creativity: the organisation of the reception area, the layout of your desk, the layout of written communications and business documents, the way in which you solve problems. We will now look more closely at the principles of good design and practise them creatively in the the Assignment which follows: 'Solving problems creatively'.

apply design and creativity

performance criteria
When you apply design and creativity you must
- appreciate the need for creative design
- recognise opportunities for innovation and creativity
- explore the use and combination of skills and techniques
- produce and evaluate creative design ideas

what this means
the need for design

It is easy to take your work environment for granted: the colour of the walls, the chair you sit on, the equipment you use (e.g. computer) because they work well (usually!) It is when things go wrong that you notice the need for design: an office repainted in a harsh colour, a chair which you gives you backache, a computer which gives you headache. You then say 'Whoever designed this? They ought to try and work here.'

opportunities for design

When can you be creative at work? More often than you realise. As mentioned above, there are a number of opportunities for design at work:

- designing a layout for your work area
- setting out a letter
- writing a notice to be displayed on the notice board
- helping to design promotional material
- thinking of a neat solution to a problem

As you will appreciate, design does not have to be large-scale. Think how successful the paperclip is.

use of skills and techniques

Not everyone is an artist, but most people have some inborn idea of design skills and techniques. If you lay the meal table at home or arrange items on your desk at work you are making decisions about how to arrange items in a given space so that the items look organised and the system works (i.e. you can eat the meal or organise your work). If you decide to put flowers on the table or a plant on your desk you are again using design creatively. In fact, the skills are used almost *without you thinking about them*. In the next section we examine some of these design techniques in more detail.

production and evaluation of design ideas

In the office environment design ideas are often produced as a result of a task given: a new letter format, a sales promotion leaflet. You do not, as the staff of an design office would, come into work, sit down and say 'Let's be creative today and think up some new designs.' Nevertheless you may well think of and evaluate ideas in groups, as a design team would. For instance your supervisor might ask 'How do you think we can rearrange these desks so that we can fit in the new trainee on Monday?' You would all think of ideas individually for reaaranging the furniture, and then discuss and evaluate them *as a group*.

what is good design? ━━━━━━━━━━━━━━━━━━━━

If you look around you in the office you will see good design and less good design in a wide range of everyday objects and pieces of equipment. What exactly are the attributes of good design? Look at your photocopier or computer and consider the following:

- *performance* - does it do its job properly and efficiently?
- *quality* - is it well made? is it smooth in operation?
- *appearance* - is it pleasing to look at? is the colour right? does it look neat and modern?
- *value* - is it good value for money?
- *durability* - is it wearing well, or is it easily marked or broken?
- *safety* - is it safe to use, or have there been accidents?

All of these qualities combine in a successful design. Sometimes some qualities are more prominent than others.   Some manufacturers concentrate on pricing and use the cheapest materials and components consistent with efficiency. Others may stress safety or appearance. You might like to apply the same principles to cars: how would you rate the Volvo, the Skoda and the Ferrari in terms of performance, quality, appearance, value, durability and safety?

We will now look at an area of design with which you are most likely to become involved: document design.

document design

Documents are used to communicate information. If the document is well designed, the message is communicated easily and clearly. Look at the two advertisements set out below. What is *wrong* with the advert at the top, and what is *right* with the advert at the bottom?

SPECIAL OFFER!

GET ALL YOUR STATIONERY REQUIREMENTS FROM
STATIONERY DESIGN OF MEREFORD

This week's special offer -
boxes of 10 computer disks: 5.25" DS/DD £5.00, 5.25" DS/HD £9.00, 3.5" DS/DD £7.00, 3.5" DS/HD £13.25.

Hurry now while stocks last!

Stationery Design
140 High Street
Mereford MR1 3RF Tel 0605 562581

 # SPECIAL OFFER!

Get your disks from Stationery Design of Mereford

This week's special offer - boxes of 10 computer disks:

5.25" DS/DD	£5.00	3.5" DS/DD	£7.00
5.25" DS/HD	£9.00	3.5" DS/HD	£13.25

Stationery Design
140 High Street
Mereford MR1 3RF Tel 0605 562581

guidelines for document design

If you look at the two advertisements on the previous page you will see that the advertisement at the top is a mess and a muddle. Why?

* the lines used are heavy and clumsy - they draw the eye away from the text
* the text itself is underlined in many places - a crude and clumsy effect
* the advertisement uses four different designs of lettering (known as fonts) which look fussy and clumsy, as below:

fussy and clumsy

fussy and clumsy

fussy and clumsy

fussy and clumsy

* the text looks messy because it is a mixture of effects:

plain text

shadowed text

outline text

* the product details are not set out in any particular format, but are strung out in one long line, and are therefore difficult to read
* there are no illustrations to show what products are on offer

The advertisement at the bottom of the previous page, on the other hand, is clear and communicates its message well. Why?

* it is simple - there is a minimum of special effects, either with the text or with lines, except for the main heading - Special Offer! - which is intended to jump out at the reader
* there are illustrations of the products
* the product details are set out clearly in columns so that they are easy to read

document design in your office

In your office you may have a special computer package which will enable you to produce documents in the style of the previous page, or you may have a word processing package which will produce similar special effects. Alternatively you may draw up documents using paper and pencil and give the task of producing the final document to your Reprographics Department or to your printer.

Although you may not have to compile complex advertisements as part of your job, you may need to draw up simple documents which require design skills:

* notices for the notice board - announcing a staff social, for instance
* simple forms relating to your work procedures

Whatever task you have to do, remember that the important point is to get the message across *simply and effectively*. In your spare time have a look at the adverts in your local paper, or documents and forms produced by other organisations. Are they successful in terms of design? Are they simple, or are they cluttered with special effects which detract from the message or information?

Common Skills Assignment 8
Applying design and creativity:
Solving problems creatively

Areas assessed

This assignment covers the following areas
- **Clerical Tasks: liaising with colleagues, health and safety**
- **Common Skills: principal skill - applying design and creativity;**
  other skills - communicating, applying numeracy

Scenario

You work as an assistant in the Administration Department of the Evening Echo, your local newspaper. During the course of a working day you are given a number of tasks which involve your design and creativity skills.

Notes on completion of the Assignment

The tasks that follow require work to be done by individuals and by small groups. Refer to your assessor for precise instructions.

Tasks

Task 1: fire precautions! - a health and safety leaflet

Your supervisor has been concerned recently because staff have been ignoring many of the basic health and safety requirements relating to fire precautions.

He asks you to design an A5 (A4 folded in half) leaflet for circulation to the staff. He wants a draft format from you which will be set out in final form and printed in-house by the Echo's advertising department. He suggests that illustrations might be a good idea, but says that if you are not able to draw, you should just make a sketch and let the advertising department provide the artwork.

He mentions a number of points which he would like you to include in the leaflet:

- staff should not wedge open internal fire doors

- staff should not obstruct the external fire exits with piles of boxes

- too much waste paper is being left around the office - a potential fire hazard

- cigarette ends are being thrown into waste bins

- plugs on electrical equipment are not being connected securely or maintained properly

Task 2:   designing a work area

You are moving into new offices next month and you have been allocated the work area illustrated below (plan not to scale).

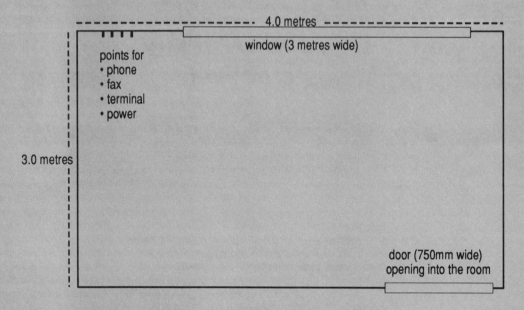

Into this area you have to fit the items of furniture listed below, *bearing in mind the Health and Safety at Work requirements*. Measurements quoted are width x depth x height (in millimetres).

- a computer workstation (1800mm x 690mm x 700mm) with computer terminal and printer (linked to a local area network)
- fax table (720mm x 690mm x 500mm) plus fax machine
- a three drawer upright filing cabinet (550mm x 600mm x 1320mm)
- telephone
- typist's chair
- a waste bin
- a set of full-height open shelves for storage (1200mm x 310mm x 1320mm)

You are to

(a)   Draw up a scale drawing of your proposed working area and mark in where you think the various items of furniture should go, bearing in mind factors such as opening doors, drawers, and the need to connect up all the relevant equipment. It is suggested that you use graph paper for the drawing as it will help you with marking in the dimensions. You might also cut out shapes (to scale) for the items of furniture and move them around on your plan of the area to obtain the best arrangement.

(b)   Suggest a possible colour for the walls (they are to be newly painted) and state the reason for your choice. The carpet is a contract job and will be a beige colour throughout the office.

(c)   Make suggestions for other items which you may need for the the working area - either to help you in your work, or to brighten up the room. Assume that you will be provided with the usual stationery items (pens, pencils, paper, disks etc.) and the filing system which will be installed in the cabinet.

(d)   Send your suggestions to items (b) and (c) on a memorandum, together with the proposed plan, to Richard Rogers, Administration Department Supervisor.

appendix 1

sample blank documents
- contract of employment
- payslip
- letterhead
- memorandum
- fax header
- message taken sheet
- cross reference cards
- index cards
- invoice
- petty cash voucher
- petty cash book
- stock record card
- inventory list

CONTRACT OF EMPLOYMENT

Particulars of Terms and Conditions of Employment pursuant to the Employment Protection (Consolidation) Act 1978

Employer..

Employee..

1. **Continuous Employment**
    You are on a fixed term contract of ....years

    Your continuous service dates from..

2. **Job Title**
    You are employed as..

3   **Salary**
    The rate of your salary is.............................per annum, paid monthly

4. **Hours of Work**
    Your normal hours of work are .... hours a week, worked over a five day period (Mondays to Fridays inclusive)

5. **Leave**
    You are entitled to.................days paid holiday per annum in addition to statutory holidays. The leave is to be taken at a time convenient to the employer.

6. **Sickness**
    Notification of absence should be made on the first day of sickness, in writing or by telephone.
    If you are absent for a period in excess of five working days, a doctor's certificate must be submitted to the employer.
    Regulations for payment during periods of sickness or injury may be inspected on request in the Administration Manager's Office.

7. **Notice**
    The length of notice for termination of employment required from employer or employee is................weeks, subject to statutory requirements.

8. **Grievance Procedure**
    In cases of dissatisfaction with disciplinary procedure you are to apply in the first instance to the Manager of the Sales Department. Details of the rules of the Company and disciplinary procedures may be obtained from the Administration Manager's Office.

9. **Pension Scheme**
    Details of the contributory Company Pension Scheme, for which you are eligible, may be obtained from the Administration Manager's Office.

    Signed this...................day of....................19...........

    T J Blake, Managing Director and Company Secretary

Wyvern (Office Products) Limited	Pay Statement	
	£	**£**
Basic Pay	Income Tax	
Overtime	National Insurance	
	Pension	
TOTAL GROSS PAY		
	TOTAL DEDUCTIONS	
	NET PAY	

CUMULATIVES
Taxable earnings
Tax to date
NI to date
Pension

NET PAY

EMPLOYEE DETAILS

Wyvern (Office Products) Limited

12, Lower Hyde Street, Mereford, MR1 2JF
Tel 0605 241851 Fax 0605 241879

MEMORANDUM

To

From   **Ref.**

Copies to   **Date**

Subject

facsimile transmission header

Wyvern (Office Products) Limited

12, Lower Hyde Street, Mereford, MR1 2JF
Tel 0605 241851 Fax 0605 241879

TO..

....

....

TELEPHONE NUMBER...FACSIMILE NUMBER...

NUMBER OF PAGES INCLUDING THIS HEADER............................DATE..

message

If you have any enquiries regarding this message please telephone the above number and

ask for extension.......................

MESSAGE

while you were out

date........................time............................taken by..

to...

from...of...

phone...

❏ telephoned

❏ returned your call

❏ will telephone again

❏ called in person

❏ please telephone

❏ wants to see you

❏ **URGENT**

> *message*

cross reference sheet ━━━━━━━━━

for

see

cross reference sheet ━━━━━━━━━

for

see

cross reference sheet ━━━━━━━━━

for

see

Name   **File no**

Tel
Fax

Date opened

Contact
Salesman

Name   **File no**

Tel
Fax

Date opened

Contact
Salesman

Name   **File no**

Tel
Fax

Date opened

Contact
Salesman

INVOICE

Wyvern (Office Products) Limited
12, Lower Hyde Street, Mereford, MR1 2JF
Tel 0605 241851 Fax 0605 241879
VAT Reg 841 1601 14

Invoice to

Invoice No
Account
Date/tax point
Your Reference

deliver to

product code	description	quantity	price	unit	total	disc %	net

Terms
Net monthly
Carriage paid
E & OE

GOODS TOTAL	
CASH DISCOUNT	
SUBTOTAL	
VAT	
TOTAL	

petty cash voucher   no.

date:

requirement	amount (£)	

signature...

authorised...

---

petty cash voucher   no.

date:

requirement	amount (£)	

signature...

authorised...

Receipts	Date	Details	Voucher No.	Total Payment	Analysis columns					
					VAT					
£				£	£	£	£	£	£	£

Receipts	Date	Details	Voucher No.	Total Payment	Analysis columns					
					VAT					
£				£	£	£	£	£	£	£

STOCK RECORD CARD

Stock Description ....

Stock units ....   Minimum ....

Stock Ref. No. ....   Maximum ....

Location ....   Re-order level ....

           Re-order quantity ....

DATE	GOODS RECEIVED		GOODS ISSUED		BALANCE
	Reference	Quantity	Reference	Quantity	

STOCK RECORD CARD

Stock Description ....

Stock units ....   Minimum ....

Stock Ref. No. ....   Maximum ....

Location ....   Re-order level ....

           Re-order quantity ....

DATE	GOODS RECEIVED		GOODS ISSUED		BALANCE
	Reference	Quantity	Reference	Quantity	

stock inventory as at					checker	
product code	item description	location	unit size	units counted	stock card balance	discrepancy

appendix 2

Wyvern (Office Products) Limited
Catalogue and Price List

Wyvern (Office Products) Limited

12 Lower Hyde Street Mereford MR1 2JF Tel (0605) 241851 Fax (0605) 241879

CATALOGUE AND PRICE LIST

WYVERN OFFICE FURNITURE

Own brand quality office furniture at economical prices. All items are made from textured finish high density melamine that is stain, heat and scratch resistant. All desks are 72 cm. high and all units have welded steel frames. All items available in light oak and teak melamine. (State colour choice when ordering.)

DESKS

Reference No.

Single Pedestal Desk with three box drawers all locking.
Large top	150 cm x 75 cm	F1006
Small top	120 cm x 65 cm	F1007

Double Pedestal Desk with two box drawers in each pedestal, all drawers lockable.
Medium top	135 cm x 75 cm	F1005

Executive Double Pedestal Desk
L.H.S. is fitted with deep filing drawer and one box drawer.
R.H.S. has three drawers, all drawers lockable.
Extra large top	450 cm x 75 cm	F1003
Large top	150 cm x 75 cm	F1004

Secretarial Unit
Large size single pedestal desk with secretarial return unit (105 cm x 48 cm), fitted complete with four stationery trays and tambour shutter.
Left hand unit	....	F1010
Right hand unit	....	F1011

TABLES

Office Table
Eight sizes of office tables are available, all have detachable steel legs for ease of transport and storage. Can also be fitted with drawer.
Office table	75 cm x 75 cm	F1022
Office table	120 cm x 60 cm	F1023
Office table	90 cm x 90 cm	F1024
Office table	120 cm x 75 cm	F1025
Office table	135 cm x 75 cm	F1026
Office table	150 cm x 75 cm	F1027
Office table	180 cm x 60 cm	F1028
Office table	180 cm x 75 cm	F1029

(If drawer is required, add D to reference number.)

Canteen Tables
A wide choice of these stackable steel frame tables in ten sizes.

Canteen table	60 cm x 60 cm	F1030
Canteen table	75 cm x 75 cm	F1031
Canteen table	90 cm x 60 cm	F1032
Canteen table	120 cm x 60 cm	F1033
Canteen table	90 cm x 90 cm	F1034
Canteen table	120 cm x 75 cm	F1035
Canteen table	135 cm x 75 cm	F1036
Canteen table	150 cm x 75 cm	F1037
Canteen table	180 cm x 60 cm	F1038
Canteen table	180 cm x 75 cm	F1039

Telephone Table
Useful table with bottom shelf to use in combination with any desk or by itself.

40 cm x 70 cm	F1040

STORAGE UNITS

Glass Front Bookcases
Glass front bookcases with glass sliding doors. Adjustable shelf height.

90 cm x 30 cm x 160 cm high	F1060
150 cm x 30 cm x 85 cm high	F1061

Open front bookcases

(Fixed shelves)	90 cm x 18 cm x 115 cm high	F1051
(Adjustable shelves)	90 cm x 21 cm x 120 cm high	F1052
(Adjustable shelves)	90 cm x 21 cm x 150 cm high	F1053
(Adjustable shelves)	90 cm x 21 cm x 195 cm high	F1054

Combination Cupboards
Fitted with adjustable shelves and double lockable doors. The cupboards can be used in multiples to create a wall unit.

A 180 cm high unit with three shelves	F1055
A 100 cm high unit with one shelf	F1056

Filing Cabinets
A matching range of filing cabinets in two, three and four drawer units
Designed to accommodate foolscap files. Lockable drawers.

4 drawer	134 cm high	F1070
3 drawer	103 cm high	F1071
2 drawer	71 cm high	F1072

Flat Storage Units
An inexpensive way of storing Artwork, Keylines, Blueprints Plans and other oversize documents. Five reinforced drawers per unit.
Choice of 4 sizes available to take up to A1 papers.

100 cm x 41 cm x 68 cm	F1080
100 cm x 41 cm x 95 cm	F1081
45 cm x 41 cm x 60 cm	F1082
65 cm x 41 cm x 75 cm	F1083

Roll Store Units
A convenient and space saving method of filing rolled documents. Each unit has sixteen compartments and comes in three different sizes with a tambour roller door.

43 cm x 43 cm x 68 cm long	F1090
43 cm x 43 cm x 100 cm long	F1091
43 cm x 43 cm x 135 cm long	F1092

OFFICE CHAIRS

Wood Framed Chairs
A quality hardwood framed chair, upholstered in tweed for comfort. Available in either teak or mahogany finish with peat or charcoal fabric. Ideal for reception or general office seating. (State finish choice when ordering.)

Wooden framed chair (no arms)	C1010
Wooden framed chair with arms	C1011
Wooden framed swivel armchair	C1012

Metal Framed Chairs
Welded steel frame in black with foam padded seat and back.
Available in peat or charcoal fabric finish.   (State finish choice when ordering.)

Metal frame chair (no arms)	C1020
Metal frame chair with arms	C1021

Metal Stacking Chairs
Welded steel frame with one piece polypropylene seat, available in grey, orange, charcoal or brown (State colour when ordering) C1025

Typist Posture Chair
All chairs have black enamelled steel 5 star bases fitted with heavy duty easy glide castors, manual height and back adjustment. Upholstered in either charcoal or peat.
(State colour when ordering)

Typist posture chair (no arms)	C1030
Typist posture chair with arms	C1031
Typist posture chair, gas lift	C1032
Typist posture, arms with gas lift	C1033

Quality Executive Chairs
Quality made executive chairs which provide day long comfort. Each chair is craftsman made and upholstered in either black leather or charcoal or peat quality tweed. Chairs can either be fixed stainless steel frame based or five star chromed base with castors.
All chairs are standard 53 cm wide. (State colour of tweed when ordering.)

Low back leather, fixed base	C1040
High back, tweed, fixed base	C1041
Medium back, tweed, fixed base	C1042
Low back, tweed, fixed base	C1043
High back, leather, swivel base	C1044
Medium back, leather, swivel base	C1045
Low back, leather, swivel base	C1046
High back, tweed, swivel base	C1047
Medium back, tweed, swivel base	C1048
Low back, tweed, swivel base	C1049

THE "FISLEY" RANGE
Superior Quality Products at Competitive Prices

Fisley storage cabinets are excellent quality and stylish. These all steel cabinets are available in two finish colours, Coffee & Cream and Goose Grey.
(State colour when ordering.)

Filing cabinets

All steel available with 2, 3 and 4 drawers, fitted with anti-tilt mechanism and lock.
Takes standard size foolscap suspension files.

Two Drawer	70 cm high	S1010
Three Drawer	100 cm high	S1011
Four Drawer	130 cm high	S1012

Storage cupboards

All steel cupboards fitted with flush front doors, magnetic door catch and two point locking mechanisms.

Size	180 cm x 90 cm x 45 cm	S1020
Size	100 cm x 90 cm x 45 cm	S1021

Multidrawer cabinets

Multidrawer cabinets provide the most versatile answer to information storage problems.
All models are mounted on black plinths except desk top cabinet.
All cabinets are 11 ins wide and 17 ins deep.

Series 12, Desk Top Five	5 cm drawers, 32 cm high	S1030
Series 29, Multidrawer Ten	5 cm drawers, 68 cm high	S1031
Series 29, Multidrawer Six	7.5 cm drawers, 68 cm high	S1032
Series 39, Multidrawer Fifteen	5 cm drawers, 95 cm high	S1033
Series 39, Multidrawer Nine	7.5 cm drawers, 95 cm high	S1034

THE WYVERN RANGE OF STATIONERY

PAPER

A great selection of quality cut products from one of the UK's leading paper manufacturers.

Sherman Paper A symbol of elegance in this range of high quality water marked wove.
In 80 and 100 gsm weights, the perfect choice of paper to fulfill all business and
promotional requirements. The colour range offered is White, Dark blue, Amber,
Light blue, Oyster, Buttermilk and Grey. (State colour when ordering.)
Paper is packed in smart black boxes with 500 sheets (1 ream) per box.

Sherman White wove	A4, 80 gsm	P1010
Sherman White wove	A4, 100 gsm	P1011
Sherman Coloured wove	A4, 80 gsm	P1012
Sherman Coloured wove	A4, 100 gsm	P1013
Sherman White, laid	A4, 80 gsm	P1014
Sherman White, laid	A4, 100 gsm	P1015
Sherman Coloured, laid	A4, 80 gsm	P1016
Sherman Coloured, laid	A4, 100 gsm...............................	P1017

Sceptre Paper: A selection of cut paper for general office use, lightweight 45 gsm
bank papers 70 and 80 gsm bond papers, 80 gsm copier bond and 70 gms duplicator paper.
In a variety of colours all packed in strong boxes of 500 sheets to protect paper
Colour range, Blue, Green, Pink and Yellow. (State colour when ordering.)

Sceptre Bank, White	A4, 45 gsm	P1020
Sceptre Bank, Coloured	A4, 45 gsm	P1021
Sceptre Bond, White	A4, 70 gsm	P1022
Sceptre Bond, White	A4, 85 gsm	P1023
Sceptre Bond, Coloured	A4, 70 gsm	P1024
Sceptre Bond, Coloured	A4, 85 gsm	P1025
Sceptre Copier Bond, White	A4, 80 gsm	P1026
Sceptre Copier Bond, Coloured	A4, 80 gsm	P1027
Sceptre Duplicator, White	A4, 70 gsm	P1028
Sceptre Duplicator, Coloured	A4, 70 gsm	P1029

Fax Machine Rolls

We supply these high quality thermal paper rolls in two basic sizes to suit the following four
groups. FR1-399 A4, FR1-338 A4, FR1-316 A4, all 210 mm W x 100 m L with 25 mm core
and FR1-396 A4 210 mm W x 100 m L with 50 mm core. Check your machine against our
Fax Roll. Packed in boxes of four per group.

Fax Roll	FR1-399 A4	P1040
Fax Roll	FR1-338 A4	P1041
Fax Roll	FR1-316 A4	P1042
Fax Roll	FR1-396 A4	P1043

Adding Machine Rolls

Quality wood free paper rolls in three popular widths to suit most of today's
desk top adding machines. Packed in boxes of twenty per group.

Machine Roll	57 mm x 57 mm Grade A	P1050
Machine Roll	57 mm x 86 mm Grade A	P1051
Machine Roll	57 mm x 70 mm Grade A	P1052
Machine Roll	37.5 mm x 35 mm Grade A	P1053
Machine Roll	70 mm x 70 mm Grade A	P1054

ENVELOPES

High quality envelopes to match the **Sherman** range of paper. Packed in boxes of 500.

Sherman matching self seal	wove white	E1010
Sherman matching self seal	wove coloured	E1012
Sherman matching self seal	laid white	E1014
Sherman matching self seal	laid coloured	E1016

Banker: Business gummed envelopes available in White and Brown Manilla, windowed
and plain. Packed in boxes of 1 000.

Brown manilla plain	90 mm x 150 mm	E1020
Brown manilla window	90 mm x 150 mm	E1021
White plain	90 mm x 150 mm	E1022
White window	90 mm x 150 mm	E1023
Brown manilla plain	110 mm x 160 mm	E1030
Brown manilla window	110 mm x 160 mm	E1031
White plain	110 mm x 160 mm	E1032
White window	110 mm x 160 mm	E1033
Brown manilla plain	100 mm x 220 mm	E1040
Brown manilla window	100 mm x 220 mm	E1041
White plain	100 mm x 220 mm	E1042
White window	100 mm x 220 mm	E1043

PENCILS

Gainsborough 'Chemi-sealed' pencils available for both general and drawing office use. Packed in boxes of 12.

General Office	range: 4B to B, HB, H to 4H	W1010
Drawing Office	range: HB, B to 8B, H to 7H	W1011
Quote hardness quality with order.		
General Office Rubber topped	HB only	W1012

Gainsborough Automatic pencils in both general office and professional quality; featuring fine line rapid refill cassette system. Professional, suitable for drawing office work, offers constant lead thickness range of 0.3, 0.5 & 0.9 mm.

General Office	packed in boxes of 10	W1020
Drawing Office	packed singly	W1021

ERASERS

Wipeout White Plastic Eraser   packed in boxes of 20 ....   W1090
     Suitable for detail on paper or film.

Felix range of Erasers

Standard white (for soft pencils)	packed in boxes of 10	W1091
Medium green (for H pencils)	packed in boxes of 20	W1092
Ink/pencil (for soft and ball pen)	packed in boxes of 20	W1093

PENS

Ball point pens available in two qualities.
Banmate 2000, long lasting tungsten carbide ball, and the famous *Rocoball* pen, the clear crystal barrel with medium point. Available in black, blue, red and green.
(Packed in boxes of 12.)

Banmate 2000	fine point	W1030
Banmate 2000	medium point	W1031
Rocoball	....	W1032

Fibre Tip Marker Pens
Heavy duty felt tipped, ideal for display work. Available in waterproof ink and dry wipe form. Colour choice Black, Blue, Red and Green. State colour when ordering.
(Packed in boxes of 12 except where specifically stated.)

Board Marker C60	hard wearing, chisel point, permanent marker	W1040
Board Marker C61	hard wearing, chisel point, dry wipe marker	W1041
Board Marker B60	hard wearing, bullet point, permanent marker	W1042
Board Marker B61	hard wearing, bullet point, dry wipe marker	W1043
Board Marker C60	hard wearing, chisel point, permanent marker	W1040
Giant Board Marker C80	chisel point, permanent marker	W1044
(packed 4 per box)		
Giant Board Marker C81	chisel point, dry wipe marker	W1045
(packed 4 per box)		

Fibre Tip Highlighters
A superb range of board tip fluorescent ink highlighters for attracting attention to important points. Available in Yellow, Green, Orange, Pink, Blue and Red.
(State colours when ordering.)

Single highlighter	packed 10 per box	W1050
Wallet of 4 different colours	Blue, Green, Orange, Red	W1051
Wallet of 6 different colours	Complete range	W1052

CLEAR PLASTIC RULES

Graduated in both imperial and metric.

150 mm	clear plastic rule	W1080
300 mm	clear plastic rule	W1081
300 mm	clear shatterproof rule	W1082
450 mm	clear shatterproof rule	W1083

OFFICE SUNDRIES

CORRECTION PAPER AND FLUID

Wippex Correction paper	50 strips	D1010
Wippex Correction fluid	available in white, yellow, blue, pink or green	D1011
Wippex Thinner	....	D1012
Wippex Twin Set	Correction and thinner fluid	D1013

HOLE PUNCHES

Available in red or yellow. State colour when ordering.

Economy 2 hole punch	capacity 12 sheets	H1010
Medium 2 hole punch	capacity 28 sheets	H1012
Heavy Duty 2 and 4 hole punch	capacity 50 sheets	H1013

STAPLERS

Available in Black and Red. State colour when ordering.

Mercury, pocket size	No. 25 staples	M1010
Mars, standard arm	No. 56 staples	M1012
Titan, long arm	No. 56 staples	M1013
Hercules, heavy duty lever arm	No. 56 staples	M1014
Electra 5000, electronic	240 volt power supply	M1015

STAPLES

Refill staples, 5000 per box	No. 25	M1090
Refill staples, 5000 per box	No. 56	M1091

PAPER CLIPS

Full range covers three standard sizes, plain and coloured in green, red and blue.
State colour when ordering.

Small plain	packed in boxes of 1000	M1080
Medium plain	packed in boxes of 1000	M1081
Giant plain	packed in boxes of 100	M1082
Small coloured	packed in boxes of 1000	M1083
Medium coloured	packed in boxes of 1000	M1084
Giant coloured	packed in boxes of 100	M1085

Wyvern (Office Products) Limited

12 Lower Hyde Street Mereford MR1 2JF Tel (0605) 241851 Fax (0605) 241879

PRICE LIST

Catalogue Number	Pack Quantity	Price £	Catalogue Number	Pack Quantity	Price £
C1010	1	52.95	F1003	1	124.95
C1011	1	57.95	F1004	1	144.50
C1012	1	95.95	F1005	1	104.95
C1020	1	41.00	F1006	1	99.95
C1021	1	48.95	F1007	1	89.50
C1025	1	8.75	F1010	1	175.00
C1030	1	31.95	F1011	1	175.00
C1031	1	47.50	F1022	1	55.75
C1032	1	46.50	F1022D	1	64.75
C1033	1	63.25	F1023	1	58.50
C1040	1	142.50	F1023D	1	67.50
C1041	1	144.95	F1024	1	61.50
C1042	1	128.00	F1024D	1	70.50
C1043	1	122.95	F1025	1	65.50
C1044	1	169.50	F1025D	1	74.50
C1045	1	153.50	F1026	1	68.95
C1046	1	147.50	F1026D	1	77.95
C1047	1	149.95	F1027	1	76.25
C1048	1	133.00	F1027D	1	85.25
C1049	1	127.95	F1028	1	80.50
D1010	50 pack	1.20	F1028D	1	89.50
D1011	1	0.78	F1029	1	84.95
D1012	1	0.55	F1029D	1	93.95
D1013	1 set	1.20	F1030	1	29.95
E1010	500	29.95	F1031	1	34.50
E1012	500	30.95	F1032	1	36.25
E1014	500	29.95	F1033	1	42.50
E1016	500	30.95	F1034	1	47.75
E1020	1000	8.60	F1035	1	49.95
E1021	1000	10.95	F1036	1	53.95
E1022	1000	14.35	F1037	1	55.75
E1023	1000	16.50	F1038	1	55.75
E1030	1000	17.25	F1039	1	64.95
E1031	1000	21.20	F1040	1	53.95
E1032	1000	18.75	F1051	1	39.95
E1033	1000	29.15	F1052	1	49.95
E1040	1000	20.25	F1053	1	58.95
E1041	1000	24.95	F1054	1	67.95
E1042	1000	24.70	F1055	1	134.95
E1043	1000	30.95	F1056	1	104.95

Catalogue Number	Pack Quantity	Price £	Catalogue Number	Pack Quantity	Price £
F1060	1	95.95	P1029	500	6.25
F1061	1	99.95	P1040	4	33.00
F1070	1	159.95	P1041	4	40.00
F1071	1	139.95	P1042	4	33.00
F1072	1	124.50	P1043	4	36.00
F1080	1	114.95	P1050	20	4.00
F1081	1	144.95	P1051	20	10.95
F1082	1	69.95	P1052	20	7.75
F1083	1	79.95	P1053	20	4.50
F1090	1	41.95	P1054	20	10.75
F1091	1	45.95	S1010	1	89.95
F1092	1	48.95	S1011	1	94.95
H1010	1	2.80	S1012	1	99.95
H1012	1	7.95	S1020	1	99.95
H1013	1	19.45	S1021	1	89.95
M1010	1	1.35	S1030	1	29.95
M1012	1	6.25	S1031	1	49.95
M1013	1	20.65	S1032	1	39.95
M1014	1	79.99	S1033	1	72.95
M1015	1	74.95	S1034	1	72.95
M1080	1000	0.95	W1010	12	1.95
M1081	1000	1.60	W1011	12	3.95
M1082	100	0.45	W1012	12	2.25
M1083	1000	4.25	W1020	10	9.30
M1084	1000	6.40	W1021	1	1.85
M1085	100	2.25	W1030	12	0.85
M1090	5000	1.70	W1031	12	0.80
M1091	5000	0.90	W1032	12	1.25
P1010	500	10.60	W1040	12	8.25
P1011	500	12.60	W1041	12	7.85
P1012	500	11.60	W1042	12	8.25
P1013	500	13.60	W1043	12	7.85
P1014	500	10.60	W1044	4	6.60
P1015	500	12.60	W1045	4	6.10
P1016	500	11.60	W1050	10	7.75
P1017	500	13.60	W1051	4	3.10
P1020	500	4.40	W1052	6	4.65
P1021	500	3.95	W1080	1	0.18
P1022	500	6.25	W1081	1	0.35
P1023	500	7.50	W1082	1	0.40
P1024	500	5.60	W1083	1	1.20
P1025	500	7.10	W1090	20	7.95
P1026	500	3.25	W1091	10	3.75
P1027	500	4.95	W1092	20	4.15
P1028	500	6.25	W1093	20	5.30

index